Ultimate Milvus Vector Database for AI Apps

Master Vector Search, Distributed Data Management, and GPU-Accelerated AI Systems with Milvus

Prashanth Raghu

www.orangeava.com

First Published: April 2026

Published By: Orange Education Pvt Ltd, AVA®

Address: 9, Daryaganj, Delhi, 110002, India

275 New North Road Islington Suite 1314 London,
N1 7AA, United Kingdom

ISBN (PBK): 978-93-49887-18-3
ISBN (E-BOOK): 978-93-49887-58-9

Scan the QR code to explore our entire catalogue

www.orangeava.com

Get a Free eBook

We hope you're enjoying your recent book purchase! Your feedback is incredibly valuable to us and helps other readers discover books that truly make a difference.

If you found this book useful or enjoyable, we'd greatly appreciate it if you could leave a short review with a 5-star rating on Amazon. Your review supports our work and allows us to reach more learners worldwide.

As a thank-you, we're happy to offer you a **free digital copy of this book** plus a **30% discount code** for your next purchase on our official websites:

www.orangeava.com

www.orangeava.in (For the Indian Subcontinent).

☑ **How it works:**

Leave your review on Amazon, take a screenshot of the confirmation or use the following link to submit the claim and email it to **info@orangeava.com.** Once received the required detail, we will send your rewards within 24 hours, **along with one month free subcription to the book on AVA SkillShelf!**

Claim Form
https://rebrand.ly/4d2477

Thank you for your support—it truly means a lot to us.

Downloading the code bundles and colored images

Please follow the links or scan the QR codes to download the ***Code Bundles and Images*** of the book:

https://github.com/ava-orange-education/-Ultimate-Milvus-Vector-Database-for-AI-Apps

The code bundles and images of the book are also hosted on ***https://rebrand.ly/f2931d***

In case there's an update to the code, it will be updated on the existing GitHub repository.

Errata

We take immense pride in our work at **Orange Education Pvt Ltd,** and follow the best practices to ensure the accuracy of our content to provide an indulging reading experience to our subscribers. Our readers are our mirrors, and we use their inputs to reflect and improve upon human errors, if any, that may have occurred during the publishing processes involved. To let us maintain the quality and help us reach out to any readers who might be having difficulties due to any unforeseen errors, please write to us at:

errata@orangeava.com

Your support, suggestions, and feedback are highly appreciated.

Dedicated to

My Beloved Parents:
Smt. Anuradha Raghu and Late Raghu Sampath.
And My Grandparents:
Late Sri G Sampath and Late G S Srirangamma,
Late Srinivasa Iyengar and Jayalakshmi.
And My Brother,
Jayanth Raghu and Family.

About the Author

Prashanth Raghu works at the intersection of semiconductor architecture, artificial intelligence, and foundational logic systems.

As the CEO of Sudarshana Semiconductors, he focuses on building original compute and reasoning architectures, spanning ASIC design, ML acceleration, and next-generation processing paradigms. Prashanth's work emphasizes first-principles thinking, long-horizon engineering, and technologies that are difficult to replicate without deep technical grounding.

Prashanth has been an active open source contributor, with contributions to Python, Memcached, NodeJs, and Redis to name a few in which he is also completing his doctoral thesis. His works have been nominated as the best seller on Amazon India in its category.

Prashanth is an avid Carnatic flutist, and performs concerts outside his professional commitments. He is also an avid writer and artist with interest in Mandala and other Indian art forms.

About the Technical Reviewer

Satvik has over 11 years of experience in architecting and deploying impactful AI/ML web-based solutions, with expertise in enterprise-grade software, distributed data processing, and cloud-native deployments. He worked across various technologies, including scaled Java-based backend services and engineering data pipelines using Apache Spark that are supported by containerization and orchestration through Docker and Kubernetes. With a commitment to driving efficiency and enhancing productivity through cutting-edge AI-driven solutions, Satvik later worked on vector databases, where he engineered semantic search, hybrid search, and retrieval architectures that combine vector similarity with metadata filtering, including multi-vector and multimodal retrieval (text and images).

At the moment, Satvik works as a Senior Software Engineer at DigiCert Security, where he designs and deploys scalable AI/ML solutions aligned with digital trust, including customer-facing chatbots powered by NLP and GenAI techniques. His work also includes implementing RAG pipelines and MCP-based integrations that enable LLM-driven clients to interact with APIs, and retrieve curated knowledge through semantic search. He also works on blending ML with AI using Databricks to extract domain-aware, context-rich AI insights that can be scaled and integrated with any digital trust product.

Acknowledgments

There are a few people I want to thank for their continued support during the writing of this book. First and foremost, I would like to thank my parents and grandparents for continuously encouraging me to write the book.

I extend my sincere thanks to my support systems, Dayananda Sagar College of Engineering, Dr. Vibha MB, Dr. Smitha Sasi, and my colleagues, for their support during this tenure. I also thank my family, friends, and well-wishers for their encouragement. I am especially grateful to my mentors, Krishna Kumar Pooloth Sir and Madhu Krishna Iyengar Sir, who have helped me during critical times.

I would like to extend my heartfelt gratitude to Naresh Pai and Ramachandra Sir for their wholehearted support. I thank all my professors and mentors who have guided me time and again during this journey. I am also grateful to all my academic institutes and workplaces that have supported me in my journey.

I offer my sincere gratitude to the publishing team at Orange Education Pvt. Ltd. for being supportive enough to provide me ample time to complete the book. I also extend my heartfelt gratitude to the technical reviewer who guided me throughout the writing process. Their input has made this book more insightful and invaluable for readers.

Preface

Chapter 1 aims to provide a comprehensive introduction to vector databases, an emerging technology in the field of data management and machine learning. The objective is to elucidate the fundamental concepts, architectures, and applications of vector databases, making this chapter a valuable resource for both novices and experienced professionals.

Chapter 2 embarks on a comprehensive exploration of vectors and their pivotal roles in AI, from fundamental properties to advanced applications within LLMs. Starting with the core mathematical principles of vectors, we will traverse through concepts like vector spaces, projection, similarity measures, and transformations. These foundational insights will set the stage for understanding vectors as not only mathematical abstractions but also as tools driving complex AI systems. This intersection of linear algebra and machine learning ultimately forms the bedrock of modern AI, enabling the translation of raw, unstructured data into structured, meaningful representations that fuel intelligent systems.

Chapter 3 discusses Milvus, a scalable vector database that follows a micro-services architecture, and how its components are divided into core micro-services as well as third-party dependencies, and how this architecture ensures modularity, scalability, and flexibility, especially in distributed environments like Kubernetes.

Chapter 4 explains how Milvus manages and stores vector data at scale. The readers will gain insights into the different types of indexes, the importance of metadata, the system's partitioning and sharding strategies, and how the decoupling of compute and storage enhances the scalability and flexibility of the system. These capabilities make Milvus a powerful tool for managing high-dimensional data across a wide range of industries and applications.

Chapter 5 examines how Milvus efficiently balances the need for indexing accuracy with the constraints of system resources, helping users to choose the best indexing strategy for their specific use cases. Thus, whether you are building a recommendation system, a semantic search engine, or a machine learning pipeline, understanding these indexing mechanisms is crucial for leveraging Milvus's full potential.

Chapter 6 delves deeper into the mechanisms behind these three types of indexes—sparse, binary, and GPU—exploring their respective use cases, implementation details, and performance considerations within Milvus. By understanding the strengths and limitations of each index type, developers can make informed decisions about the most appropriate indexing strategy for their specific application, ultimately achieving optimal search performance and resource efficiency.

Chapter 7 explores the distributed data management features of Milvus in detail, including its storage, indexing, and querying mechanisms. We will cover how Milvus handles data partitioning and replication, ensuring scalability and fault tolerance. Additionally, we will dive into the processes involved in setting up and managing a distributed Milvus deployment, examining the key components that work together to deliver high-performance results in production environments.

Chapter 8 discusses Distributed Index Management, which involves splitting the index across multiple machines or nodes in a distributed system. This enables the system to handle vast amounts of data, and perform faster searches by leveraging parallelism, load balancing, and fault tolerance.

Chapter 9 delves into the various aspects of the Proxy in Milvus, examining its architecture, responsibilities, and how it enables the system to scale and perform efficiently in a distributed environment. We will also explore how the Proxy ensures fault tolerance, high availability, and load balancing, crucial for distributed vector search applications. Milvus is also used in fraud detection and cybersecurity, where outlier or anomaly vectors are indexed and queried to identify unusual patterns or behaviors.

Chapter 10 explores how Milvus harnesses the power of GPUs to optimize vector searches. We will delve into the architecture of GPU acceleration within Milvus, the different types of optimizations applied, and how these optimizations enhance the performance of common operations such as similarity searches, indexing, and retrieval in a variety of use cases.

Chapter 11 explores the crucial roles of Kafka, and Pulsar in enabling Milvus to scale, ensure consistency, and efficiently manage metadata, configuration, and inter-node communication. These technologies work in concert to support Milvus' distributed operations, ensuring that it can handle large-scale data ingestion, search, and real-time analytics, while maintaining high performance and reliability.

Chapter 12 highlights how Milvus is a high-performance, open-source vector database for large-scale similarity search across billions of data points. It underpins real-time applications such as machine learning pipelines, recommendation systems, and search engines. Efficient, reliable client connections are critical to achieving low-latency, high-throughput performance. Milvus supports multiple interaction methods, including language-specific SDKs and network protocols like gRPC and RESTful APIs. Through these, clients can insert data, run vector searches, and perform real-time updates. This chapter explains how connections are established, which protocols are involved, how various SDKs and tools integrate with Milvus, and the best practices for managing connections from setup through query execution and ongoing system maintenance.

DID YOU KNOW

Did you know that Orange Education Pvt Ltd offers eBook versions of every book published, with PDF and ePub files available? You can upgrade to the eBook version at **www.orangeava.com** and as a print book customer, you are entitled to a discount on the eBook copy. Get in touch with us at: **info@orangeava.com** for more details.

At **www.orangeava.com**, you can also read a collection of free technical articles, sign up for a range of free newsletters, and receive exclusive discounts and offers on Print Books and eBooks.

PIRACY

If you come across any illegal copies of our works in any form on the internet, we would be grateful if you would provide us with the location address or website name. Please contact us at **info@orangeava.com** with a link to the material.

ARE YOU INTERESTED IN AUTHORING WITH US?

If there is a topic that you have expertise in, and you are interested in either writing or contributing to a book, please write to us at **business@orangeava.com**. We are on a journey to help developers and tech professionals to gain insights on the present technological advancements and innovations happening across the globe and build a community that believes Knowledge is best acquired by sharing and learning with others. Please reach out to us to learn what our audience demands and how you can be part of this educational reform. We also welcome ideas from tech experts and help them build learning and development content for their domains.

REVIEWS

Please leave a review. Once you have read and used this book, why not leave a review on the site that you purchased it from? Potential readers can then see and use your unbiased opinion to make purchase decisions. We at Orange Education would love to know what you think about our products, and our authors can learn from your feedback. Thank you!

For more information about Orange Education, please visit **www.orangeava.com**.

Table of Contents

Chapter 1
Introduction to Vector Databases

Introduction

As data escaped the neat rows and columns of classical databases and began to live as text, images, audio, code, and graphs of relationships, a new geometry became necessary. Vector databases emerged to meet this shift. They store meaning rather than labels by representing data as high-dimensional vectors produced by embeddings. In this space, similarity becomes a distance problem, not a keyword match. This makes vector databases indispensable for modern AI systems like semantic search, recommendation engines, RAG pipelines, fraud detection, and multimodal assistants, where relevance depends on context and intent rather than exact matches. Their rise mirrors the transition from rule-based software to representation-based learning, where understanding emerges from proximity in latent space.

Mastery of vector databases is mastery of AI at scale because they sit at the junction of models, data, and systems. Knowing how vectors are generated, indexed, sharded, compressed, and queried allows engineers to reason about latency, recall, drift, and cost, not just accuracy. At scale, naive similarity search collapses under its own weight, and only a deep understanding of approximate nearest neighbor algorithms, embedding lifecycle management, and feedback loops keeps systems reliable and adaptive. In short, models think, but vector databases remember and retrieve meaning efficiently. Understanding these turns AI from a clever demo into an industrial, evolving intelligence. In this chapter, we aim to provide a comprehensive introduction to vector databases, an emerging technology in the field of data management and machine learning. Our objective is to elucidate the fundamental concepts, architectures, and applications of vector databases, making this chapter a valuable resource for both novices and experienced professionals.

Structure

In this chapter, we will cover the following topics:

- Introduction to Vector Databases
- Exploring Use Cases
- Understanding the Architecture
- Indexing Techniques
- Scalability and Performance

Introduction to Vector Databases

A vector database is designed to store and manage high-dimensional data, which traditional Database Management Systems (DBMS) struggle to handle effectively. This innovative type of database utilizes mathematical representations known as vectors, which can consist of numerous dimensions, typically ranging from tens to thousands, depending on the complexity of data. These vectors are generated from various forms of data, including text, images, audio, and video, allowing for sophisticated analysis and retrieval capabilities that go beyond simple keyword matching. Vector databases facilitate fast and precise similarity searches, making them essential for applications in machine learning, natural language processing, and computer vision. They also support the integration of Large Language Models (LLMs), enhancing the capabilities for tasks such as semantic search, real-time knowledge retrieval, and reducing inaccuracies often encountered in LLM outputs, commonly referred to as "hallucination".

Differences between Vector and Relational and NoSQL DBMS

Let us understand the differences between Vector and Relational Databases with an example. Consider a scenario where a user wants to find images similar to a specific photo. In a vector database, the user can input the photo, and the database will retrieve images based on their visual features represented as high-dimensional vectors. In contrast, a traditional database would require the user to search using keywords or exact matches, which may not yield the desired results based on similarity.

The following table demonstrates the key differences:

Vector Databases	Relational Databases
Store data as high-dimensional vectors that represent features or attributes of complex data types (like images, text).	Use structured data formats that fit rigid schemas, typically handling rows and columns.
Vector databases use a special methodology called as Semantic Search to perform the Search Capability. By using, Semantic Search, Vector Databases find the items based on the similarity and not just the exact matches. This is particularly useful for applications like recommendation systems or natural language processing.	Traditional Databases typically perform searches based on exact terms or defined criteria, limiting their ability to understand context.
Vector Databases can handle unstructured and complex data types such as images, audio and video, which are transformed into vectors for storage and retrieval.	Traditional Databases mainly support structured data, making them less effective for handling diverse data types.
Vector Databases are commonly used in applications requiring real-time knowledge search, semantic search, and machine learning integration.	Traditional Databases are often struggle with high-dimensionality due to dimensionality catastrophe.

Table 1.1: *RDBMS versus Vector Databases*

Exploring Use Cases

Vector databases have become increasingly important due to the rise of machine learning, AI, and other advanced computational tasks that require the processing and retrieval of high-dimensional data. These databases are optimized for storing and querying vector representations of data, typically generated by models such as embeddings from deep learning models. The detailed use cases of the Vector Databases are as following;

Search and Information Retrieval

Search and information retrieval form one of the core essence of the needs of the data management systems where users data is sliced and managed according to the needs of the individual applications.

In this section, we delve into the fundamentals of such systems and how vectors play such an important role in the storage and management of such data retrieval systems.

Semantic Search: What is Semantic Search

Semantic search retrieves information based on meaning and intent rather than exact keywords, using embeddings to understand context. It enables systems to find what you mean, not just what you type, even when the words differ.

For example, if a user searches for "how to cool a room without AC," a keyword-based system might prioritize documents containing "cool," "room," and "AC," even if they are irrelevant. A semantic search system, however, recognizes the goal of the user—finding alternative cooling methods—and could surface results about fans, cross-ventilation, or thermal curtains, even if those terms are not explicitly mentioned in the query.

Instead of relying solely on keyword matching, vector databases enable semantic search by allowing text embeddings to be stored. This enables search engines to better understand the context and meaning of queries and documents, resulting in more relevant search results. Instead of relying solely on keyword matching, vector databases enable semantic search by allowing text embeddings to be stored. This enables search engines to better understand the context and meaning of queries and documents, resulting in more relevant search results.

On an e-commerce platform, various product descriptions are embedded into vectors representing their semantic meaning. When a user searches for "comfortable running shoes," the query is also converted into a vector. The vector database then retrieves products with similar vector representations, ensuring that items such as "Lightweight sneakers for jogging" are included in the search results, even if they do not explicitly mention "running shoes."

This approach ensures that the search is more context-aware, improving the relevance of the results and enhancing the user experience.

Image and Video Search

By having visual embeddings from images and videos stored in vector databases, searches based on visual similarity are enabled. Users are allowed to search for images or videos that are visually similar to a given input, even if the metadata does not explicitly match.

On a media platform, embeddings of images and videos are created based on their visual content and stored as vectors in a vector database. When a user provides an image of a "red sports car" as an input, the query is converted into a vector that captures the visual characteristics of the car. The vector database then retrieves images or videos with similar visual embeddings, ensuring that other visually similar "red sports cars" are included in the search results, even if they are labeled differently.

This approach allows for a more intuitive and accurate search experience, as users can visualize the related content without relying solely on metadata.

Recommendation Systems

A subset of search and retrieval systems, recommendation engines slice the data by understanding repeated patterns according to multiple cross sections of filters enabling the system to predict and suggest patterns to users or to use business management teams.

- **Content-Based Recommendations:** Embeddings of user preferences and item attributes can be stored in vector databases. Recommendations are generated by identifying the nearest neighbors (similar vectors) in this high-dimensional space, resulting in personalized content delivery.

  On a streaming platform, user preferences and content attributes are embedded into vectors and stored in a vector database. When a user interacts with a particular movie or series, the platform retrieves similar content by finding vectors that are close to the preferred vector of the user. For instance, if a user frequently watches "action thrillers," the platform recommends other action-packed titles with similar thematic elements, even if the titles are not explicitly labeled as "action thrillers."

  This approach ensures that recommendations are more aligned with the tastes of the user, enhancing the overall user experience through personalized content suggestions.

- **Collaborative Filtering:** By embedding users and items into the same vector space, vector databases enable the efficient computation of similarity scores. Recommendations are made based on the preferences of other users with similar tastes.

  In an online shopping platform, user behavior and product attributes are embedded into a shared vector space. When a user interacts with certain products, the system identifies other users with similar behavior patterns by finding vectors close to the vector of the user in the space. The platform then recommends products that these similar users have liked or purchased.

  This approach allows for personalized recommendations based on collective user behavior, ensuring that users discover products they are likely to enjoy based on the preferences of others with similar tastes.

Anomaly Detection

Systems which understand undesirable usage patterns leading to abuse of either the systems, business or users and try to prevent them are called Anomaly Detection and Management Systems.

- **Fraud Detection:** In financial transactions, network security, and other domains, embeddings of typical behavior can be stored in vector databases. Anomalous activities are detected by measuring the distance of new data points from these embeddings, allowing potential fraud or irregularities to be identified.

  In a banking system, typical transaction behaviors are embedded into vectors and stored in a vector database. When a new transaction occurs, its vector is compared against the stored vectors representing normal behavior. If the vector of the new transaction is significantly distant from the typical behavior vectors, it is flagged as potentially fraudulent.

  This approach enables the early detection of suspicious activities, helping to prevent fraud by identifying irregular patterns that deviate from the norm.

- **Industrial Monitoring:** In manufacturing or other industries, sensor data can be embedded and stored in a vector database. Anomalies in machine operations or production processes are detected by identifying deviations from the norm in the vector space.

  In a manufacturing plant, sensor readings from machines are continuously embedded into vectors and stored in a vector database. These vectors represent normal operating conditions. When new sensor data is received, its vector is compared to the stored vectors. If a significant deviation from the normal pattern is detected, the system flags it as an anomaly, indicating potential issues in the operation of the machine.

  This approach allows for proactive maintenance by identifying irregularities early, reducing downtime and improving the overall efficiency of industrial operations.

Natural Language Processing (NLP)

Bringing computation for all users has the implicit need for computers to understand language data. However, simple the problem statement might look has captured the interest of the global community.

- **Text Classification:** By having text embeddings stored in vector databases, the classification of documents, emails, or other text data is facilitated. This is particularly useful in applications such as spam detection, sentiment analysis, and topic categorization.

  In an email system, emails are embedded into vectors based on their content and stored in a vector database. When a new email arrives, its vector is compared against pre-labeled vectors representing categories such as "spam," "important," or "promotional." The system then classifies the email accordingly. For instance, if the vector closely aligns with the "spam" vectors, the email is flagged as spam.

This approach improves the accuracy of text classification tasks, ensuring that documents or messages are correctly categorized based on their content.

- **Large Language Models (LLMs):** By having text and other data embeddings stored in vector databases, the retrieval of relevant information during text generation or query handling is facilitated. This enhances the ability of LLMs to produce accurate, contextually aware, and coherent outputs.

  In a chatbot system, user queries are embedded into vectors and stored in a vector database. When a new query is received, its vector is compared against stored vectors representing similar queries or relevant information. The LLM then generates a response based on the most relevant retrieved content, improving the accuracy and relevance of its answers.

  This approach allows LLMs to handle complex queries more effectively by leveraging stored embeddings that capture the semantic meaning of the data.

- **Retrieval-Augmented Generation (RAG):** By storing embeddings of external knowledge in vector databases, the retrieval of relevant information to augment text generation is enabled. This allows RAG systems to generate more informed and contextually accurate content.

  In a research assistant application, external documents and datasets are embedded into vectors and stored in a vector database. When the system is tasked with generating a report on a specific topic, it retrieves the most relevant information by comparing vectors in the database. The retrieved data is then used to inform the generative process, ensuring the output is up-to-date and contextually rich.

  This approach improves the quality and relevance of content generated by RAG systems, particularly when specific or recent information is required.

Drug Discovery and Drug Prediction

Drug discovery is the scientific process of identifying new compounds that can treat or prevent diseases. Researchers study biological targets such as proteins or genes and screen thousands of molecules to find those that interact effectively with them. Promising compounds are then optimized and tested through laboratory studies and clinical trials to ensure safety and effectiveness before becoming medicines.

Molecular Similarity Search

By representing molecules as high-dimensional vectors based on their properties and storing these embeddings in vector databases, the search for similar molecules is facilitated. This capability is particularly valuable in drug discovery, where finding molecules with similar properties can accelerate the development of new treatments.

In a drug discovery project, the chemical structures of various compounds are embedded into vectors and stored in a vector database. When researchers identify a molecule with desirable properties, they can query the database to find other molecules with similar vector representations. This enables them to quickly identify potential drug candidates that share similar characteristics with the molecule of interest.

This approach significantly speeds up the drug discovery process by allowing researchers to efficiently explore chemical space and identify promising compounds.

Financial Services

AI in financial services enables institutions to analyze vast amounts of financial data to detect patterns, risks, and opportunities in real time. It powers applications such as fraud detection, credit scoring, algorithmic trading, and personalized financial recommendations.

- **Credit Scoring:** By storing and processing embeddings of financial histories, behaviors, and transactions in vector databases, more accurate and real-time credit scoring is enabled. This enhances the ability to evaluate creditworthiness based on a comprehensive analysis of the financial data of an individual.

  In a credit scoring system, embeddings representing various aspects of the financial history of a person, such as transaction patterns, credit usage, and repayment behavior, is stored in a vector database. When a new credit application is evaluated, the system retrieves and compares the financial embeddings of the applicant with those of similar profiles stored in the database. This allows for a nuanced assessment of the credit risk of the applicant, leading to more accurate and timely credit scores.

  This approach improves the precision of credit scoring by leveraging detailed embeddings, allowing for better-informed lending decisions and enhanced risk management.

- **Portfolio Management:** By representing financial portfolios as vectors based on asset characteristics and storing these embeddings in vector databases, quick comparisons and optimizations are facilitated. This approach helps in improving returns and reducing risks associated with portfolio management.

  In a portfolio management system, different portfolios are embedded into vectors that capture asset characteristics such as risk levels, returns, and market correlations. When evaluating or optimizing a portfolio, the system queries the vector database to find similar portfolios or benchmark against optimal vectors. This allows for efficient analysis and adjustment of asset allocations to enhance portfolio performance and mitigate risks.

This approach streamlines the process of portfolio optimization, enabling more informed decision-making and better alignment with investment goals.

Content Moderation

- **Detection of Harmful Content:** By storing embeddings of flagged content, such as hate speech or adult content, in vector databases, real-time detection and moderation of harmful content are enabled. This allows for the effective identification and management of inappropriate content by comparing embeddings of new content against stored flagged embeddings.

  In a content moderation system, various types of harmful content are embedded into vectors and stored in a vector database. When new user-generated content is submitted, its vector is compared to the stored vectors representing harmful content. If the vector of the new content is found to be similar to flagged embeddings, it is flagged for review or automatically moderated to prevent its dissemination.

  This approach enhances content moderation by enabling prompt and accurate detection of harmful material, ensuring a safer and more compliant online environment.

- **Automatic Tagging and Categorization:** By embedding content metadata into vectors and storing these embeddings in vector databases, the process of automatically tagging and categorizing user-generated content on social platforms is facilitated. This approach streamlines content organization and enhances discoverability.

  On a social media platform, content such as posts, images, and videos are embedded into vectors based on their metadata, like themes, topics, and user interactions. When new content is uploaded, its vector is compared to stored vectors representing various tags and categories. The system then automatically assigns relevant tags or categories to the new content based on the closest matches, improving the efficiency of content management and user experience.

  This approach ensures that user-generated content is systematically organized, making it easier for users to discover and engage with relevant material.

Knowledge Graphs and Ontologies

Knowledge graphs and ontologies use AI to organize information into interconnected entities, relationships, and concepts, creating structured representations of knowledge. AI techniques help automatically extract relationships from large datasets and continuously enrich these graphs.

- **Entity Linking:** By storing entity embeddings in vector databases, linking entities in knowledge graphs is facilitated through comparison of these embeddings. This aids in integrating data from various sources, ensuring consistency and enriching the knowledge graph.

  In a knowledge graph, entities such as people, organizations, or concepts are represented by embeddings and stored in a vector database. When integrating data from different sources, the system compares the embeddings of new entities with those in the database to identify and link equivalent entities. For instance, if two data sources refer to the same person with slightly different names, their embeddings are compared to determine they represent the same entity, allowing for unified and comprehensive data integration.

  This approach enhances the accuracy and completeness of knowledge graphs by effectively linking related entities across diverse datasets.

- **Relationship Discovery:** By storing and analyzing vector representations of entities and their relationships, vector databases assist in discovering hidden relationships and insights within knowledge graphs. This enables the identification of previously unknown connections and patterns.

  In a knowledge graph, entities and their relationships are represented as vectors and stored in a vector database. By analyzing these vectors, the system can uncover hidden relationships between entities that were not explicitly documented. For instance, if the vectors of two entities are found to be closely related in the vector space, the system might reveal an implicit connection between them, such as a shared affiliation or influence. This discovery can lead to new insights and enhance the depth of the knowledge graph.

  This approach improves the ability to explore and understand complex networks of relationships, uncovering valuable insights and enhancing data analysis.

Understanding the Architecture

At its core, Milvus combines vector indexes with metadata filtering and coordination services, allowing it to scale horizontally while maintaining consistency and performance. This architecture makes it well-suited for production-grade semantic search, recommendations, and retrieval-augmented generation systems.

- **Data Representation:** Data is converted into high-dimensional vectors using embedding functions, such as machine learning models or feature extraction algorithms. This transformation allows the database to handle diverse data types, including text, images, audio, and video.

- **Storage Techniques:**
    - **Sharding:** Data is distributed across multiple machines or clusters (shards) to enhance scalability and performance. Sharding can be done through hash-based or range-based methods to balance load and avoid hotspots.
    - **Partitioning:** The database is divided into smaller, manageable segments based on specific criteria (like geographic location or category) to improve usability and query performance.
- **Caching:** Caching strategies, such as Least Recently Used (LRU) or partitioned caching, are implemented to optimize resource utilization by storing frequently accessed vector data.
- **Data Replication:** Multiple copies of data are created across different nodes to ensure availability and durability. Replication methods include leaderless and leader-follower approaches, each balancing consistency and performance differently.
- **Indexing and Search:** Efficient indexing is crucial for handling high-dimensional vector data. Techniques like Approximate Nearest Neighbor (ANN) search and graph-based search methods facilitate quick and accurate similarity searches.
- **Support for Diverse Vector Types:** Vector databases accommodate various vector types (for example, dense, sparse, binary) and their unique characteristics, necessitating a flexible indexing system.
- **Distributed Processing:** To manage large-scale data and queries, vector databases support distributed parallel processing, addressing challenges like load balancing and fault tolerance.
- **Integration with Machine Learning Frameworks:** Seamless integration with popular machine learning frameworks (like TensorFlow, PyTorch) is essential for generating and utilizing vector embeddings, requiring robust APIs and connectors.
- **Cross-Modal Support:** Vector databases enable cross-modal searches, allowing users to retrieve relevant data across different formats (text, images, and the like.), thus enhancing the richness of search results.
- **Real-Time Knowledge Retrieval:** Real-time search capabilities are supported, providing access to the latest information and minimizing the chances of generating inaccurate results (hallucination).

Indexing Techniques

Vector similarity search is computationally expensive by nature. A naive brute-force search compares a query vector against every stored vector, an approach that collapses under scale. Milvus addresses this by supporting **Approximate Nearest Neighbor (ANN)** indexing techniques that trade a small amount of accuracy for massive gains in speed, memory efficiency, and scalability.

Milvus is architected to support **multiple index types**, allowing practitioners to choose the right geometric shortcut based on data size, dimensionality, latency requirements, recall targets, and hardware availability. These index types broadly fall into **CPU-optimized** and **GPU-accelerated** families.

CPU-Based Indexing Techniques in Milvus

CPU indexes are the most widely used in production due to their maturity, flexibility, and lower infrastructure cost. They are implemented primarily using FAISS and custom Milvus logic.

FLAT (Brute Force)

Category:CPU

Type: Exact search

FLAT indexing performs a full linear scan over all vectors, computing exact distances. There is no approximation, no compression, and no clever geometry.

Characteristics:

- Highest recall (100%)
- No preprocessing or training
- Extremely high latency at scale
- Linear growth in compute cost

Use cases:

- Small datasets
- Ground truth evaluation
- Debugging or benchmarking other indexes

FLAT is the philosophical baseline, the Platonic ideal of similarity, but impractical beyond modest data sizes.

IVF (Inverted File Index)

Category:CPU

Type: Coarse quantization + ANN

IVF partitions the vector space into clusters using k-means. Each vector is assigned to a centroid, and searches only probe a subset of clusters (nprobe) instead of the entire dataset.

Key parameters:

- nlist: number of clusters
- nprobe: number of clusters searched at query time

Characteristics:

- Significant speedup over FLAT
- Tunable recall versus latency
- Requires training phase
- Performance degrades if clusters are poorly balanced

Use cases:

- Medium to large datasets
- When latency matters but recall can be tuned
- General-purpose semantic search

IVF turns the search problem from "search everywhere" into "search where it makes sense."

IVF_PQ (Inverted File + Product Quantization)

Category:CPU

Type: ANN + vector compression

IVF_PQ builds on IVF by compressing vectors using **Product Quantization (PQ)**. Vectors are split into subspaces, each quantized separately, dramatically reducing memory usage.

Characteristics:

- Much lower memory footprint
- Faster cache-friendly search
- Lower recall than IVF_FLAT
- Training complexity is higher

Use cases:

- Very large datasets (hundreds of millions to billions)
- Memory-constrained environments
- Recommendation systems at scale

IVF_PQ is where geometry meets thrift, squeezing vectors into compact symbolic representations.

HNSW (Hierarchical Navigable Small World Graph)

Category:CPU

Type: Graph-based ANN

HNSW builds a multi-layer graph where vectors are nodes connected by proximity edges. Search becomes a greedy graph traversal rather than a partitioned lookup.

Key parameters:

- M: graph connectivity
- efConstruction: build-time accuracy
- efSearch: query-time accuracy

Characteristics:

- Very high recall with low latency
- No clustering step
- High memory usage
- Slower index build time

Use cases:

- High-recall semantic search
- RAG pipelines
- Interactive AI systems

HNSW behaves like a well-designed city map: local roads, highways, and shortcuts—all working together.

SCANN (Selective Search, Limited Support)

Category:CPU

Type: Hybrid ANN

SCANN combines tree partitioning with asymmetric hashing. Despite being powerful, its support in Milvus is more limited compared to IVF and HNSW.

Characteristics:

- Good speed-recall tradeoff
- Complex tuning
- Less commonly deployed

GPU-Based Indexing Techniques in Milvus

GPU indexing is designed for **extreme throughput** and **real-time workloads**, trading hardware cost for massive parallelism.

GPU_FLAT

Category:GPU

Type: Exact search

GPU_FLAT performs brute-force search using CUDA cores. While still O(N), it exploits GPU parallelism to reduce latency dramatically.

Characteristics:

- Exact results
- Very high throughput
- High GPU memory usage
- Limited by GPU VRAM

Use cases:

- Real-time exact search
- Small to medium datasets
- Latency-critical applications

GPU_IVF_FLAT

Category:GPU

Type: ANN

This is the GPU-accelerated version of IVF_FLAT. Clustering and probing are executed on the GPU.

Characteristics:

- Orders-of-magnitude faster than CPU IVF
- Requires careful memory management
- GPU memory bound

Use cases:

- Large-scale semantic search
- Real-time recommendation systems
- Streaming inference pipelines

GPU_IVF_PQ

Category:GPU

Type: ANN + compression

It combines GPU parallelism with PQ compression.

Characteristics:

- Best for massive datasets
- Excellent throughput
- Slightly lower recall
- More complex deployment

Use cases:

- Billion-scale vector databases
- Enterprise-grade AI platforms
- Multitenant AI systems

CPU versus GPU Indexing: A Strategic View

CPU indexing processes data sequentially or with limited parallelism, making it efficient for complex logic and smaller datasets. GPU indexing uses massive parallel cores to build and query indexes across large datasets much faster. As a result, GPUs excel in high-throughput tasks like vector search, large-scale analytics, and AI workloads

Dimensions	CPU Indexes	GPU Indexes
Cost	Lower	Higher
Latency	Moderate	Very low
Throughput	Limited	Extremely high
Memory	RAM-based	VRAM-limited
Deployment	Easier	More complex
Use Case	General production	Real-time, hyperscale

Table 1.2: *CPU versus GPU Indexing*

In practice, many Milvus deployments adopt **hybrid architectures**, using CPU indexes for long-term storage and GPU indexes for hot or frequently queried data.

Scalability and Performance

Scalability is the ability of a system to handle increasing workloads by efficiently adding resources such as compute, memory, or storage. Performance measures how quickly and efficiently the system processes tasks under a given load. Well-designed systems balance both, ensuring that performance remains stable even as scale grows.

Indexing Techniques

- **Description:** Efficient indexing is crucial for fast retrieval of high-dimensional vectors. Techniques such as Approximate Nearest Neighbor (ANN) search and graph-based indexing improve search speed and accuracy.
- **Mechanism:** Indexing structures like HNSW (Hierarchical Navigable Small World) graphs or LSH (Locality Sensitive Hashing) are used to quickly locate nearest neighbors in high-dimensional space.

Caching Strategies

- **Description:** Caching frequently accessed vectors or query results reduces the need for repetitive computations, improving response times.
- **Mechanism:** Implementations like Least Recently Used (LRU) or partitioned caching store recent queries and vector results in memory, enabling faster access.

Efficient Query Processing

- **Description:** Vector databases optimize query processing through techniques such as vector quantization and dimensionality reduction, which enhance performance without compromising accuracy.
- **Mechanism:** Methods like Product Quantization (PQ) or Principal Component Analysis (PCA) reduce the complexity of similarity searches by approximating high-dimensional vectors with lower-dimensional representations.

Real-Time Data Handling

- **Description:** For applications requiring real-time updates and queries, vector databases are optimized to handle rapid data ingestion and querying.
- **Mechanism:** Stream processing frameworks and in-memory data structures enable real-time analytics and quick retrieval of newly added vectors.

Fault Tolerance and High Availability

- **Description:** To ensure continuous operation and reliability, vector databases implement fault tolerance and high availability strategies.

- **Mechanism:** Data replication and redundancy mechanisms ensure that data is preserved across failures, and failover strategies allow for uninterrupted service.

Conclusion

Vector databases have emerged as a foundational component of modern AI systems, reshaping how machines store, search, and reason over unstructured data. As intelligence shifted from rule-driven logic to representation learning, data began to be encoded as high-dimensional vectors that capture semantic meaning rather than explicit structure. Traditional relational and keyword-based databases struggle in this regime, as they are optimized for exact matches and fixed schemas. Vector databases address this gap by enabling efficient similarity search over embeddings, making them indispensable in an era dominated by large language models, multimodal AI, and context-aware applications.

From an application standpoint, vector databases serve as the backbone for a wide range of intelligent systems. They power semantic search engines that understand intent beyond keywords, recommendation systems that learn taste and behavior, and retrieval-augmented generation pipelines that ground language models in external knowledge. Their relevance spans domains such as enterprise search, customer support automation, healthcare, finance, robotics, defense, and scientific discovery. Any system that must reason over meaning, relationships, or perception rather than rigid identifiers naturally benefits from vector-based storage and retrieval. As embeddings become the universal interface between data and models, vector databases act as the connective tissue that binds learning to memory.

Performance and scalability are where vector databases distinguish themselves as production-grade infrastructure rather than experimental tools. By employing approximate nearest neighbor indexing techniques, intelligent partitioning, compression, and distributed execution, they can handle millions to billions of vectors while maintaining low latency and high throughput. Modern vector databases are designed to scale horizontally, decouple compute from storage, and adapt to evolving data distributions without retraining entire systems. This ability to sustain semantic performance under massive data growth transforms AI from a laboratory artifact into a reliable, industrial capability. In essence, vector databases are not just faster storage engines; they are enablers of scalable intelligence in the data-rich world.

The upcoming chapter will focus on the basics of the mathematical principles of Vectors and how it forms the building block of AI systems to later investigate how Vector systems handle this data form which is the interjection of the development of the next generation of computing applications.

CHAPTER 2
Fundamentals of Vectors and AI

Introduction

Vectors serve as the foundational building blocks of artificial intelligence, enabling the transformation of complex data into structured, mathematical forms that machines can interpret and process. In essence, a vector is a fundamental element within a vector space, defined by properties such as linearity, dimensionality, and orientation. These attributes allow vectors to represent not only simple numeric values but also rich, multidimensional relationships within data. In the context of artificial intelligence and, more specifically, Large Language Models (LLMs), vectors facilitate the nuanced representation of linguistic and contextual information.

At the heart of any machine learning model lies the need for data representation. In Natural Language Processing (NLP), data representation is particularly challenging, given the inherent complexity of human language. Here, vectors are essential in transforming words, phrases, and even entire texts into embeddings—dense, high-dimensional vectors that capture semantic relationships. This vectorized approach allows LLMs to recognize and interpret relationships between words, such as similarity, analogy, and context, thereby bridging raw linguistic input with computational understanding. By representing each word or phrase as a vector in an embedding space, these models can harness geometric properties like distance, angle, and direction to perform operations that resemble linguistic intuition.

Vectors in artificial intelligence extend beyond mere representation. They enable key operations central to machine learning, such as calculating distances to determine similarity, projecting data into lower-dimensional spaces for efficiency, and transforming inputs using linear mappings. For instance, in large-scale models like transformers, vectors enable the model to attend selectively to specific parts of an input, enhancing its ability to understand context across long sequences. This capacity is crucial in the "attention mechanism," where vectors known as queries, keys, and values facilitate weighted focus on relevant data points within a sequence.

This chapter embarks on a comprehensive exploration of vectors and their pivotal roles in AI, from fundamental properties to advanced applications within LLMs. Starting with the core mathematical principles of vectors, we will traverse through concepts like vector spaces, projection, similarity measures, and transformations. These foundational insights will set the stage for understanding vectors as not only mathematical abstractions but also as tools driving complex AI systems. This intersection of linear algebra and machine learning ultimately forms the bedrock of modern AI, enabling the translation of raw, unstructured data into structured, meaningful representations that fuel intelligent systems.

Structure

In this chapter, we will cover the following topics:

- Representation of Data in AI Systems
- Need for Vector Embeddings in the Growth of Precision AI Models
- Mathematics of Vector Operations
- Recurrent Neural Networks
- Transformer Based Neural Networks

Background: Representing Language in AI Systems

In AI, representing human language in a way that machines can understand is crucial but challenging. Over time, language representation methods have evolved from simple frequency-based approaches to sophisticated embeddings that capture deep semantic meanings. This section explores the progression of these techniques, highlighting their advantages, limitations, and the reasons for transitioning to embeddings.

Early Methods of Text Representation

Traditional text representation methods focused primarily on the presence and frequency of words, without considering relationships, context, or meaning. Here are two foundational approaches:

Bag of Words (BoW)

The **Bag of Words (BoW)** model represents a document as a collection (or "bag") of words. This approach creates a vocabulary from all unique words across documents and counts the occurrence of each word in each document. Although straightforward, BoW suffers from significant drawbacks:

- **No Order**: BoW disregards the order of words, losing the structure of the sentence. This means "I reset my password" and "My password reset I" appear identical.
- **Sparse Vectors**: For large vocabularies, the resulting vectors are high-dimensional and sparse (containing many zeros), requiring substantial memory and computation.
- **Lack of Context**: Each word is treated as an independent feature, so "good" and "bad" have no inherent relation even though they convey opposite sentiments.

Example: If the sentence is "Reset my password," and the vocabulary includes ["reset," "password," "update", "shipping"], the BoW vector might look like:

Vector: [1, 1, 0, 0]

This vector simply indicates the presence of "reset" and "password," but it does not capture the purpose or context of the sentence.

Term Frequency-Inverse Document Frequency (TF-IDF)

TF-IDF improves on BoW by weighting terms based on their importance within a document relative to a larger set of documents. It combines **Term Frequency (TF)** (how often a word appears in a document) with **Inverse Document Frequency (IDF)** (how common the word is across all documents), assigning higher weights to rarer words that appear frequently in a specific document.

TF-IDF Vector Calculation: For a term ttt in a document ddd within a collection DDD:

- TF(t) = (Number of times term ttt appears in document ddd) / (Total number of terms in ddd)
- IDF(t) = log(Total number of documents in DDD / Number of documents containing ttt)

For example, in a customer support dataset, "password" might receive a higher TF-IDF score in documents discussing login issues and a lower score in general discussions. Despite being an improvement, TF-IDF shares several limitations with BoW, such as ignoring word order and context.

Limitations of Traditional Methods

Both BoW and TF-IDF approaches have limitations that affect their ability to capture the depth of language:

- **High-Dimensionality and Sparsity**: As vocabulary grows, the feature vectors become larger and sparser, slowing down processing and increasing memory requirements.
- **Context Insensitivity**: Neither BoW nor TF-IDF accounts for word context or relationships. They treat "good" and "bad" as independent terms, missing nuances such as sarcasm or sentiment.
- **Semantic Similarity**: These methods cannot recognize similarity between semantically related words or phrases, like "happy" and "joyful" or "reset my password" and "change my password."

These limitations led researchers to explore new ways to represent language more meaningfully, resulting in a shift toward embeddings.

Embeddings: A Paradigm Shift in Language Representation

To overcome the limitations of traditional methods, **embeddings** were introduced, marking a breakthrough in NLP and AI. Embeddings are dense, fixed-size vectors that capture the semantic meaning of words or sentences in a continuous vector space. Unlike sparse, high-dimensional BoW or TF-IDF vectors, embeddings use smaller dimensions (often hundreds) where each dimension represents learned features capturing context, relationships, and meaning.

Word Embeddings

Early embedding techniques like **Word2Vec** (developed by Google) and **GloVe** (by Stanford) revolutionized NLP by capturing relationships between words based on their context in large text corpora.

- **Word2Vec** uses a neural network to predict a word based on its surrounding words (or vice versa). Words used in similar contexts are placed closer in the vector space.
- **GloVe** represents words based on the global statistical co-occurrence of words in a corpus, ensuring words with similar meanings are embedded close to each other.

Example: For instance, "king" and "queen" are closely related, and Word2Vec models capture this by learning that king–man+woman=queen\text{king} - \text{man} + \text{woman} = \text{queen}king–man+woman=queen, demonstrating embeddings' ability to encode analogies.

Sentence Embeddings

With advancements in deep learning, especially **Transformer-based models** like **BERT** and **Sentence-BERT**, embeddings evolved to capture the meaning of entire sentences and even paragraphs. Sentence embeddings account for not only individual words but also their relationships, context, and position, producing a vector representation that is sensitive to the full sentence structure and meaning.

- **Contextual Encoding**: Words in a sentence influence the meaning of each other, so "bank" in “river bank” has a different vector representation than "bank" in “savings bank.”

- **Fine-Tuned Representations**: These models are pre-trained on massive corpora and fine-tuned for specific tasks, ensuring that the embeddings align closely with the task at hand.

Example: The sentence “How can I reset my password?” is converted to a dense vector, say, [0.12, -0.34, 0.56, ..., 0.87], capturing the full context of the request. This allows the system to compare it meaningfully to similar sentences, such as “Can you help me change my password?”

Why Embeddings are Essential in Modern AI

Embeddings brought a new level of sophistication to language representation by:

- **Capturing Context and Semantic Similarity**: Unlike BoW and TF-IDF, embeddings understand relationships between words and phrases, allowing for nuanced understanding and comparison.

- **Efficient Dimensionality**: Embeddings reduce dimensionality while retaining semantic richness, making them efficient for processing and storage.

- **Application Versatility**: Embeddings are used across a range of applications, including semantic search, recommendation engines, language translation, and conversational AI.

Vector Space and Similarity

Embeddings place words or sentences in a **high-dimensional vector space**, where **cosine similarity** is often used to measure the “closeness” or similarity between vectors. Vectors that are close together in this space have similar meanings, enabling powerful capabilities like semantic search and recommendation.

Cosine Similarity

- **Definition**: Cosine similarity measures the cosine of the angle between two vectors in a multi-dimensional space. It evaluates how closely aligned the vectors are, regardless of their magnitude.
- **Formula**:

$$\text{Cosine Similarity} = \frac{\sum_{i=1}^{n} A_i B_i}{\sqrt{\sum_{i=1}^{n} A_i^2} \times \sqrt{\sum_{i=1}^{n} B_i^2}}$$

Interpretation: The resulting value ranges from -1 to 1. A value of 1 indicates that the vectors are identical, 0 indicates orthogonality (no similarity), and -1 indicates opposite directions.

Euclidean Distance

- **Definition**: Euclidean distance measures the straight-line distance between two vectors in the vector space. It provides a simple way to quantify the distance or dissimilarity between vectors.
- **Formula**:

$$d(A,B) = \|A - B\|_2 = \sqrt{(A_1 - B_1)^2 + (A_2 - B_2)^2 + \cdots + (A_n - B_n)^2}$$

$$d(A,B) = \sqrt{\sum_{i=1}^{n} (A_i - B_i)^2}$$

Manhattan Distance (L1 Distance)

- **Definition**: Manhattan distance, also known as L1 distance, calculates the distance between two points by summing the absolute differences of their coordinates. It is named for the grid-like street geography of Manhattan.
- **Formula**:

$$d(A,B) = \|A - B\|_1 = |A_1 - B_1| + |A_2 - B_2| + \cdots + |A_n - B_n|$$

$$d(A,B) = \sum_{i=1}^{n} |A_i - B_i|$$

- **Interpretation**: Like Euclidean distance, a smaller Manhattan distance indicates higher similarity, but it can be more robust to outliers.

Jaccard Similarity

- **Definition**: Jaccard similarity is a measure of similarity between two sets, calculated as the size of the intersection divided by the size of the union of the sets.

- **Formula**:

$$J(A,B) = \frac{|A \cap B|}{|A \cup B|}$$

$$J(A,B) = \frac{\text{Number of common elements}}{\text{Total unique elements in } A \text{ and } B}$$

- **Interpretation**: Values range from 0 to 1, where 1 indicates complete similarity (the same set) and 0 indicates no overlap.

Hamming Distance

- **Definition**: Hamming distance measures the number of positions at which the corresponding elements of two vectors of equal length differ. It is often used in coding theory.
- **Formula**:

$$d(A,B) = \sum_{i=1}^{n} \mathbf{1}(A_i \neq B_i)$$

$$d(A,B) = |\{\, i \mid A_i \neq B_i \,\}|$$

- **Interpretation**: A lower Hamming distance indicates higher similarity between the two vectors.

Summary of Similarity Measures

- **Cosine Similarity** compares the **angle between vectors**, making it useful when magnitude does not matter, such as in text analysis.
- **Euclidean Distance** measures the **straight-line distance between two points**, capturing absolute differences in values.
- **Jaccard Similarity** compares **overlap between sets**, focusing on shared elements relative to the total unique elements.
- **Hamming Distance** counts the **number of positions where two strings or binary vectors differ:**

Measure	Range	Interpretation
Cosine Similarity	-1 to 1	Angle between vectors
Euclidean Distance	0 to ∞	Straight-line distance
Manhattan Distance	0 to ∞	Sum of absolute differences
Jaccard Similarity	0 to 1	Ratio of intersection to union
Hamming Distance	0 to n	Number of differing elements

Table 2.1: *Summary of Similarity Measures*

Applications of Vector Representation and Similarity Measures

Before we move into the working of the state-of-the-art transformer models, we will first look into the machine learning approaches in the field of Language modeling. Let us first consider an example of the next word prediction. We may see this application in modern language models like GPT, Llama, Gemma and many more. But before the invention of the transformers, this task was almost impossible without an advanced computer.

Background on N-gram Models

N-gram models are a statistical framework used in natural language processing (NLP) to predict the next item in a sequence based on the previous n−1n-1n−1 items. An n-gram is defined as a contiguous sequence of nnn items (words, characters, and so on) from a given text or speech sample. These models leverage the principle of conditional probability to capture the relationships between consecutive words in a language.

Definition

or a given sequence of words w1,w2,...,wnw_1, w_2, \ldots, w_nw1,w2,...,wn:

- A **unigram** model considers individual words without context, focusing solely on the probability of each word:

  P(wi)P(w_i)P(wi)

- A **bigram** model considers pairs of consecutive words, calculating the probability of a word given its immediate predecessor:

  P(wi|wi−1)P(w_i | w_{i-1})P(wi|wi−1)

- A **trigram** model extends this to triples, considering the two preceding words:

  P(wi|wi−2,wi−1)P(w_i | w_{i-2}, w_{i-1})P(wi|wi−2,wi−1)

How It Works

The core idea behind n-gram models is to estimate the conditional probabilities of words based on their observed frequencies in a training corpus. The model is built by counting how often each n-gram appears in the text and normalizing these counts to create probabilities. This process involves two key steps:

- **Frequency Counting**: For a given corpus, the model counts occurrences of each n-gram. For example, in a bigram model, we would count how many times each pair of words appears together.
- **Probability Estimation**: The probability of a word given its context is estimated using the formula:

$$P(w_n \mid w_1, w_2, \ldots, w_{n-1}) = \frac{C(w_1, w_2, \ldots, w_n)}{C(w_1, w_2, \ldots, w_{n-1})}$$

These models are advantageous for their simplicity and efficiency, providing a foundational approach to various NLP tasks, including next word prediction, text generation, and language modeling. However, they also have limitations, such as the inability to capture long-range dependencies beyond nnn words and issues related to data sparsity.

Next Word Prediction Using N-gram Model

Next word prediction is a fundamental task in natural language processing, aiming to estimate the probability of a word given its preceding context. Formally, let w1,w2,...,wnw_1, w_2, \ldots, w_nw1,w2,...,wn represent a sequence of words. The goal is to predict the next word wn+1w_{n+1}wn+1 using the conditional probability:

$$w_{n+1} = \arg\max_{w} \; P(w \mid w_1, w_2, \ldots, w_n)$$

To simplify this computation, we employ an n-gram model. Specifically, in a bigram model, the prediction can be reduced to:

P(wn+1|wn)P(w_{n+1} | w_n)P(wn+1|wn)

Example: Consider the sentence "The cat sat on the." We aim to predict the next word following "the," which can be expressed as:

P(w6|w5="the")P(w_6 | w_5 = \text{"the"})P(w6|w5="the")

The estimation of this probability is based on frequency counts derived from a training corpus.

Limitations of N-gram Models

While N-gram models have been widely used in Natural Language Processing due to their simplicity and effectiveness, they also present several limitations that can hinder their performance, especially in complex language tasks.

Contextual Limitations

N-gram models rely on a fixed-length context (n-1 previous words), which restricts their ability to capture long-range dependencies. Language often contains intricate relationships and dependencies that extend beyond the local context. For example, understanding the meaning of a word can depend on several preceding words or even entire sentences. Consequently, N-gram models may struggle to predict words that require knowledge of context beyond the immediate N-gram.

Data Sparsity

As the value of nnn increases, the number of possible N-grams grows exponentially. This phenomenon leads to data sparsity issues, where many N-grams may not appear in the training corpus. The absence of sufficient training data for certain n-grams can result in unreliable probability estimates, negatively impacting the performance of the model in real-world applications.

Limited Generalization

N-gram models often rely heavily on memorization rather than generalization. Because they are based on observed frequencies, they may perform well on training data but poorly on unseen data. This reliance on specific word combinations limits their ability to adapt to variations in language, such as synonyms, paraphrases, or different sentence structures.

High Dimensionality

As the vocabulary size increases, the feature space for N-gram models expands significantly. The high dimensionality can lead to computational inefficiencies, requiring substantial memory and processing power. This challenge becomes particularly pronounced in large-scale applications, where the model must handle vast vocabularies and numerous n-grams.

Lack of Semantic Understanding

N-gram models treat words as discrete entities without understanding their semantic relationship. They do not capture the meaning of words or the relationships between them, which can limit their effectiveness in tasks that require a deeper understanding of language, such as sentiment analysis or text generation.

Inflexibility

The fixed nature of N-gram models makes them inflexible in adapting to new language constructs or evolving vocabulary. As language changes over time, n-gram models may require retraining or modification to remain relevant, which can be a resource-intensive process.

As we can see, the n gram models had a lot of limitations. In order to address these, Recurrent Neural Networks, or, RNNs were used for better accuracy.

Background on Recurrent Neural Networks (RNNs)

Recurrent Neural Networks (RNNs) is a class of artificial neural networks designed to process sequential data. They are particularly effective in tasks where the order and context of the input data are significant, such as time series prediction, speech recognition, and natural language processing.

Fundamental Concepts

Sequential Data: RNNs are specifically tailored to handle sequences of data where each element is dependent on the previous ones. For instance, in natural language processing, the meaning of a word is often influenced by the words that come before it.

Hidden State: At the core of RNNs is the hidden state, which serves as a memory mechanism. This hidden state captures information from previous inputs, allowing the network to maintain context across time steps. The hidden state is updated as the network processes each input sequentially.

Mathematical Formulation

The RNN processes a sequence of inputs (x1,x2,…,xT)(x_1, x_2, \ldots, x_T)(x1,x2,…,xT) over TTT time steps. At each time step ttt, the network performs the following operations:

- **Input Representation**: The input at time ttt, denoted as xtx_txt, is typically represented as a dense vector using techniques like word embeddings or one-hot encoding.
- **Hidden State Update**: The hidden state hth_tht at time ttt is computed using the previous hidden state ht−1h_{t-1}ht−1 and the current input xtx_txt:

  $$h_t = \tanh(W_h h_{t-1} + W_x x_t + b)$$

  where:

  - WhW_hWh is the weight matrix for the hidden state,
  - WxW_xWx is the weight matrix for the input,

- bbb is a bias term, and
- fff is a non-linear activation function (commonly the hyperbolic tangent function or ReLU).

- **Output Generation**: The output yty_tyt at each time step can be derived from the hidden state:

  yt=g(Wyht+by)y_t = g(W_yh_t + b_y)yt=g(Wyht+by)

  where:

  WyW_yWy is the output weight matrix,

  byb_yby is the output bias, and

  ggg is typically a softmax function when dealing with classification tasks.

Training RNNs

RNNs are trained using BackPropagation through Time (BPTT), a variant of the backpropagation algorithm. In BPTT, the gradients of the loss function are calculated with respect to the weights across all time steps, allowing the network to learn from the entire sequence of inputs. The main steps in the training process include:

- **Forward Pass**: The input sequence is fed into the RNN, and the hidden states and outputs are computed iteratively.
- **Loss Calculation**: A loss function is applied to measure the difference between the predicted outputs and the actual targets.
- **Backward Pass**: The gradients are calculated and propagated back through the time steps, updating the weights accordingly.

Advantages of RNNs

- **Dynamic Sequence Length**: RNNs can handle input sequences of varying lengths, thereby, making them suitable for tasks with diverse input sizes.
- **Memory Mechanism**: The hidden state enables RNNs to maintain context over time, allowing them to capture temporal dependencies in data.
- **End-to-End Learning**: RNNs facilitate end-to-end learning, eliminating the need for extensive feature engineering.

Next Word Prediction Using Recurrent Neural Networks (RNNs)

Recurrent Neural Networks (RNNs) represent a powerful architecture for sequence prediction tasks, including next word prediction. Unlike N-gram models, which rely on fixed-length contexts, RNNs are designed to handle variable-length sequences, making them particularly suitable for Natural Language Processing.

RNN Architecture

The key feature of RNNs is their ability to maintain a hidden state that captures information from previous inputs, allowing the model to learn dependencies over time. An RNN processes a sequence of words w1,w2,...,wnw_1, w_2, \ldots, w_nw1,w2,...,wn one at a time, updating its hidden state hth_tht at each time step ttt as follows:

- **Input Layer**: At time ttt, the input word wtw_twt is transformed into a vector representation, typically using techniques such as word embeddings.
- **Hidden State Update**: The hidden state hth_tht is updated based on the previous hidden state ht−1h_{t-1}ht−1 and the current input. where WhW_hWh and WxW_xWx are weight matrices, bbb is a bias term, and fff is a non-linear activation function (often a hyperbolic tangent or ReLU).
- **Output Layer**: The output for the next word wt+1w_{t+1}wt+1 is generated by applying a softmax function over the hidden state to produce a probability distribution across the vocabulary, where WyW_yWy is the output weight matrix, and byb_yby is the output bias.

Advantages of RNNs

- **Contextual Understanding**: RNNs can maintain context across arbitrary lengths, allowing them to capture long-range dependencies in sequences. This capability is particularly beneficial in language, where the meaning of a word often relies on its context within a sentence.
- **Dynamic Input Length**: RNNs can process sequences of varying lengths, making them suitable for natural language tasks where input sizes may differ significantly.
- **End-to-End Learning**: RNNs can be trained end-to-end using backpropagation through time (BPTT), enabling the model to learn directly from the data without the need for extensive feature engineering.

Limitations of RNNs

Despite their advantages, RNNs also face challenges:

- **Vanishing and Exploding Gradients**: During training, gradients can diminish or explode, making it difficult to learn long-range dependencies. This issue is often mitigated by using specialized architectures like Long Short-Term Memory (LSTM) networks or Gated Recurrent Units (GRUs).

- **Computational Complexity**: RNNs can be computationally intensive, particularly for long sequences, due to the sequential nature of their processing.
- **Data Requirements**: RNNs typically require large amounts of training data to generalize well, especially in tasks with diverse vocabulary and syntactic structures.

As we can see, there are fewer limitations of the RNNs. But RNNs were very expensive to train and used to take a lot of time. They were sequential in nature and hence needed a lot of computation power, space and time to be fully trained.

Finally, after the introduction of the transformer, all these issues were resolved.

Background on Transformers

Transformers are a revolutionary architecture introduced in the paper "Attention is All You Need" by Vaswani et al. in 2017. They were designed to address some of the limitations of previous models, particularly Recurrent Neural Networks (RNNs), by providing a more efficient mechanism for handling sequential data. The Transformer architecture has since become the backbone of many state-of-the-art models in natural language processing (NLP) and beyond, such as BERT, GPT, and T5.

Key Concepts

- **Self-Attention Mechanism**: The core innovation of Transformers is the self-attention mechanism, which allows the model to weigh the importance of different words in a sequence when generating a representation for a specific word. Unlike RNNs, which process input sequentially, the self-attention mechanism enables the model to consider all words in a sequence simultaneously. This is mathematically represented as:

  Attention(Q, K, V) = softmax((QK^T) / √d_k) V

  where:

  - QQQ (queries), KKK (keys), and VVV (values) are input representations.
  - dkd_kdk is the dimension of the keys, used for scaling.

- **Positional Encoding**: Since Transformers do not inherently account for the order of tokens in a sequence, they use positional encodings to inject information about the relative positions of tokens. This allows the model to maintain an understanding of sequence order:

  PE(pos, 2i) = sin(pos / 10000^(2i/d))

  PE(pos, 2i+1) = cos(pos / 10000^(2i/d))

  where pospospos is the position and iii is the dimension index.

Transformer Architecture

The Transformer architecture consists of an encoder-decoder structure, each made up of multiple layers:

- **Encoder**: The encoder processes the input sequence and generates a series of hidden representations. Each encoder layer includes:
  - **Multi-Head Self-Attention**: Allows the model to focus on different parts of the input sequence simultaneously.
  - **Feed-Forward Neural Network**: Applies a non-linear transformation to each attention output.
  - **Layer Normalization and Residual Connections**: Help stabilize training and improve gradient flow.
- **Decoder**: The decoder generates the output sequence from the hidden representations of the encoder. It incorporates:
  - **Masked Multi-Head Self-Attention**: Prevents attending to future tokens during training.
  - **Multi-Head Attention over Encoder Outputs**: Allows the decoder to focus on relevant parts of the output of the encoder.
  - **Feed-Forward Neural Network**: Similar to the architecture of the encoder.

Each of these components can be summarized as follows:

Output = LayerNorm(X + FeedForward(Attention(X)))

where X represents the input to each layer.

Training Transformers

Transformers are trained using standard techniques from supervised learning, typically with a cross-entropy loss for tasks like language modeling. The training process includes:

- **Forward Pass**: Input sequences are processed through the encoder-decoder structure, generating outputs.
- **Loss Calculation**: The loss function quantifies the difference between predicted and actual outputs.
- **Backpropagation**: Gradients are calculated and propagated through all layers, updating weights accordingly.

Advantages of Transformers

- **Parallelization**: Unlike RNNs, which process sequences sequentially, Transformers can process entire sequences in parallel, significantly speeding up training and inference.
- **Long-Range Dependencies**: The self-attention mechanism allows Transformers to capture relationships between distant words in a sequence effectively, addressing the limitations of RNNs in maintaining long-term context.
- **Scalability**: Transformers scale well with increased data and model sizes, leading to improved performance on a variety of tasks.

Next Word Prediction in Transformers

Next word prediction is a fundamental task in natural language processing (NLP) where the objective is to predict the most likely subsequent word in a sequence given the preceding words. Transformers excel in this task due to their architecture, particularly the self-attention mechanism, which allows them to capture complex relationships between words in a sequence.

Mechanism of Next Word Prediction

The process of next word prediction in Transformers involves the following steps:

1. **Input Representation**: The input sequence is represented as a series of tokens (words or subwords). Each token is transformed into an embedding vector, which is further combined with positional encodings to retain information about the order of words. This results in a sequence of vectors that serve as input to the Transformer model.
2. **Self-Attention**: During the forward pass, each token attends to all other tokens in the input sequence through the self-attention mechanism. For each token xix_ixi in the input, the model calculates attention scores with every other token xjx_jxj, determining how much focus should be given to each token.
3. **Generating Contextualized Representations**: The output of the self-attention layer produces contextualized representations for each token. These representations encapsulate the meaning of the tokens in relation to each other, allowing the model to understand the context of the entire sequence.
4. **Output Layer**: The final output from the Transformer consists of a sequence of contextualized embeddings, which are passed through a linear layer followed by a softmax activation function to produce a probability distribution over the vocabulary for the next word. The predicted next word y^\hat{y}y^ is obtained by selecting the token with the highest probability:

ŷ = argmax(softmax(W_o h_T + b_o))

where WoW_oWo and bob_obo are the weight matrix and bias for the output layer, respectively, and hTh_ThT is the last hidden state corresponding to the input sequence.

Benefits of Using Transformers for Next Word Prediction

- **Contextual Awareness**: The self-attention mechanism enables Transformers to weigh the importance of each word in the context of the entire input sequence, leading to more accurate predictions. For example, in the sentence "The dog barked at the..." the model can effectively predict "cat" or "stranger" based on the attention paid to earlier words.
- **Parallel Processing**: Unlike RNNs, which process tokens sequentially, Transformers process all tokens simultaneously, allowing for faster training and inference. This parallelism is particularly beneficial when handling long sequences of text.
- **Handling Long-Range Dependencies**: Transformers excel in capturing long-range dependencies in text due to their global attention mechanism. This is critical in next word prediction, where the relevant context may be several tokens back in the sequence.

Implementation Steps

To implement next word prediction using Transformers, the following steps are typically followed:

1. **Preprocessing**: Input text data is tokenized, and each token is converted into embeddings. Positional encodings are added to these embeddings to maintain order information.
2. **Model Training**: The Transformer model is trained on a large corpus of text data using supervised learning. During training, the model is provided with input sequences and the corresponding next words, minimizing the cross-entropy loss between predicted and actual words.
3. **Inference**: During inference, the model takes a sequence of tokens as input and generates predictions for the next word. Techniques such as beam search or temperature sampling can be employed to enhance prediction quality.
4. **Fine-tuning**: For specific applications or domains, pre-trained Transformer models (such as BERT or GPT) can be fine-tuned on domain-specific data to improve performance.

Although the invention of the transformer did solve many challenges that RNNs had, it is still considered computationally intensive to train the transformer. The main advantage of the transformer was its parallel processing capability which RNNs lacked, bringing the time complexity to the quadratic power. Even today, researchers from all around the world are focusing on the optimization of the transformers. In the future chapters, we will see how to execute these concepts using the popular deep learning library, PyTorch.

Conclusion

Early AI systems relied on traditional methods of data representation such as symbolic logic, one-hot encoding, rule-based systems, and structured feature engineering. These approaches worked well when the world could be neatly described using predefined categories and explicit rules. Databases stored facts, algorithms applied logic, and intelligence was handcrafted through domain expertise. However, such representations struggled with ambiguity, context, scale, and learning from raw, unstructured data. They treated symbols as isolated entities, unable to capture relationships, nuance, or semantic continuity, leading to brittle systems that failed outside narrowly defined conditions.

The limitations of traditional representations created the need for vector embeddings, a shift that enabled AI systems to represent meaning numerically and continuously. Vector embeddings map data such as words, images, signals, or behaviors into high-dimensional spaces where similarity corresponds to semantic or functional closeness. This transformation has been central to the rise of precision AI models, as it allows systems to generalize, interpolate, and reason under uncertainty. Embeddings make learning scalable, adaptable, and transferable across tasks, enabling models to improve accuracy not by memorization, but by understanding patterns in latent space.

At the mathematical core of this paradigm lies vector algebra and geometry. Vector spaces provide the structure in which data representations live, while operations such as dot products, norms, and projections define how similarity and relevance are measured. Similarity metrics like cosine similarity, Euclidean distance, and inner products allow AI systems to compare meaning, detect clusters, and retrieve relevant information efficiently. These concepts are applied across domains, from semantic search and recommendation systems to anomaly detection and scientific modeling, making vector mathematics a universal language of modern AI.

Recurrent Neural Networks (RNNs) marked a major step forward by introducing temporal dynamics into vector representations. Designed to process sequences, RNNs maintain hidden states that evolve over time, allowing models to capture dependencies in language, time-series data, speech, and control systems. Variants such as LSTMs and GRUs addressed issues like vanishing gradients, enabling longer contextual memory.

RNNs demonstrated how vectors could represent not just static data, but evolving state, bringing sequence awareness into AI systems.

Transformer-based neural networks represent the next architectural leap, replacing recurrence with attention mechanisms that model global relationships directly. By allowing each element in a sequence to attend to every other element, transformers capture long-range dependencies more efficiently and in parallel. This architecture has become the foundation of large language models and multimodal systems, scaling vector representations across massive datasets with unprecedented performance. Together, embeddings, vector mathematics, RNNs, and transformers form a continuous narrative: the evolution of AI from symbolic reasoning to distributed, geometric intelligence that learns, adapts, and scales with data.

After understanding the role of vectors, its relations, and its importance in the current AI landscape, we will try to delve into the architecture of massive AI systems by understanding the components in Milvus and how the orchestration of these layers produces a seamless, reliable and yet scalable vector management and application database.

CHAPTER 3
Components of Milvus

Introduction

Milvus is a high-performance vector database designed for similarity search on vector datasets, supporting large amount of vectors. Milvus is optimized for embedding retrieval, and uses vector search libraries such as FAISS, HNSW, DiskANN, and SCANN for index construction and retrieval. The architecture of the platform offers a rich set of features, including data sharding, streaming data ingestion, managing schemas on the fly and support for search on hybrid and sparse vectors. Milvus employs shared-storage architecture with storage and computing disassociation, enabling horizontal scalability for compute nodes. The architecture separates the data plane and control plane, organized into four distinct layers: the access layer, coordinator service, worker nodes, and storage. The layers operate independently offering independent scalability and disaster recovery. This chapter provides an overview of the architecture and capabilities of Milvus, and will begin by laying a foundation for understanding its role in modern vector-based search and retrieval systems.

Structure

In this chapter, we will discuss the following topics:

- Components of Milvus
- Components of the Messaging Layer
- Components of the Coordination Layer
- Components of the Worker Nodes
- Components of the Storage Layer

Components of Milvus

Milvus, a scalable vector database, follows a micro-services architecture. Its components are divided into core micro-services and third-party dependencies. This architecture ensures modularity, scalability, and flexibility, especially in distributed environments like Kubernetes.

Micro-Service Components

- Milvus is built using a microservices architecture consisting of seven core services. Each service is responsible for a specific function within the vector database system. These services operate independently and communicate with each other through well-defined interfaces. They collectively manage vector data storage, indexing, query execution, and metadata handling. The architecture enables scalable processing of large volumes of high-dimensional vector data. This modular design improves reliability, flexibility, and efficient distributed computation.
- **Root Coordinator**
    - Role:
        - Serves as the central control plane.
        - Manages metadata for collections, partitions, and indexes.
        - Coordinates other components to ensure smooth operations.
    - Responsibilities:
        - Handles schema creation and management.
        - Oversees the lifecycle of collections and partitions.
        - Synchronizes metadata across other components.
- **Proxy**
    - Role:
        - Acts as the entry point for client requests.
        - Ensures load balancing and request routing.
    - Responsibilities:
        - Validates and forwards queries to the appropriate components.
        - Handles authentication and basic preprocessing.
        - Aggregates query results from multiple nodes.
- **Query Coordinator**
    - Role:
        - Manages and optimizes query execution.

  - Responsibilities:
    - Allocates tasks to Query Nodes.
    - Maintains an overview of query workload distribution.
    - Monitors the health and status of Query Nodes.

- **Query Node**
  - Role:
    - Executes query operations on vector data.
  - Responsibilities:
    - Processes search and retrieval requests.
    - Computes similarities and distances between vectors.
    - Retrieves results from storage or in-memory data.
- **Data Coordinator**
  - Role:
    - Oversees data management and persistence.
  - Responsibilities:
    - Orchestrates the flow of data between Data Nodes and storage layers.
    - Tracks data versions and ensures consistency.
    - Handles data compaction and garbage collection.
- **Data Node**
  - Role:
    - Handles data ingestion and storage.
  - Responsibilities:
    - Processes data insertions, deletions, and updates.
    - Writes vector data to the storage layer.
    - Streams data for real-time updates.
- **Index Node**
  - Role:
    - Responsible for indexing vector data to accelerate query performance.
  - Responsibilities:
    - Creates and maintains vector indexes such as IVF, HNSW, and so on.

        - Updates indexes when new data is added or modified.
        - Ensures indexes are optimized for efficient querying.

Third-Party Dependencies

Milvus relies on several external systems to support its distributed architecture. These systems provide essential capabilities such as storage, metadata management, and cluster coordination. Object storage services are used to persist large volumes of vector data and index files. Coordination services help manage distributed nodes and maintain system consistency. Message queue systems enable communication and task scheduling between different services.

Together, these external components enhance scalability, reliability, and high-performance vector search.

These dependencies are:

- Etcd
    - Role:
        - Distributed key-value store for metadata and configuration management.
    - Responsibilities:
        - Stores and synchronizes metadata across components.
        - Ensures consistency and availability in a distributed environment.
- Pulsar/Kafka
    - Role:
        - Distributed messaging system for real-time communication.
    - Responsibilities:
        - Facilitates data streaming between components.
        - Ensures reliable and scalable data ingestion pipelines.
- Storage Backend
    - Role:
        - Provides persistent storage for vector data, indexes, and metadata.
    - Responsibilities:
        - Stores large-scale vector data in formats like S3, HDFS, or MinIO.

Handles backups and disaster recovery.

The micro-services architecture of Milvus allows independent deployment and scaling of its components on container platforms such as Kubernetes. This modular approach provides the following advantages:

- **Scalability:**
  - Each component can scale independently based on workload.

    For example, Query Nodes can be scaled horizontally for increased query throughput.
- **High Availability:**
  - Deploying multiple instances of critical services (such as Root Coord or Proxy) ensures fault tolerance.
- **Isolation and Customization:**
  - Resource allocation (CPU, memory) can be customized for each micro-service.
  - Services can be updated or replaced without disrupting the entire system.
- **Monitoring and Logging:**
  - Kubernetes makes it easier to monitor resource usage and system health using tools such as Prometheus and Grafana.

Components of the Messaging Layer

In Milvus, Kafka serves as a robust message queue system, facilitating efficient data ingestion, synchronization, and communication between various components. Its integration into Milvus enhances the ability of the database to handle large-scale, real-time data streams, ensuring scalability and reliability.

Key Roles of Kafka in Milvus

- **Data Ingestion and Streaming:**

  Kafka enables seamless streaming of vector data into Milvus, allowing for real-time data processing and analysis. By acting as an intermediary, it decouples data producers from consumers, ensuring efficient and scalable data ingestion pipelines.
- **Message Queue Management:**

  As a message broker, Kafka manages logs of recent changes, outputs stream logs, and provides log subscriptions. This functionality is crucial for maintaining data consistency and integrity across distributed systems.

- **Change Data Capture (CDC):**

  Kafka facilitates capturing and synchronizing incremental data changes within Milvus instances. This capability ensures that any data modifications are reliably propagated, supporting tasks like incremental backups and disaster recovery.

- **Integration with External Systems:**

  Through connectors such as the Kafka Connect Milvus Sink, Kafka allows for streaming vector data from Kafka topics directly into Milvus. This integration simplifies the process of connecting various data sources to Milvus, enhancing its versatility in handling diverse data ingestion scenarios.

- **Scalability and Fault Tolerance:**

  The distributed architecture of Kafka ensures that Milvus can handle high-throughput data streams while maintaining fault tolerance. This design supports the requirements of Milvus for scalability and reliability in large-scale deployments.

- **Configuration Flexibility:**

  Milvus provides configurable options for integrating with Kafka, allowing users to tailor the message queue settings to their specific needs. This flexibility ensures optimal performance and resource utilization based on the deployment environment.

Thus, by leveraging Kafka, Milvus enhances its capabilities in real-time data processing, ensuring efficient data flow and robust system performance. This integration positions Milvus as a powerful vector database solution capable of meeting the demands of modern data-intensive applications.

In Milvus, Apache Pulsar serves as the default message storage system, playing a crucial role in managing logs of recent changes, outputting stream logs, and providing log subscription services.

Key Roles of Pulsar in Milvus

- **Write-Ahead Logging (WAL):**

  Pulsar supports the Write-Ahead Logging mechanism of Milvus, ensuring secure data processing by recording every operation before execution. This feature allows the system to recover by replaying these logs in case of unexpected failures.

- **Message Queue Management:**

  As a message broker, Pulsar manages logs of recent changes, outputs stream logs, and provides log subscription services, which are essential for maintaining data consistency and integrity across distributed systems.

- **Scalability and Flexibility:**

  Pulsar's multi-layered architecture, which separates the serving and storage layers, enhances scalability and simplifies cluster management. It supports dynamic scaling, allowing the system to adapt to changing workloads seamlessly.

- **Integration with Apache BookKeeper:**

  Pulsar integrates with Apache BookKeeper, ensuring the persistent storage and management of data. This integration is particularly important when dealing with large datasets and scenarios that require high fault tolerance.

- **Configuration Flexibility:**

  Milvus provides configurable options for integrating with Pulsar, allowing users to tailor the message queue settings to their specific needs. This flexibility ensures optimal performance and resource utilization based on the deployment environment.

Therefore, by leveraging Pulsar, Milvus enhances its capabilities in real-time data processing, ensuring efficient data flow and robust system performance. This integration positions Milvus as a powerful vector database solution capable of meeting the demands of modern data-intensive applications.

Components of the Coordinators

In the Milvus architecture, coordinators play a crucial role in managing and overseeing the operations of different aspects of the distributed system. Coordinators are responsible for the efficient management of resources, task distribution, and system state across the various nodes in the Milvus cluster. There are several types of coordinators in Milvus, each managing a specific aspect of the system's operation. In the following sub-section, there is an expanded explanation of the roles of the key coordinators in Milvus.

Root Coordinator

The Root Coordinator is the central management component in Milvus that coordinates high-level cluster management activities and ensures the overall system's consistency. It acts as the primary authority for cluster-wide resource management.

The responsibilities of the Root Coordinator are as follows:

- **Cluster-wide Management:** It is responsible for managing the state of the entire Milvus cluster, including monitoring the status of various nodes (For example, Query Nodes, Data Nodes, Index Nodes) and ensuring their coordination.

- **Metadata Management:** The Root Coordinator maintains metadata related to collections, partitions, and indexes. It handles operations such as creating, dropping, and retrieving metadata for different components in the system.
- **Task Coordination:** It schedules and dispatches tasks to the appropriate nodes. These tasks may include data insertion, query execution, indexing, and balancing resources across nodes.
- **State Management:** It keeps track of the overall system state, including which nodes are active, the health status of services, and resource usage. If any node fails or becomes unreachable, the Root Coordinator will reassign tasks or resources to other available nodes to ensure minimal service disruption.
- **Fault Tolerance:** In case of node failures, the Root Coordinator can trigger recovery processes, such as rescheduling or redistributing tasks, ensuring that the system maintains its availability and consistency.

Query Coordinator

The Query Coordinator is responsible for managing the query execution process within the Milvus cluster. It plays a vital role in ensuring that client queries are executed efficiently, distributed, and optimized for performance.

The responsibilities of the Query Coordinator are as follows:

- **Query Parsing:** The Query Coordinator receives queries from the Proxy and parses them to identify the necessary steps to retrieve data from the system. This parsing includes breaking down complex queries into smaller operations.
- **Query Distribution:** It is responsible for distributing query tasks to the appropriate Query Nodes based on the workload and resource availability. This process involves deciding how to divide the query into smaller subqueries that can be processed in parallel across multiple Query Nodes.
- **Load Balancing:** The Query Coordinator ensures that queries are evenly distributed across the available Query Nodes, balancing the system's load and preventing any single node from becoming overwhelmed with too many queries.
- **Query Optimization:** It may perform optimizations on incoming queries, such as adjusting the query structure to enhance performance, minimizing the data scanned, or implementing filtering strategies to reduce resource consumption.
- **Aggregation of Results:** Once the Query Nodes process subqueries, the Query Coordinator aggregates the results and returns the final response to the client. This may involve merging partial results, handling scoring and ranking, and filtering based on query conditions.

Data Coordinator

The Data Coordinator is responsible for managing the data-related operations in Milvus. It handles the organization, storage, and retrieval of vector data across the system's data nodes.

The responsibilities of the Data Coordinator are as follows:

- **Data Distribution:** The Data Coordinator manages how vector data is distributed across Data Nodes. It ensures that data is partitioned appropriately and placed on different nodes to balance the storage load.
- **Data Migration:** It handles data migration when needed, such as moving data between nodes to optimize resource usage, storage capacity, or when adding new nodes to the cluster.
- **Data Consistency:** The Data Coordinator ensures that data is consistent across the system. This may include monitoring synchronization between different Data Nodes and ensuring that no data is lost or corrupted during migrations or failures.
- **Data Replication:** In Milvus, data may be replicated across different nodes for redundancy. The Data Coordinator manages this replication to ensure high availability and fault tolerance.
- **Backup and Recovery:** The Data Coordinator is involved in performing data backups and managing recovery processes in case of data loss. It works with other components to ensure that the database can be restored to a consistent state in the event of a failure.

Index Coordinator

The Index Coordinator is responsible for managing the creation, maintenance, and distribution of indexes in the Milvus cluster. Indexes are essential for optimizing the performance of vector searches by allowing faster query execution.

The responsibilities of the Index Coordinator are as follows:

- **Index Management:** The Index Coordinator is in charge of creating and managing indexes for various collections in Milvus. This includes selecting the appropriate index type, such as IVF, HNSW, or others, based on the use case and data characteristics.
- **Index Distribution:** Once an index is created, the Index Coordinator ensures it is properly distributed across the relevant Index Nodes. It tracks the status of indexes and ensures they are updated and synchronized when data changes occur.

- **Index Rebuilding:** If there are changes in the data (For example, new vectors are inserted or deleted), the Index Coordinator ensures that the associated indexes are updated accordingly. It may trigger index rebuilds to maintain search accuracy and performance.
- **Performance Optimization:** The Index Coordinator monitors the performance of index structures and may make adjustments, such as rebalancing or refreshing indexes, to ensure fast and efficient vector searches.
- **Fault Tolerance:** If an Index Node fails, the Index Coordinator is responsible for reallocating indexing tasks to other available nodes and recovering the index as needed.

Proxy (Coordination Role)

While not a "coordinator" in the traditional sense, the Proxy component plays a critical coordination role in Milvus. It acts as the intermediary between client requests and the internal components of the system, directing requests to the appropriate coordinator or node.

The responsibilities of the Proxy are as follows:

- **Request Forwarding:** The Proxy receives client requests and forwards them to the appropriate coordinators or backend services, such as the Query Coordinator or Data Coordinator.
- **Load Balancing:** The Proxy helps distribute client requests evenly across the available nodes, ensuring that no single node is overwhelmed with requests. This contributes to system efficiency and ensures high availability.
- **Authentication and Authorization:** The Proxy is involved in verifying the identity of clients and ensuring that they have the appropriate permissions to execute specific operations.

Each coordinator in Milvus is responsible for a specific aspect of the system's operation, working together to manage data, queries, indexing, and cluster-wide operations. The Root Coordinator oversees the entire system, the Query Coordinator manages query execution, the Data Coordinator handles data storage and distribution, and the Index Coordinator focuses on indexing. These components enable Milvus to operate efficiently in a distributed and scalable environment, ensuring high availability, fault tolerance, and performance across large-scale deployments.

Components of the Worker Nodes

In the context of Milvus, **worker nodes** are crucial for processing and handling specific tasks related to data storage, indexing, and querying within the distributed environment. They are responsible for executing the workload assigned by the coordinators (such as Root Coordinator, Query Coordinator, Data Coordinator, and so on). These nodes are typically the components that actually perform the heavy lifting in the Milvus architecture. Depending on the type of task (data insertion, query execution, index building), different worker nodes are responsible for different functions. An expanded explanation of the roles of the various types of worker nodes in Milvus is mentioned in the following sub-section.

Types of Worker Nodes in Milvus

There are primarily five types of worker nodes in Milvus:

- **Query Node**
- **Data Node**
- **Index Node**
- **Proxy (Worker Role)**
- **Query Coordinator Nodes** (sometimes directly involved in the task execution in certain configurations)

Each of these worker nodes plays a specific role in the distributed architecture of Milvus.

Query Node

The **Query Node** is a key worker node in Milvus responsible for executing vector search queries and processing retrieval requests.

The responsibilities of the Query Node are as follows:

- **Query Execution**: The Query Node executes the actual search operations. Upon receiving a query from the Proxy (via the Query Coordinator), the Query Node processes the query, performs the vector search, and retrieves the relevant data. This involves comparing query vectors with stored vectors using indexing and searching techniques.

- **Result Processing**: After performing the search, the Query Node processes the results. This may include filtering, ranking, or scoring the results to match the query conditions. If necessary, the Query Node splits complex queries into smaller parts for parallel processing across multiple nodes.

- **Distributed Query Execution**: When a query involves large-scale data or multiple partitions, the Query Node coordinates with other Query Nodes to distribute the query load, ensuring that the system processes the query efficiently in parallel.

- **Optimization**: The Query Node optimizes query execution by utilizing indexing structures, such as IVF, HNSW, or PQ (Product Quantization), to speed up search operations and reduce computational complexity.
- **Data Retrieval**: After processing the query and filtering results, the Query Node retrieves the required data from the Data Nodes or caches and sends the final results back to the client, via the Proxy.

The key characteristics are:

- **High Throughput**: Query Nodes need to support high throughput for serving large volumes of search requests.
- **Low Latency**: Since they handle real-time queries, minimizing latency is crucial.
- **Scalability**: Query Nodes can be scaled horizontally to distribute the query load in large-scale systems.

Data Node

The **Data Node** in Milvus is responsible for storing and managing the actual vector data (vectors and metadata). It is the fundamental unit for handling data storage and retrieval.

The responsibilities of the Data Node are as follows:

- **Data Storage**: The Data Node is responsible for physically storing vectors in a distributed manner. Each Data Node stores a portion of the vector data (or specific partitions) on disk, ensuring that large datasets are spread across multiple nodes.
- **Data Retrieval**: When a Query Node requires specific vectors or data for query execution, the Data Node retrieves the data from its local storage and sends it to the Query Node. This can involve retrieving vectors for similarity search or any metadata associated with those vectors.
- **Data Replication**: In a highly available system, Data Nodes ensure that data is replicated across different nodes for fault tolerance. The Data Node works with the Root Coordinator to maintain and synchronize data across nodes, ensuring data consistency.
- **Data Insertion**: Data Nodes are responsible for handling data insertions, where vectors and associated metadata are stored. When new data is inserted into Milvus, the Data Node stores this data and may initiate updates to indexes or partitions to accommodate the new entries.
- **Partition Management**: Data Nodes manage the partitioning of datasets, where each partition can be independently indexed and queried. Data Nodes handle operations such as splitting, merging, or reorganizing partitions to optimize data retrieval and storage.

The key characteristics are:

- **Efficient Storage**: Data Nodes must be optimized for storing large amounts of vector data and supporting high throughput for data insertion and retrieval.
- **Fault Tolerance**: Data Nodes work with replication systems to ensure that data is available even in the case of hardware or node failures.
- **Scalability**: Data Nodes can be scaled out horizontally as data volumes grow to ensure that the system remains performant and efficient.

Index Node

The **Index Node** is responsible for creating and maintaining vector indexes that enable fast search and retrieval operations. Indexing is a key part of Milvus' performance optimization for high-dimensional vector searches.

The responsibilities of the Index Node are as follows:

- **Index Creation**: The Index Node is responsible for creating the indexes used by the system to speed up search queries. This includes the creation of vector indexes such as IVF (Inverted File), HNSW (Hierarchical Navigable Small World), and others depending on the configuration and use case.
- **Index Maintenance**: Index Nodes maintain and update indexes as new data is inserted into the system. When new vectors are added or deleted, the corresponding indexes need to be updated. This could involve recalculating and rebuilding indexes for the affected data.
- **Index Updates and Refresh**: When changes in the data occur, such as the insertion of new vectors or updates to existing ones, the Index Node handles the necessary updates to the indexes, ensuring that they remain accurate and efficient.
- **Index Deletion**: Index Nodes also handle the removal of data from indexes, ensuring that outdated or deleted data is properly removed from the index to avoid unnecessary computations during search queries.
- **Index Optimization**: To ensure query performance remains optimal, Index Nodes may perform periodic optimizations to the indexes, such as compacting, balancing, or refreshing index structures to adapt to changes in data distribution.

The key characteristics are:

- **Performance Optimization**: The Index Node is critical for ensuring that vector searches are performed efficiently. It significantly reduces the time and resources required for large-scale similarity search.

- **Scalability**: Like the other worker nodes, Index Nodes can be scaled horizontally to support larger datasets and more complex indexing tasks.

Proxy (Worker Role)

While the **Proxy** is typically a coordinator in Milvus, it can also play a worker role by distributing tasks and managing connections. In some scenarios, the Proxy can be responsible for forwarding requests to appropriate worker nodes.

The responsibilities of the Proxy (Worker Role) are:

- **Request Distribution**: When working in the worker capacity, the Proxy helps in routing requests to the appropriate Query Nodes, Data Nodes, or Index Nodes, ensuring that client requests are processed efficiently.
- **Task Assignment**: The Proxy assigns specific tasks, such as data insertion or querying, to the relevant worker nodes based on the current system load and availability.
- **Load Balancing**: The Proxy ensures that worker nodes are not overwhelmed with excessive load by balancing client requests across the available nodes.
- **Client Communication**: It ensures seamless communication between the clients and the backend worker nodes. The Proxy receives client requests, processes them, and forwards them to the relevant worker nodes, then returns the results to the client.

Proxy Nodes

Act as the entry point for all client requests, including insert, delete, search, and query operations.

The key Responsibilities of the Proxy Nodes are to:

- Validate client requests, enforce schema constraints, and perform basic request preprocessing.
- Route search and query requests to the appropriate Query Nodes based on metadata and routing rules.
- Forward data mutation operations such as inserts and deletes to the data management layer.
- Aggregate and post-process results returned from Query Nodes before responding to clients.
- Handle request-level load balancing to distribute traffic evenly across the cluster.
- Manage authentication, authorization, and access control where configured.

- Maintain session state and track request lifecycle for observability and debugging.
- Shield clients from internal topology changes, providing a stable and consistent API surface.
- Serve as the coordination gateway that decouples client logic from the internal execution architecture of Milvus.

Query Coordinator Nodes

Query Nodes are the execution engines that transform stored vector data into actionable similarity results. While storage and indexing determine how vectors are organized and persisted, Query Nodes determine how effectively the system responds to real-world questions. They sit on the critical path of every search and retrieval request, making them central to latency, throughput, and user experience. In large-scale AI systems where semantic search and retrieval-augmented generation must operate in real time, Query Nodes are where abstract embeddings become concrete answers.

The Key Responsibilities of Query Coordinator Nodes in Milvus are to:

- Coordinate and manage the overall lifecycle of query execution across the cluster.
- Assign, release, and rebalance data segments among Query Nodes based on load and availability.
- Maintain global metadata about which Query Nodes hold which segments and indexes.
- Monitor the health and status of Query Nodes and trigger failover when nodes become unavailable.
- Orchestrate the loading and eviction of segments to ensure efficient memory utilization.
- Ensure query consistency by controlling visibility of sealed and growing segments.
- Optimize query routing decisions in collaboration with Proxy Nodes.
- Support horizontal scalability by dynamically adapting to changes in data volume and query traffic.
- Enforce cluster-level policies related to performance, resource usage, and availability.
- Act as the control plane that keeps distributed query execution coherent, balanced, and resilient.

Worker nodes in Milvus, such as **Query Nodes**, **Data Nodes**, and **Index Nodes**, are responsible for the critical tasks of data storage, query execution, and indexing. These nodes work in conjunction with the coordinators to ensure that Milvus operates as a scalable, efficient, and high-performance vector database. Thus, by distributing the workload among these worker nodes, Milvus can handle complex, large-scale vector search operations while maintaining low latency and high throughput.

Components of the Storage Layer

The storage architecture of Milvus is further enriched by mechanisms for managing **log snapshots**, **index files**, and **delta files**, which ensure consistency, efficiency, and reliability. Here is how they fit into the storage architecture:

- **Log Snapshots:**
  - **Purpose**: Capture the state of the database at specific points in time for data consistency and recovery.
  - **Description**:
    - Milvus uses Write-Ahead Logging (WAL) to record changes to data before they are applied.
    - Periodically, snapshots of the database are created to record its state, which includes vector data, metadata, and indexes.
  - **Key Characteristics**:
    - **Durability**: Ensures data integrity in the event of system failures by allowing recovery from the last consistent snapshot.
    - **Checkpointing**: Snapshots act as recovery points to minimize replaying WAL logs during recovery.
  - **Storage Layer**:
    - Stored in persistent storage, often alongside delta files and index files in cold storage.
- **Index Files:**
  - **Purpose**: Improve query performance by reducing the computational complexity of vector searches.
  - **Description**:
    - Index files store precomputed data structures (For example, IVF, HNSW, ANNOY) to accelerate nearest neighbour search operations.
    - Milvus generates these files during data ingestion or as part of offline index-building tasks.

- **Key Characteristics**:
  - **Storage Location**: Persisted in cold storage (For example, object storage such as S3 or MinIO).
  - **Usage**: Loaded into memory (hot storage) during query execution for fast retrieval.
  - **Reusability**: Once built, index files remain valid unless the underlying data changes.
- **Indexing Process**:
  - Large datasets are first ingested.
  - Indexes are built asynchronously to minimize query disruptions.

- **Delta Files**
  - **Purpose**: Track deletions and updates to ensure database consistency without frequent rewriting of entire datasets.
  - **Description**:
    - Delta files store "soft delete" markers or modifications for vectors.
    - Instead of physically removing or updating data immediately, these operations are logged in delta files.
    - During queries, Milvus applies the delta files to exclude deleted vectors or reflect updates.
  - **Key Characteristics**:
    - **Efficiency**: Avoids the overhead of rewriting entire datasets when changes occur.
    - **Compactness**: Regular compaction operations merge delta files to optimize storage and performance.
    - **Storage Location**: Persisted in object storage alongside vector data and index files.
  - **Delta Management**:
    - Periodic compaction ensures that changes from delta files are applied to the main dataset and old delta files are removed.

Workflow Incorporating Log Snapshots, Index Files, and Delta Files

In Milvus, data operations follow a workflow involving log snapshots, index files, and delta files. When new vectors are inserted, they are first recorded in **log**

files to ensure durability and recovery. Periodic **snapshots** capture the current state of the data for efficient restoration and checkpointing. **Index files** are then generated from the stored vectors to accelerate similarity search operations. **Delta files** record updates and deletions that occur after the snapshot is taken. During queries, the system combines snapshots, index files, and delta files to reconstruct the most up-to-date dataset.

- **Data Ingestion**:
  - Vectors are ingested into memory and logged in the WAL.
  - Snapshots periodically save the state of the data and metadata.
  - Delta files record any subsequent deletions or updates.
- **Index Building**:
  - Indexes are built asynchronously and stored in cold storage.
  - Index files are loaded into memory during query execution.
- **Query Execution**:
  - Queries access memory (hot storage) for active data and indexes.
  - Delta files are applied in real time to ensure deleted or updated vectors are correctly handled.
- **Data Compaction**:
  - Delta files are merged with the main dataset during compaction.
  - Snapshots ensure a consistent state before and after compaction.

Summary of Relationships

By leveraging log snapshots, index files, and delta files, Milvus ensures high performance, data integrity, and efficient storage utilization, enabling it to meet the demands of large-scale vector search applications.

Component	Purpose	Location	Managed By
Log Snapshots	Data recovery and consistency	Cold storage	WAL and checkpointing
Index Files	Accelerate vector searches	Cold storage (loaded into memory as needed)	Index builder
Delta Files	Track deletions and updates	Cold storage (merged during compaction)	Data compactor

Table 3.1: *Summary of Relationships*

Components of the Storage Layer

Milvus, employs a layered storage tiered architecture to efficiently manage vector data and metadata. The architecture separates compute and storage layers to improve scalability and system performance.

Hot data used for frequent queries is maintained in faster storage or memory layers. Cold or historical data is stored in distributed object storage for cost-efficient persistence.

The storage layers in Milvus include the following:

- **Hot Storage (Memory)**
    - **Purpose**: Primarily used for active data processing and query execution.
    - **Description**:
        - Data in the hot storage layer resides in memory, enabling fast query execution.
        - Recent data inserts or frequently accessed data are cached here to provide low-latency responses.
        - The QueryNode in Milvus is responsible for handling in-memory data operations.
    - **Key Characteristics**:
        - Volatile: Data in memory may not persist across restarts.
        - Designed for speed, ensuring sub-second query performance.
- **Warm Storage (Local or Remote Disk)**
    - **Purpose**: Stores data files temporarily before being consolidated into long-term storage.
    - **Description**:
        - This layer manages intermediate data during ingestion or compaction.
        - It works closely with memory to offload less frequently accessed data or process large-scale operations.
    - **Key Characteristics**:
        - Data may persist on local SSDs or high-performance disks.
        - Acts as a staging area for data that is being compacted or processed.

- **Cold Storage (Object Storage)**
  - **Purpose**: Long-term and large-scale storage for vector data and metadata.
  - **Description**:
    - Data in this layer is stored persistently in an object store, such as AWS S3, MinIO, or HDFS.
    - Index files, vector data, and other metadata are stored here for durability and scalability.
  - **Key Characteristics**:
    - Scalable and cost-effective storage for large volumes of data.
    - Supports redundancy and fault tolerance.
    - Data is retrieved into memory or local disk only when needed for querying.

Workflow across Layers

- **Data Ingestion**:
  - New data is first ingested into the memory layer (hot storage).
  - If the data exceeds memory capacity or becomes less active, it is flushed to the local disk (warm storage).
  - Data is then compacted and organized before being uploaded to object storage (cold storage).
- **Query Execution**:
  - Queries are primarily served from the hot storage layer for active datasets.
  - If data resides in cold storage, it is fetched, temporarily cached in warm storage, and loaded into memory as needed.

Benefits of Milvus Storage Layering

This architecture enables Milvus to handle diverse workloads, from real-time data searches to large-scale batch processing, while maintaining a balance between performance, scalability, and cost.

- **Performance**:

  Hot storage ensures low-latency query execution for real-time analytics.

- **Scalability**:
  Cold storage enables handling massive datasets cost-effectively.
- **Durability**:
  Persistent storage layers ensure data reliability and fault tolerance.
- **Flexibility**:
  Layered storage allows for efficient data movement and lifecycle management, optimizing resource usage.

Conclusion

The architecture of Milvus is designed to support large-scale, low-latency vector similarity search while remaining flexible, fault-tolerant, and cloud-native. At a high level, Milvus follows a distributed, decoupled architecture where compute and storage are separated, and responsibilities are clearly divided across specialized nodes. This separation allows the system to scale independently along data volume, query load, and indexing complexity, which is essential for production-grade AI systems operating on millions or billions of embeddings.

At the front of the system sit the Proxy Nodes, which serve as the stable interface between clients and the Milvus cluster. Proxy Nodes handle all incoming requests such as inserts, deletes, searches, and queries. They validate schemas, preprocess requests, manage authentication where applicable, and route operations to the appropriate internal services. By abstracting the internal topology, Proxy Nodes ensure that clients remain unaffected by scaling events, node failures, or rebalancing activities within the cluster. They also aggregate results returned from downstream nodes, providing a clean and consistent API layer.

The Query Coordinator functions as the control plane for query execution. It maintains global metadata about data distribution, tracks which Query Nodes hold which segments and indexes, and makes intelligent decisions about segment assignment and rebalancing. When data grows or query patterns shift, the Query Coordinator dynamically redistributes segments to maintain optimal performance and memory utilization. It also monitors Query Node health, enabling failover and recovery without disrupting client-facing operations. In essence, the Query Coordinator ensures that query execution across a distributed system remains coherent, balanced, and resilient.

The Query Nodes form the execution layer where actual vector search happens. These nodes load vector segments and indexes into memory and execute similarity search, filtering, and ranking operations. Query Nodes handle both sealed segments (historical data) and growing segments (recent inserts), ensuring that newly ingested data becomes searchable with minimal delay. By executing searches in parallel across multiple segments and nodes, Query Nodes deliver low-latency responses even under heavy workloads. Their design directly impacts recall, throughput, and real-time responsiveness, making them central to the user-perceived performance of Milvus.

On the data ingestion side, Data Nodes manage incoming writes, including inserts and deletes. They handle buffering, segment creation, and persistence of vector data to durable storage. Data Nodes ensure that write-heavy workloads are absorbed efficiently while maintaining consistency and durability. Once data segments are sealed, they become candidates for indexing and query serving, creating a clean pipeline from ingestion to retrieval.

Index Nodes are responsible for building vector indexes such as IVF, HNSW, or PQ based on sealed data segments. Index construction is compute-intensive and decoupled from query execution to avoid performance interference. After indexes are built, they are stored in object storage and later loaded by Query Nodes as needed. This separation allows Milvus to scale indexing capacity independently and rebuild indexes without disrupting live queries.

Underlying all these components is a shared storage and metadata layer. Object storage provides durable, scalable persistence for vectors, indexes, and logs, while metadata services track schemas, segment states, and cluster topology. This foundation enables Milvus to recover from failures, support elastic scaling, and operate reliably in cloud and on-prem environments.

Hence, together these architectural components form a system where each node type has a focused responsibility, yet all cooperate to deliver fast, scalable, and reliable vector search. The Milvus architecture reflects a broader shift in AI infrastructure: from monolithic databases to distributed and semantic-aware systems where memory, computation, and coordination are engineered explicitly for embedding-driven intelligence.

CHAPTER 4

Data, Storage and Cluster Management

Introduction

Milvus, with its ability to manage compute and storage, provides robust vector storage capabilities while offering a sophisticated architecture that facilitates efficient data management. This chapter delves into the core aspects of data management in Milvus, focusing on index management, metadata management, data storage, and the innovative approach to compute-storage disaggregation. These components work in tandem to enable scalable, efficient, and high-performance data management for large-scale vector data. By the end of this chapter, readers will have a deep understanding of how Milvus manages and stores vector data at scale. They will gain insights into the different types of indexes, the importance of metadata, the partitioning and sharding strategies of the system, and how the decoupling of compute and storage enhances the scalability and flexibility of the system. These capabilities make Milvus a powerful tool for managing high-dimensional data across a wide range of industries and applications.

Structure

In this chapter, we will discuss the following topics:

- Compute/Storage Disaggregation
- Implementation of Compute Storage Disaggregation and High availability Using K8s
- Implementation of the Data Coordinator
- Implementation of the Root Coordinator
- Implementation of the Index Coordinator
- Implementation of the Data Node

Compute-Storage Disaggregation and Its Implementation in Kubernetes in Milvus

As data workloads continue to scale exponentially, traditional monolithic architectures, where compute and storage resources are tightly coupled, struggle to keep up with the demands of modern distributed systems. The concept of compute-storage disaggregation has emerged as a solution to decouple compute (the resources required for processing queries and operations) from storage (the resources needed to store massive datasets), offering greater flexibility, scalability, and cost efficiency. Milvus, a high-performance vector database, has adopted this approach to effectively manage high-dimensional data in large-scale distributed environments. This section explores the concept of compute-storage disaggregation and how it is implemented in Kubernetes to enhance the scalability, performance, and resilience of Milvus.

Understanding Compute-Storage Disaggregation

Compute-storage disaggregation refers to the separation of compute resources, responsible for executing data operations such as query processing, from storage resources, which handle data persistence. This separation allows each resource type to be scaled independently, based on workload requirements.

In traditional, tightly coupled architectures, compute and storage are often treated as a single unit, meaning that scaling one typically involves scaling the other. For example, increasing storage to handle larger datasets would often require an increase in compute capacity, even if the query load remains constant. Similarly, expanding compute resources to handle more queries would result in unnecessary storage provisioning, even though the data itself has not grown.

By decoupling these resources, Milvus can achieve several key benefits:

- **Independent Scaling:** Compute and storage can be scaled independently, based on specific demands. For example, if there is a surge in query volume but the dataset size remains relatively constant, only compute resources need to be scaled up, avoiding unnecessary overhead in storage.

- **Improved Resource Efficiency:** Resources are allocated more efficiently. For example, if storage grows significantly, compute resources can remain static until the query load increases, leading to cost savings.

- **Fault Isolation:** Failures in one resource type (say storage failure) do not impact the other, improving system resilience.

Implementation in Kubernetes

The Kubernetes configurations to accommodate the distributed architecture of Milvus involves several types of roles for managing compute resources, such as Data Coordinator, Root Coordinator, Index Coordinator, Data Worker, Index Worker, and Query Worker. Each component will have its own role within Milvus to manage distributed data and perform specific functions like query processing, data coordination, index building, and storage management The Kubernetes configurations tailored for each of these roles are as following:

Data Coordinator (`data-coord`) Deployment Configuration

The Data Coordinator is responsible for managing the data-related operations such as data partitioning, replication, and storage management. It coordinates the data worker nodes.

```
milvus-data-coord-deployment.yaml
apiVersion: apps/v1
kind: Deployment
metadata:
  name: milvus-data-coord
  labels:
    app: milvus
spec:
  replicas: 1  # Typically, you only need 1 data coordinator
  selector:
matchLabels:
      app: milvus
      role: data-coord
  template:
    metadata:
      labels:
        app: milvus
        role: data-coord
    spec:
      containers:
        - name: milvus-data-coord
          image: milvusdb/milvus:v2.0.0
          ports:
            - containerPort: 8080
          env:
            - name: MILVUS_ROOT_COORDINATOR_HOST
```

```
            value: "milvus-root-coord"  # Root coordinator service hostname
            - name: MILVUS_STORAGE_HOST
              value: "milvus-storage"  # Storage service hostname
milvus-data-coord-service.yaml
apiVersion: v1
kind: Service
metadata:
  name: milvus-data-coord
  labels:
    app: milvus
spec:
  ports:
    - port: 8080
targetPort: 8080
  selector:
    app: milvus
    role: data-coord
```

Root Coordinator (`root-coord`) Deployment Configuration

The Root Coordinator is responsible for managing the overall orchestration of the Milvus system, including service discovery and scheduling. It is the highest-level coordinator in the Milvus architecture.

```
milvus-root-coord-deployment.yaml
apiVersion: apps/v1
kind: Deployment
metadata:
  name: milvus-root-coord
  labels:
    app: milvus
spec:
  replicas: 1  # Typically, only 1 root coordinator is needed
  selector:
matchLabels:
      app: milvus
      role: root-coord
  template:
    metadata:
      labels:
        app: milvus
        role: root-coord
    spec:
```

```
      containers:
        - name: milvus-root-coord
          image: milvusdb/milvus:v2.0.0
          ports:
            - containerPort: 8081
          env:
            - name: MILVUS_DATA_COORDINATOR_HOST
                value: "milvus-data-coord"  # Data coordinator service
hostname
            - name: MILVUS_QUERY_COORDINATOR_HOST
              value: "milvus-query-coord"  # Query coordinator service
hostname
milvus-root-coord-service.yaml
apiVersion: v1
kind: Service
metadata:
  name: milvus-root-coord
  labels:
    app: milvus
spec:
  ports:
    - port: 8081
targetPort: 8081
  selector:
    app: milvus
    role: root-coord
```

Index Coordinator (index-coord) Deployment Configuration

The Index Coordinator is responsible for managing index creation, indexing operations, and coordinating the workers that perform indexing tasks.

```
milvus-index-coord-deployment.yaml
apiVersion: apps/v1
kind: Deployment
metadata:
  name: milvus-index-coord
  labels:
    app: milvus
spec:
  replicas: 1  # Typically, only 1 index coordinator is needed
  selector:
matchLabels:
      app: milvus
```

```
      role: index-coord
  template:
    metadata:
      labels:
        app: milvus
        role: index-coord
    spec:
      containers:
        - name: milvus-index-coord
          image: milvusdb/milvus:v2.0.0
          ports:
            - containerPort: 8082
          env:
            - name: MILVUS_ROOT_COORDINATOR_HOST
                value: "milvus-root-coord"  # Root coordinator service
hostname
            - name: MILVUS_STORAGE_HOST
              value: "milvus-storage"  # Storage service hostname
milvus-index-coord-service.yaml
apiVersion: v1
kind: Service
metadata:
  name: milvus-index-coord
  labels:
    app: milvus
spec:
  ports:
    - port: 8082
targetPort: 8082
  selector:
    app: milvus
    role: index-coord
```

Data Worker (data-worker) Deployment Configuration

The Data Workers handle the data operations, including managing partitions and handling large-scale data storage across nodes.

```
milvus-data-worker-deployment.yaml
apiVersion: apps/v1
kind: Deployment
metadata:
  name: milvus-data-worker
  labels:
```

```
    app: milvus
spec:
  replicas: 3  # Scale the number of data worker pods
  selector:
matchLabels:
      app: milvus
      role: data-worker
  template:
    metadata:
      labels:
        app: milvus
        role: data-worker
    spec:
      containers:
        - name: milvus-data-worker
          image: milvusdb/milvus:v2.0.0
          ports:
            - containerPort: 19530
          env:
            - name: MILVUS_DATA_COORDINATOR_HOST
                value: "milvus-data-coord"  # Data coordinator service
hostname
            - name: MILVUS_STORAGE_HOST
              value: "milvus-storage"  # Storage service hostname
milvus-data-worker-service.yaml
apiVersion: v1
kind: Service
metadata:
  name: milvus-data-worker
  labels:
    app: milvus
spec:
  ports:
    - port: 19530
targetPort: 19530
  selector:
    app: milvus
    role: data-worker
```

Index Worker (index-worker) Deployment Configuration

The Index Workers perform indexing operations, responsible for building and managing the indexes for the dataset.

```
milvus-index-worker-deployment.yaml
apiVersion: apps/v1
kind: Deployment
metadata:
  name: milvus-index-worker
  labels:
    app: milvus
spec:
  replicas: 2  # Scale the number of index worker pods
  selector:
matchLabels:
      app: milvus
      role: index-worker
  template:
    metadata:
      labels:
        app: milvus
        role: index-worker
    spec:
      containers:
        - name: milvus-index-worker
          image: milvusdb/milvus:v2.0.0
          ports:
            - containerPort: 19531
          env:
            - name: MILVUS_INDEX_COORDINATOR_HOST
               value: "milvus-index-coord"  # Index coordinator service
hostname
            - name: MILVUS_STORAGE_HOST
              value: "milvus-storage"  # Storage service hostname
milvus-index-worker-service.yaml
apiVersion: v1
kind: Service
metadata:
  name: milvus-index-worker
  labels:
    app: milvus
spec:
  ports:
    - port: 19531
targetPort: 19531
  selector:
    app: milvus
    role: index-worker
```

Query Worker (query-worker) Deployment Configuration

The Query Workers handle query processing, serving the end-user queries related to vector searches.

```
milvus-query-worker-deployment.yaml
apiVersion: apps/v1
kind: Deployment
metadata:
  name: milvus-query-worker
  labels:
    app: milvus
spec:
  replicas: 3  # Scale the number of query worker pods
  selector:
matchLabels:
      app: milvus
      role: query-worker
  template:
    metadata:
      labels:
        app: milvus
        role: query-worker
    spec:
      containers:
        - name: milvus-query-worker
          image: milvusdb/milvus:v2.0.0
          ports:
            - containerPort: 19532
          env:
            - name: MILVUS_ROOT_COORDINATOR_HOST
              value: "milvus-root-coord"  # Root coordinator service
hostname
            - name: MILVUS_QUERY_COORDINATOR_HOST
              value: "milvus-query-coord"  # Query coordinator service
hostname
milvus-query-worker-service.yaml
apiVersion: v1
kind: Service
metadata:
  name: milvus-query-worker
  labels:
    app: milvus
```

```
spec:
  ports:
    - port: 19532
targetPort: 19532
  selector:
    app: milvus
    role: query-worker
```

Deploying the Configuration Files

To deploy the services for the Milvus distributed system, run the following commands:

```
# Apply the coordinator configurations
kubectl apply -f milvus-root-coord-deployment.yaml
kubectl apply -f milvus-root-coord-service.yaml
kubectl apply -f milvus-data-coord-deployment.yaml
kubectl apply -f milvus-data-coord-service.yaml
kubectl
apply -f milvus-index-coord-deployment.yamlkubectl apply -f milvus-
index-coord-service.yaml
```

Apply the worker configurations

```
kubectl apply -f milvus-data-worker-deployment.yamlkubectl apply -f
milvus-data-worker-service.yamlkubectl apply -f milvus-index-worker-
deployment.yamlkubectl apply -f milvus-index-worker-service.yamlkubectl
apply -f milvus-query-worker-deployment.yamlkubectl apply -f milvus-
query-worker-service.yaml
```

Cluster Management in Milvus: The Role of Data Coordinator

In a distributed system like **Milvus**, managing the coordination between various components is essential for ensuring that data is efficiently stored, accessed, and processed. The **Data Coordinator** plays a critical role in this process, particularly in managing data nodes, channels, and data flow throughout the system. One of the key elements of this management is the **Cluster** interface and its implementation, **ClusterImpl**, which is responsible for handling the interactions between data nodes in the Milvus cluster.

The Cluster Interface

The **Cluster Interface** is central to managing the communication and operations between Milvus data nodes. It defines a set of methods that enable adding, removing, and interacting with the nodes in the cluster. These methods include:

- **Startup**: This method initializes the cluster by adding the data nodes and preparing the necessary channels for data distribution.
- **Register/Unregister**: These methods handle the addition and removal of data nodes, ensuring the cluster is dynamically adaptable to changes in the system.
- **Watch**: This function adds channels to data nodes, allowing the coordinator to track and manage data flowing through specific channels.
- **Flush**: The flush method asynchronously sends requests to flush data segments to the data nodes, ensuring data consistency across the cluster.
- **PreImport** and **ImportV2**: These methods manage the import of data into the system, preparing it for processing or importing new data into the nodes.
- **QueryPreImport** and **QueryImport**: These methods are used to query the status of pre-imported or imported data, allowing the system to monitor and manage data import operations.
- **QuerySlots**: This method retrieves information about the number of slots (resource allocations) available on each node, providing insights into the resource distribution of the system.
- **GetSessions**: It returns a list of all active sessions in the cluster, providing an overview of the currently running processes.
- **Close**: It ensures that all resources are released when the cluster is no longer in use.

ClusterImpl: Implementing the Cluster Interface

The **ClusterImpl** struct provides the concrete implementation of the **Cluster** interface. It manages two key components that enable the functionality of the cluster:

- **sessionManager**: It is responsible for managing the sessions of the data nodes, ensuring that they are properly tracked and maintained.
- **channelManager**: It manages the channels through which data is distributed to the nodes and ensures data consistency throughout the system.

By interacting with these components, **ClusterImpl** handles the core responsibilities of managing data nodes, channel allocation, and data flow across the cluster.

Core Methods in ClusterImpl

- **Startup**: When the system starts, **Startup** initializes the cluster by adding data nodes and preparing the necessary communication channels. It categorizes nodes into "legacy" and "all" nodes ensure that each node is properly connected to the channel manager. This setup is crucial for establishing the network of data nodes within Milvus.

- **Register/Unregister**: These methods allow new data nodes to be added to or removed from the cluster. When a node is registered, it is added to the session manager and channel manager, enabling it to participate in data operations. When a node is unregistered, it is properly removed from both managers, ensuring that the system remains consistent.
- **Flush**: The **Flush** method is one of the most critical functions in Milvus, as it handles the data flushing operations. It sends requests to the data nodes to flush data segments to storage. The request is sent asynchronously, ensuring that the system can continue operating while the data is flushed. This method ensures that the data remains consistent and up-to-date across all nodes.
- **QuerySlots**: To manage resources effectively, Milvus queries the available slots on each node. This method uses concurrency to query multiple nodes in parallel, allowing the system to efficiently retrieve slot information for all nodes in the cluster. This feature is essential for understanding resource usage and ensuring that the system can handle workloads appropriately.
- **PreImport/Import**: These methods manage the data import process, allowing Milvus to pre-process data or import new data into the system. They facilitate the integration of external datasets into the Milvus database and allow for efficient data management and processing.
- **Close**: The **Close** method ensures that all resources and connections are properly released when the cluster is no longer needed. This ensures that the system remains in a clean state and can be safely shut down or reconfigured.

Concurrency and Resource Management

Milvus employs efficient concurrency mechanisms to handle tasks like querying node slots. In the **QuerySlots** method, the system queries the slots of each node in parallel using goroutines, ensuring that the operation is scalable and responsive. This design allows Milvus to handle large-scale distributed workloads without compromising performance.

The **ClusterImpl** component is a cornerstone of the distributed architecture of Milvus, as it is responsible for managing the data nodes, communication channels, and various data operations in the system. By implementing the **Cluster** interface, **ClusterImpl** ensures that the system is scalable, resilient, and capable of handling large datasets with low latency. Whether it is managing data imports, flushing data, or querying resources, the **ClusterImpl** plays an essential role in maintaining the integrity and performance of the Milvus database.

For more detailed information and source code, please refer to the Cluster Implementation in Milvus. (https://github.com/milvus-io/milvus/blob/2.0/internal/datacoord/cluster.go)

Milvus Compaction Management

The `compaction.go` file in Milvus is responsible for managing the compaction process, which involves the merging and optimizing of data stored across various segments. This is important for improving performance and resource efficiency in the Milvus system.

The key methods are as follows:

- **StartCompaction**: It initiates the compaction process, which merges multiple data segments into fewer ones for optimization.
    - **Parameters**: It accepts details related to the segments that need to be compacted.
    - **Return Values**: It returns an error if the compaction process encounters issues.
- **StopCompaction**: It stops an ongoing compaction process if required, typically when certain conditions are met or if forced to halt.
    - **Parameters**: There are none.
    - **Return Values**: It returns an error if it fails to stop the compaction.
- **TriggerCompaction**: It triggers the compaction process for specific data segments based on predefined criteria or triggers.
    - **Parameters**: It defines which segments need to undergo compaction.
    - **Return Values**: It returns an error if it fails to trigger the process.
- **CompactionStatus**: It retrieves the status of ongoing or completed compaction tasks, useful for monitoring.
    - **Parameters**: It accepts identifiers for segments whose compaction status is required.
    - **Return Values**: It provides the status of the compaction.
- **GetCompactionProgress**: It provides progress details about the ongoing compaction task.
    - **Parameters**: There are none.
    - **Return Values**: It returns progress information as a percentage or similar indicator.

Source:

For more details, you can access the full code on GitHub: Milvus compaction.go - GitHub (https://github.com/milvus-io/milvus/blob/2.0/internal/datacoord/compaction.go)

Milvus Garbage Collection for Data Coordinator

The garbage_collector.go file in Milvus manages the cleanup and removal of obsolete or unused data from the system, optimizing storage and system performance by ensuring that unnecessary data is periodically purged.

The key methods are as follows:

- **StartGarbageCollection**: It initiates the garbage collection process, marking data as eligible for deletion when it is no longer needed.
  - **Parameters**: There are none.
  - **Return Values**: It returns an error if garbage collection fails to start.
- **StopGarbageCollection**: It stops the garbage collection process, typically when a stop condition or manual interruption is required.
  - **Parameters**: There are none.
  - **Return Values**: It returns an error if stopping fails.
- **CollectGarbage**: It actively removes unused data segments from the system to free up resources.
  - **Parameters**: It defines which data segments should be considered for removal.
  - **Return Values**: It returns an error if the garbage collection process encounters issues.
- **CheckGarbageCollectionStatus**: It provides the status of ongoing or completed garbage collection tasks.
  - **Parameters**: There are none.
  - **Return Values**: It returns a status report on the collection process.

Source:

For more details, you can access the full code on GitHub:

Milvus garbage_collector.go - GitHub (https://github.com/milvus-io/milvus/blob/2.6/internal/datacoord/garbage_collector.go)

Milvus Index Service Management

The index_service.go file in Milvus is responsible for handling operations related to the indexing of data, allowing for more efficient searches and retrievals within the system. This file defines methods that deal with index creation, management, and updates, ensuring that the data is indexed properly across various nodes in the Milvus cluster.

The key methods are:

- **CreateIndex**: It creates an index for the specified collection. This operation is crucial for accelerating search and retrieval operations on the data stored within Milvus.
    - **Parameters**: It takes collection and index creation configurations.
    - **Return Values**: It returns an error if index creation fails.
- **DropIndex**: It removes an existing index from a collection. This might be done to optimize performance or in case an index is no longer needed.
    - **Parameters**: It accepts collection details and index configuration.
    - **Return Values**: It returns an error if the index cannot be dropped.
- **GetIndex**: It retrieves information about an existing index within a collection, typically used for auditing or configuration management.
    - **Parameters**: It specifies the collection and index to query.
    - **Return Values**: It returns index details or an error if retrieval fails.
- **UpdateIndex**: It modifies the settings or configurations of an existing index. This is useful for improving search performance based on evolving query patterns.
    - **Parameters**: It includes the index configuration and collection details.
    - **Return Values**: It returns an error if updating the index fails.
- **GetIndexState**: It checks the status of an index, such as whether it is ready, being built, or encountering issues.
    - **Parameters**: It accepts the identifier for the index to check.
    - **Return Values**: It returns the status of the index.

Source:

For more details, you can access the full code on GitHub:

Milvus index_service.go - GitHub (https://github.com/milvus-io/milvus/blob/master/internal/datacoord/index_service.go)

Milvus Segment Management

The `segment_manager.go` file in Milvus is responsible for managing the lifecycle of segments, which are the basic unit of storage in Milvus. This file includes methods that handle segment creation, retrieval, and deletion, ensuring that data is efficiently segmented and managed within the Milvus system.

The key methods are:

- **CreateSegment**: It creates a new segment for storing data. This method handles the initialization of the segment, ensuring that it is properly set up for data insertion.
    - **Parameters**: It takes parameters related to the collection and the data to be stored in the new segment.
    - **Return Values**: It returns an error if the segment cannot be created.
- **DropSegment**: It drops a specified segment from the system, freeing up storage resources. This is typically used when a segment is no longer needed.
    - **Parameters**: It accepts the segment identifier and collection details for the segment to be dropped.
    - **Return Values**: It returns an error if the segment cannot be dropped.
- **GetSegment**: It retrieves information about an existing segment, such as its status, size, and other relevant details.
    - **Parameters**: It accepts the segment ID to query.
    - **Return Values**: It returns the segment information or an error if retrieval fails.
- **LoadSegment**: It loads the segment into memory for use in queries and other operations. This is important for performance, ensuring that frequently queried data is quickly accessible.
    - **Parameters**: It accepts segment identifiers and the conditions for loading the segment.
    - **Return Values**: It returns an error if the segment fails to load.
- **FlushSegment**: It ensures that the data in a segment is persisted to storage, typically when the segment is no longer actively used in memory.
    - **Parameters**: It accepts segment-specific information to determine when to flush.
    - **Return Values**: It returns an error if the flushing process fails.

- **MergeSegment**: It merges multiple segments into a single larger segment, often used for optimizing data storage and query performance.
    - **Parameters**: It accepts the list of segments to be merged.
    - **Return Values**: It returns an error if the merge process encounters issues.

Source:

For more details, you can access the full code on GitHub:

Milvus segment_manager.go - GitHub (https://github.com/milvus-io/milvus/blob/master/internal/datacoord/segment_manager.go)

Implementation of the Root Coordinator in Milvus

The **Root Coordinator in Milvus** is responsible for managing and coordinating various key tasks related to system operations, such as handling requests for creating and modifying collections, managing tasks, and overseeing garbage collection operations. A detailed explanation is as following:

- **Handling Requests and Workflow Management:**

  The Root Coordinator processes high-level system requests and manages workflows, including:

    - **Create Collection**: It handles the creation of new collections in the Milvus system, setting up necessary configurations and metadata.
    - **Alter Collection**: It manages changes to an existing collection, such as modifying collection schemas, configurations, or other parameters.
    - **Create Task**: It initiates background tasks like index building, data compaction, or other system operations that are essential for maintaining the performance and efficiency of the system.
    - **Alter Task**: It modifies or updates the existing tasks, such as adjusting parameters for ongoing processes (for example altering the configuration of an index-building task or adjusting task priorities).

- **Metadata Management:**

  The Root Coordinator is responsible for managing and storing critical metadata for collections, indexes, and tasks, which includes:

    - Tracking and storing collection schemas.
    - Managing index configurations.

    - Monitoring the state and status of ongoing tasks (such as whether tasks are pending, in progress, or completed).
    - Ensuring the consistency of metadata across the system to ensure smooth query routing and data management.

- **Task Management:**

  The Root Coordinator is also involved in managing the lifecycle of background tasks, such as:

    - **Scheduling Tasks**: It assigns tasks like index creation, data compaction, and garbage collection.
    - **Monitoring Tasks**: It oversees the status of tasks, ensuring that they are executed correctly and efficiently across the distributed system.
    - **Task Prioritization**: It helps in prioritizing certain tasks to ensure smooth operations and optimal system performance.

- **Garbage Collection**

  The Root Coordinator plays a role in managing **garbage collection** tasks, which involve cleaning up and removing outdated or unnecessary data from the system to free up resources.

    - **Schedule and Monitor Garbage Collection**: It initiates the garbage collection process, ensuring old or irrelevant data (like stale segments or deleted data) is cleaned up efficiently.
    - **Optimize Storage**: It ensures that storage resources are optimized by removing unused or obsolete data to maintain performance.

In summary, the **Root Coordinator** in Milvus manages high-level tasks related to:

- Handling requests like creating or altering collections and tasks.
- Managing metadata for collections, tasks, and system configurations.
- Overseeing task management, including task creation, monitoring, and prioritization.
- Garbage collection, which involves cleaning up unused data to optimize storage and system performance.

Understanding the Create Partition Task in Root Coordinator

In this section, we will dive into the internals of Milvus, specifically the file `create_partition_task.go`, which is a part of the root coordinator module. This file plays an essential role in handling the creation of partitions within a collection, a fundamental operation in Milvus when managing large datasets. Let us break down the core elements of this file to understand how the partition creation task works.

Overview of the `create_partition_task.go` File

The `create_partition_task.go` file is part of the internal logic of Milvus, a high-performance vector database designed for managing unstructured data. This file specifically deals with the creation of partitions, which are used to organize data within a collection for improved management and performance. The code defines a task that is responsible for processing partition creation requests and ensuring that the necessary steps are followed for a successful partition addition.

The main task here is handled by the `createPartitionTask` struct, which contains necessary information such as the partition creation request and the collection metadata. This struct will be responsible for verifying the request, interacting with the metadata system, and eventually executing the partition creation.

Key Components of the Code

- **The `createPartitionTask` Struct:**

  At the core of this functionality is the `createPartitionTask` struct. This struct encapsulates the logic required to handle the partition creation process. It inherits from a parent struct baseTask, which likely contains common functionality for task execution within Milvus. The `createPartitionTask` struct includes two critical fields:

  - **CreatePartitionRequest**: This is the request object that contains all the necessary information to create a new partition, such as the partition name and collection name.

  - **collMeta**: This field holds metadata related to the collection in which the partition will be created. It is vital for understanding the current state of the collection, including whether any partitions already exist or if there are limitations.

- **The Prepare Method:**

  The Prepare method is responsible for the preliminary checks and preparations needed before executing the partition creation task. It performs the following tasks:

  - **Validates the Request**: The method ensures that the request is valid and of the correct type. Specifically, it checks if the task is indeed a CreatePartition request, confirming that the action being performed is appropriate.

- **Fetches Collection Metadata**: The method interacts with the metadata system of Milvus to retrieve the current metadata of the collection specified in the request. This is crucial because it provides information about the existing partitions of the collections, thereby, allowing the system to check for potential issues before proceeding with the creation of a new partition.
- **Checks for Capacity Issues**: The Prepare method also looks into whether there are any capacity limitations that would prevent the partition from being created. This might include checking the current number of partitions or resource constraints.

- **The Execute Method:**

  Once the preliminary checks are completed, the Execute method is called to carry out the actual partition creation process. Here is what happens:

  - **Partition Duplication Check**: The method first checks if a partition with the same name already exists. If it does, a warning is logged, and the task is halted. This prevents the system from trying to create duplicate partitions, which could cause errors or inconsistencies.
  - **Proceeding with Partition Creation**: If the partition name is unique and no errors were found, the method proceeds with the creation of the partition. This step involves interacting with the underlying database or metadata system to physically create the new partition.
  - **Logging and Handling of Execution Flow**: Throughout the execution, the method logs important events (for example, warnings when a partition already exists) and, also ensures that the task is completed successfully.

Practical Implications

Understanding how the `create_partition_task.go` works is essential for anyone looking to modify or extend the functionality of Milvus, especially those involved in managing large-scale datasets. This task ensures that partitions are created correctly, and it safeguards against common errors like attempting to create a partition with a name that already exists. Furthermore, by interacting with the collection metadata, it ensures that the system remains consistent and resource-efficient.

For further details on the full implementation, refer to the source code available on GitHub: create_partition_task.go on GitHub.

Overview of Creating a Database Task in Root Coordinator

In this section, we explore the `create_collection_task.go` file within the Milvus codebase, which defines the logic for handling database creation tasks. A database in Milvus serves as a container for collections, and the ability to create databases efficiently is crucial for managing large-scale data operations. This file encapsulates the task logic for creating a new database, checking constraints, and handling potential conflicts. Let us walk through the key components of this file.

Overview of the `create_db_task.go` File

The `create_collection_task.go` file is responsible for handling requests to create new databases in Milvus. It defines a task that is executed whenever a new database is requested. This task involves several critical steps, such as validating the request, checking whether the maximum number of allowed databases has been reached, and allocating a unique ID for the new database. It also interacts with the metadata system to persist the new database details.

The main structure of the code is encapsulated in the `createDatabaseTask` struct, which contains the necessary information to execute the database creation operation. This task also ensures that the database creation process follows the internal constraints and limitations of Milvus.

Key Components of the Code

- **`createCollectionTaskStruct`:**

  The createCollectionTaskstruct defines the core structure for the database creation operation. It holds the following important fields:

  - **Req**: This field contains the request data for creating the database. It includes details like the database name and any other configuration necessary to initialize the database.
  - **dbID**: This is a unique identifier for the database. It will be assigned dynamically when a new database is created, ensuring that each database can be tracked individually within Milvus.
  - **Inheritance from baseTask**: The struct inherits from baseTask, indicating that it shares common properties and methods with other tasks in Milvus. This inheritance suggests that there is a general pattern for tasks in the Milvus codebase, where each task follows the same structure but performs specific operations.

- **Prepare and `validateSchemaMethod`:**

  The Prepare method is called before the main execution of the task. It performs several important checks and setups:

  - **Check for the Existing Databases**: The method queries the metadata store to retrieve the list of currently existing databases. This check ensures that the system is aware of all the databases present before attempting to create a new one.
  - **Validate Schema**: It checks if the provided schema for the collection confirms to the aforementioned requirements in Milvus.
  - **Limits Check**: Milvus enforces a maximum number of databases that can be created. The Prepare method checks whether this limit (MaxDatabaseNum) has been exceeded. If the number of databases is already at its maximum, the task will return an error, preventing the creation of new databases beyond the allowed limit. This helps to ensure that resources are not overwhelmed.
  - **Allocate a Database ID**: A unique identifier is needed for the new database. The Prepare method allocates this ID using the idAllocator component, ensuring that no two databases share the same ID. This allocation process is essential for maintaining the integrity of database operations.

- **The Execute Method:**

  The Execute method performs the actual creation of the database. After the preparation checks are complete, this method carries out the following actions:

  - **Create a New Database Object**: A new database object is instantiated using the allocated ID, the name from the request, and other necessary properties. This database object represents the new database within the system.
  - **Persist the Database**: The new database is saved into the metadata store, making it part of the persistent state of Milvus. This ensures that the database is available for further operations, such as creating collections within it.

  The Execute method ensures that the database creation process is completed successfully and that all required metadata is updated accordingly.

- **`GetLockerKey` Method:**

  The `GetLockerKey` method returns a key that is used to lock the database creation process. This lock is necessary to prevent multiple concurrent operations that could lead to conflicts. By using a lock key, Milvus ensures that only one process can create a database at a time, preventing race conditions or other inconsistencies during the database creation process.

Practical Implications

Understanding the `create_collection_task.go` file is critical for those working with the database management features of Milvus. This task is central to the creation of databases, and the logic ensures that resources are allocated efficiently, constraints are respected, and database operations remain consistent.

For example, the check for the maximum number of databases (MaxDatabaseNum) is a key aspect of resource management in Milvus, ensuring that the system does not run into capacity issues. Additionally, the process of allocating a unique database ID guarantees that each database can be individually tracked and managed.

By understanding this file, developers and system administrators can better manage database creation, extend the functionality of Milvus, or troubleshoot any issues related to database operations.

The `create_db_task.go` file defines the task logic for creating new databases within Milvus. From validating the request and checking system constraints to allocating a unique database ID and ensuring the task is executed correctly, this file plays an essential role in the database management system of Milvus. By examining the structure and flow of this task, we gain insight into the internal mechanisms that power the ability of Milvus to handle large datasets in a scalable and efficient manner.

For further details, refer to the full source code: https://github.com/milvus-io/milvus/blob/2.6/internal/rootcoord/create_collection_task.go.

Overview of the Index Coordinator

In Milvus, the **Index Coordinator** plays a crucial role in managing and overseeing the indexing operations of collections. Indexes are vital for efficient searching and retrieval of high-dimensional data, which is one of the core strengths of Milvus. The Index Coordinator is responsible for ensuring that the appropriate indexing strategies are applied to collections, managing index creation, maintenance, and deletion processes, and optimizing the performance of data retrieval operations.

This write-up delves into the key functions of the Index Coordinator, explaining its role within the Milvus architecture, how it interacts with other components, and the various responsibilities it handles.

Understanding Index Coordinator

The Index Coordinator is a component within Milvus that is responsible for managing the lifecycle of indexes for collections and partitions. When users request indexing for a collection (or partition), the Index Coordinator coordinates the creation, deletion, and maintenance of these indexes. It ensures that indexes are built on the relevant data, updated when necessary, and properly managed throughout their lifespan.

An index in Milvus is used to speed up query performance, particularly for high-dimensional vector data. Depending on the type of queries and data, different index types may be applied (for example, IVF, HNSW, and the like). The Index Coordinator ensures that the most efficient index types are chosen and managed for each collection.

Key Functions of the Index Coordinator

- **Index Creation Management:**

  One of the primary responsibilities of the Index Coordinator is managing the creation of indexes. This includes:

  - **Handling Index Requests**: When a user or system component requests an index for a collection or partition, the Index Coordinator coordinates the process. It communicates with the relevant backend components (such as the IndexNode), making sure that the request is fulfilled.

  - **Choosing the Right Index Type**: The Index Coordinator ensures that the appropriate index type is chosen based on the data and query requirements. It can choose from different index types like **IVF (Inverted File Index)**, **HNSW (Hierarchical Navigable Small World)**, or **Flat Index**, each of which has distinct advantages for various search operations.

  - **Defining Index Parameters**: For index creation, the Index Coordinator might also define and enforce certain parameters (like nlist, m, and so on) that dictate the index creation behavior, allowing for optimization based on the properties of the collection.

- **Index Deletion and Cleanup:**

  Another critical function of the Index Coordinator is managing the deletion and cleanup of indexes. When an index is no longer needed or when a collection is dropped, the Index Coordinator ensures that the index is properly removed from the system, freeing up resources. This includes:

  - **Dropping Indexes**: When a user requests to drop an index for a collection or partition, the Index Coordinator ensures that the operation is executed successfully. It ensures that all related resources are freed up and that no remnants of the index remain in the system.

- **Cleanup After Collection Deletion**: If a collection is deleted, the Index Coordinator handles the removal of associated indexes, ensuring that no orphaned index data remains, which might otherwise cause unnecessary resource consumption.

- **Index Maintenance and Updates:**

  The Index Coordinator is responsible for maintaining indexes over time. This includes ensuring that they remain up-to-date with the latest data and optimally serve queries:

  - **Rebuilding Indexes**: In cases where the index structure becomes suboptimal (due to updates, deletions, or other data modifications), the Index Coordinator may trigger the rebuilding of indexes.

  - **Optimizing Indexes**: It can also be involved in tasks that optimize the index for better query performance, like merging segments or adjusting the index parameters.

  - **Handling Dynamic Changes**: As collections grow or shrink, the Index Coordinator ensures that indexes are maintained and adjusted to reflect these changes, guaranteeing consistent performance across various data sizes.

- **Coordination with Other Milvus Components:**

  The Index Coordinator does not work in isolation. It interacts with other Milvus components, ensuring smooth workflows:

  - **Interaction with RootCoord**: The Root Coordinator is responsible for managing high-level system tasks, including database and collection management. The Index Coordinator coordinates with the Root Coordinator to ensure that indexing operations are aligned with the overall system state.

  - **Interaction with QueryNode**: Since indexing is tightly coupled with search queries, the Index Coordinator works with the QueryNode to ensure that the indexes are used effectively during query execution. This helps achieve faster and more accurate search results by utilizing the best index available for a query.

  - **Interaction with IndexNode**: The IndexNode is directly responsible for performing the actual indexing operations (like building and updating indexes). The Index Coordinator delegates tasks to the IndexNode and ensures that indexing jobs are distributed properly across the cluster.

- **Monitoring and Reporting:**

  The Index Coordinator also plays a role in monitoring the status and health of indexing tasks. It keeps track of indexing operations, such as:

  - **Index Build Progress**: The Index Coordinator tracks the progress of index creation, providing feedback and updates on the status of the process. If the process fails, it can trigger error handling or retries.
  - **Performance Metrics**: The Index Coordinator may collect and report on various performance metrics, such as the time taken for index creation or the efficiency of the indexing strategy, helping to optimize future operations.

- **Ensuring Index Consistency:**

  Index consistency is crucial in distributed systems, and the Index Coordinator ensures that indexes remain consistent even when the system is under heavy load or in the case of node failures. It coordinates index creation and updates to avoid conflicts and ensures that indexes reflect the latest data.

  - **Distributed Indexing**: In a distributed environment, the Index Coordinator ensures that indexing tasks are properly distributed across different nodes, minimizing the risk of inconsistent or incomplete indexes.

Benefits of the Index Coordinator in Milvus

- **Efficient Query Performance**: By managing the indexing process and selecting the optimal index types, the Index Coordinator plays a key role in enhancing the performance of queries, particularly for large-scale datasets.
- **Scalability**: The Index Coordinator ensures that indexing can scale across a distributed system, making Milvus capable of handling large volumes of high-dimensional data.
- **Resource Optimization**: It helps optimize the use of system resources by managing index creation, deletion, and maintenance efficiently, freeing up resources when they are no longer needed.
- **Fault Tolerance**: The Index Coordinator enhances the fault tolerance of the indexing process by ensuring consistency and recovering from failures, maintaining high availability for indexing tasks.

The Index Coordinator is a vital component in the architecture of Milvus, handling the creation, management, maintenance, and deletion of indexes. It ensures that indexing operations are efficient, consistent, and scalable, directly impacting the query performance and resource utilization of the system. By seamlessly coordinating with other components, the Index Coordinator helps Milvus manage large-scale vector data and ensures that the system can scale effectively while providing high-performance search capabilities.

In the following subsection, there is a more accurate and detailed explanation of the **Index Node** functionality based on the real code.

Overview of the Indexing Operations

The `indexnode.go` file in Milvus defines the functionality of the **Index Node**. This component is responsible for performing index-related operations on a distributed cluster of Milvus nodes, such as index creation, index maintenance, and responding to queries that involve indexed data. It is essential for ensuring that vector data is indexed correctly to speed up query processing.

The key responsibilities of the Index Node are as follows:

- **Index Creation**: The Index Node listens for requests to create indexes for collections or partitions. It ensures that the right type of index (for instance **IVF**, **HNSW**) is created according to the data and query requirements.
- **Index Deletion**: It also manages the removal of indexes when they are no longer needed, freeing up resources and ensuring that deleted indexes do not remain in the system.
- **Index Management**: Besides creation and deletion, the Index Node may also be responsible for handling updates or optimizations to indexes to ensure that the indexing mechanism is always efficient and up-to-date.

The key components of `indexnode.go` are as follows:

- **IndexNode Struct**: The IndexNode struct in the `indexnode.go` file encapsulates the properties of an index node in Milvus. This struct manages:
    - **Server ID**: It is a unique identifier for the index node.
    - **Address**: It is the information about the network address of the node, allowing communication with other Milvus components.
    - **Index Manager**: This manager is responsible for the actual creation and maintenance of indexes for collections.
- **Index Creation Flow**: Instead of a specific method like `HandleIndexCreation()`, the flow for handling index creation involves multiple steps across different methods:
    - When an index creation request is received, the Index Node will receive the request via its API and then delegate the task to the **IndexManager**.

    - The **IndexManager** will handle the actual building of the index, depending on the requested index type, such as IVF, HNSW, and so on

  The creation flow also involves communicating with other nodes, such as the **RootCoordinator** and **QueryNode**, to ensure that the index is created and used properly within the system.

- **API Handlers**: The Index Node listens for specific API calls to trigger actions like index creation or deletion. Some of the key API handlers include:
    - `CreateIndex`: This function is used to handle requests for creating new indexes.
    - `DropIndex`: This function listens for requests to remove indexes when they are no longer needed.
    - `GetIndexState`: It is a function that checks and returns the current state of an index, such as whether it is being built or has already been completed.
- **Task Management**: The Index Node defines a task management system where it can schedule and execute indexing tasks. The tasks are handled asynchronously, allowing the node to process indexing requests in parallel. The node will handle:
    - **Task Scheduling**: It decides when and how to begin indexing tasks based on the system's current state.
    - **Task Execution**: The primary purpose is to run the actual indexing algorithms in response to requests, managing progress, and ensuring the index is built correctly.
    - **Error Handling**: In case of errors during the indexing process, the system will attempt retries or notify other components of the failure.
- **Communication with Other Components**:
    - **RootCoordinator**: The Index Node interacts with the Root Coordinator to get updates about the collection and partition information. The Root Coordinator manages metadata and ensures that the index creation process aligns with the high-level management tasks of the system.
    - **QueryNode**: The Query Node is responsible for executing searches on indexed data. The Index Node ensures that the indexes created are available for fast querying by the Query Nodes, which use these indexes to speed up similarity searches.

- **Index Node Lifecycle**: The Index Node goes through specific phases:
    - **Startup**: When the node starts up, it initializes the necessary components, sets up connections, and prepares for indexing tasks.
    - **Shutting Down**: On shutdown, the node cleans up any active tasks and releases resources.
- **Concurrency and Resource Management**: The Index Node handles concurrent index creation tasks and ensures that system resources, such as memory and CPU, are used efficiently. It balances the indexing load across different parts of the cluster and manages resource allocation to prevent bottlenecks or overloading.

Important Functions in `indexnode.go`

While HandleIndexCreation does not exist in the code, there are other important functions that implement the indexing functionality. Some of these include:

- **Start()**: The Start() method is responsible for initializing the index node. It prepares the node to handle incoming index creation, deletion, and query requests.
- **Stop()**: The Stop() method gracefully shuts down the node, ensuring that no indexing tasks are left incomplete.
- **CreateIndex()**: This method is responsible for handling the creation of indexes. It takes in requests, processes them, and triggers the index creation process through the **IndexManager**.
- **DropIndex()**: This method handles requests to remove indexes. When invoked, it ensures that the specified index is properly deleted and resources are freed.
- **GetIndexState()**: It returns the status of an index, which could be useful for monitoring purposes to check if the indexing process has completed successfully or if it is still ongoing.
- **ExecuteTask()**: This function is used to execute indexing tasks in a distributed manner. It ensures that tasks are properly scheduled and executed, possibly across multiple Index Nodes in the cluster.
- **SyncWithRootCoord()**: This function ensures synchronization with the Root Coordinator to make sure that index creation, deletion, and maintenance align with the global state of the system.

The **Index Node** in Milvus, defined by `indexnode.go`, plays a pivotal role in ensuring that indexing tasks are executed efficiently in a distributed manner. While the node itself handles the actual building and management of indexes, it interacts closely with other Milvus components to ensure smooth indexing workflows, such as coordinating with the **RootCoordinator** and **QueryNode**. Understanding the functionality of the `indexnode.go` file is essential for anyone working with Milvus, as it helps maintain the performance and scalability of the system when handling high-dimensional data indexing.

For further details, refer to the full source code: https://github.com/milvus-io/milvus/blob/2.5/internal/indexnode/indexnode.go.

Overview of the Index Creation Manager

The `task_index.go` file in Milvus is a crucial part of the **Index Node** module. It defines the task management system for indexing operations, specifically focusing on how indexing tasks are created, executed, and managed. This file is responsible for handling the lifecycle of indexing tasks, ensuring that indexing operations are processed efficiently and distributed across the system.

This chapter provides an overview of the structure of the file, the task-related functionality it provides, and how it contributes to the overall indexing system in Milvus.

The key responsibilities of `task_index.go` are as follows:

- **Task Definition**: The primary role of `task_index.go` is to define the **indexing tasks** in Milvus. These tasks encapsulate the operations related to the creation, deletion, and maintenance of indexes for collections and partitions. This file defines how these tasks are structured, what parameters they require, and how they should be processed.

- **Task Lifecycle**: The tasks defined in `task_index.go` follow a lifecycle, starting from when they are created and scheduled to when they are executed and completed. This lifecycle ensures that indexing operations are carried out in an orderly, efficient manner. The lifecycle is managed by the Index Node, which coordinates task execution across the system.

- **Task Execution**: The `task_index.go` file defines the functions responsible for executing indexing tasks. The file ensures that indexing jobs are processed by appropriate workers or components, and that the results of indexing tasks (say the creation of an index) are properly communicated to the rest of the Milvus system.

- **Task Coordination**: This file plays a key role in task coordination, ensuring that the Index Node handles multiple tasks concurrently and efficiently. It is designed to manage the scheduling, execution, and monitoring of indexing tasks to prevent bottlenecks and ensure high performance during large-scale indexing operations.

The key Components in `task_index.go` are as follows:

- **IndexTask Struct**: The IndexTask struct defines the properties of a task related to indexing. Each IndexTask represents a specific operation, such as creating or deleting an index. The struct typically includes:
    - **Task ID**: It is a unique identifier for the task, which allows the system to track and manage the progress of the tasks.
    - **Collection Name**: It is the name of the collection for which the index is being created or managed.
    - **Partition Name**: If applicable, then it is the partition within the collection for which the index is being created.
    - **Index Type**: It is the type of index to be created (say, IVF, HNSW).
    - **Params**: These are any specific parameters required for index creation (for instance, nlist, m for HNSW).
- **Index Task Execution Methods**: `task_index.go` are defined as methods which are responsible for executing index tasks:
    - **`CreateIndex()`**: This method is invoked to create a new index for a given collection or partition. It ensures the correct index type is chosen and the required resources are allocated to build the index.
    - **`DropIndex()`**: This method handles the deletion of indexes that are no longer needed. It ensures that resources are freed up and that no traces of the index remain in the system.
    - **`UpdateIndex()`**: In some cases, an existing index may need to be updated due to changes in data or indexing parameters. This method would handle such updates.
- **Task Scheduling**: The file is responsible for scheduling indexing tasks. Indexing tasks are submitted to a queue and are executed in order based on availability of system resources. The scheduling mechanism ensures that tasks are executed efficiently, without overloading any part of the system. The task scheduler coordinates with other Milvus components to ensure that indexing tasks are executed in the correct sequence.
- **Task State Management**: Each indexing task has a state that indicates its progress through the indexing lifecycle. States include:
    - **Pending**: The task has been created but has not yet started execution.
    - **Running**: The task is currently being executed.
    - **Completed**: The task has been successfully completed.

  - **Failed**: The task has failed, possibly due to an error in the indexing process.
  - **Canceled**: The task has been canceled by the user or due to system intervention.

  The file defines methods for updating and querying the state of tasks, providing visibility into the progress of indexing operations.

- **Error Handling**: `task_index.go` handles errors that may arise during indexing tasks. This includes failures due to invalid parameters, resource constraints, or other issues during task execution. The system ensures that errors are logged and appropriate actions are taken, such as retrying the task or alerting other components.

- **Concurrency**: Since Milvus operates in a distributed environment, indexing tasks are executed concurrently across multiple nodes. `task_index.go` manages the concurrency of indexing tasks, ensuring that the system can handle large-scale indexing operations without conflicts or performance degradation.

Task Management Flow

- **Task Creation**: When an indexing request is made (such as the creation of a new index for a collection or partition), an IndexTask is created and populated with the relevant parameters (for example, collection name, index type, and configuration settings).

- **Task Scheduling**: The created task is submitted to a task queue, which is managed by the Index Node. The scheduler checks the resource availability of the system, and ensures that tasks are executed in an efficient, ordered manner.

- **Task Execution**: When resources are available, the task is executed by the appropriate worker or node. The execution of the task could involve communicating with other Milvus components like the **Root Coordinator** or **Query Node** to ensure proper index creation or deletion.

- **Task Completion**: Once an index task has been executed, the system updates the state of the task to **Completed**. If the task was successful, the index is now available for use in queries. If there was an error, the task state is updated to **Failed**, and further steps may be taken to handle the failure (like, retrying the task).

- **Error Handling and Recovery**: If an error occurs during task execution, the task will be marked as **Failed**. The system may take corrective actions, such as retrying the task, rolling back changes, or alerting the user.

The key functions and methods in `task_index.go` are as follows:

- `CreateIndexTask()`: This function creates a new IndexTask and adds it to the task queue. It is responsible for setting up the necessary parameters and ensuring the task is properly initialized.
- `ExecuteTask()`: Once a task is scheduled, the ExecuteTask() function is invoked to process it. This function is responsible for the actual creation or deletion of the index, coordinating with the **IndexManager** to perform the task.
- `GetTaskStatus()`: This function retrieves the current status of a given task, allowing other components or users to monitor the progress of indexing operations.
- `RetryTask()`: If a task fails, the `RetryTask()` function can be used to attempt the task again. It ensures that transient errors or temporary issues do not result in permanent task failures.

The `task_index.go` file is a crucial component in Milvus that defines and manages the lifecycle of indexing tasks. It ensures that indexing operations are executed efficiently, with proper task scheduling, state management, and error handling. By handling tasks such as index creation, deletion, and updates, it enables Milvus to manage large-scale vector data efficiently and provides the necessary mechanisms to ensure the scalability and fault tolerance of the system. Understanding how indexing tasks are managed in Milvus is vital for optimizing indexing workflows and ensuring high performance in high-dimensional vector search.

For further details, refer to the full source code: https://github.com/milvus-io/milvus/blob/2.5/internal/indexnode/task_index.go.

Conclusion

In this chapter, we have explored the key components of Milvus responsible for managing and coordinating indexing, data storage, and overall system coordination: the **Root Coordinator**, the **Index Coordinator**, and the **Data Coordinator**. Each of these coordinators plays a crucial role in ensuring the efficient operation of Milvus, which is designed to manage high-dimensional vector data at scale.

The **Root Coordinator** is the cornerstone of the distributed architecture of Milvus, which is responsible for managing metadata and coordinating tasks across different components. It acts as a central control unit, overseeing the management of collections, partitions, and other critical metadata that drive the overall functionality of Milvus. The source code within the **Root Coordinator** typically handles the creation, modification, and deletion of collections and partitions, orchestrating metadata operations in a distributed environment.

The **Index Coordinator** is responsible for overseeing indexing tasks within Milvus. Indexes are a core part of the ability of Milvus to perform fast similarity searches on high-dimensional data. The source code of the **Index Coordinator** typically defines the processes that initiate index creation, track index status, and manage the lifecycle of index tasks across different nodes. It ensures that indexing operations are carried out in parallel across the system, optimizing performance for large-scale datasets.

The **Data Coordinator** is focused on the storage and management of the actual vector data. It handles the allocation, retrieval, and management of data partitions across the Milvus system

The source code for the **Data Coordinator** manages the organization and storage of vectors, partitions, and other data-related tasks. It works closely with the **Root Coordinator** to ensure that data is allocated efficiently and with the **Index Coordinator** to ensure that indexing is properly handled.

Together, the **Root Coordinator**, **Index Coordinator**, and **Data Coordinator** collaborate to provide a seamless and scalable environment for Milvus. Each coordinator has specialized roles, yet they interact and communicate to support the overall lifecycle of vector data processing. The efficient orchestration between these three coordinators allows Milvus to scale and handle the massive amounts of high-dimensional vector data required for real-time similarity search.

The **Root**, **Index**, and **Data Coordinators** are central to the distributed architecture of Milvus. Each coordinator serves a distinct function, but they rely on each other to maintain system coherence and high performance in managing, indexing, and querying large-scale vector data. By understanding the source code of these components, developers and system administrators can gain deeper insights into how Milvus efficiently handles the challenges of high-dimensional vector data, from storage and indexing to query processing. As Milvus continues to evolve, these coordinators will remain key elements of its infrastructure, ensuring the scalability and performance of the system across diverse use cases.

In the following chapters, we will dive deeper into specific indexing algorithms and the architecture of the **Query Node** and **Data Node**, which further complement the work of these coordinators in delivering fast and accurate search results.

Chapter 5
Indexing Schemes

Introduction

In modern data retrieval systems, efficient indexing is critical for optimizing performance, especially when working with large-scale, high-dimensional data. Milvus, an open-source vector database, is designed to handle massive amounts of unstructured data, making it a go-to solution for applications in machine learning, artificial intelligence, and data science. One of the key factors behind the high performance of Milvus is its powerful and flexible indexing mechanisms.

In this chapter, we explore the various indexing techniques employed by Milvus to improve the speed and accuracy of vector searches. By transforming high-dimensional vectors into searchable representations, these indexing structures enable fast retrieval even in massive datasets. The chapter will delve into the different types of indexes available in Milvus, including IVF (Inverted File Index), HNSW (Hierarchical Navigable Small World), and others, providing insight into their underlying algorithms, use cases, and trade-offs.

We will also examine how Milvus efficiently balances the need for indexing accuracy with the constraints of system resources, helping users to choose the best indexing strategy for their specific use cases. Whether you are building a recommendation system, a semantic search engine, or a machine learning pipeline, understanding these indexing mechanisms is crucial for leveraging the full potential of Milvus.

Structure

In this chapter, we will discuss the following topics:

- Overview of the Indexing Types
- Implementation of the Flat Indexing Scheme
- Implementation of the IVF Scheme
- Implementation of the HNSW Scheme

Overview of the Indexing Types

Milvus offers several indexing mechanisms, each designed to optimize vector search for specific use cases. These indexing methods can be broadly categorized into **Floating-Type Indexes**, **Sparse Indexes**, and **GPU-Based Indexes**. Each category serves different data types and performance needs, allowing Milvus to efficiently handle a wide variety of search tasks.

Floating-Type Indexes

These indexes are designed for dense vectors, typically represented as floating-point numbers. These are the most common type of vectors used in machine learning, image recognition, and other high-dimensional data applications.

- **IVF (Inverted File Index)**:
    - **Concept**: It divides the vector space into clusters and performs a search within the most relevant cluster.
    - **Use Case**: It is best for large-scale datasets where approximate search results are acceptable. Balances speed and accuracy.
    - **Advantages**: It reduces search complexity by narrowing down the search space to relevant clusters.
- **HNSW (Hierarchical Navigable Small World)**:
    - **Concept**: It is a graph-based index that uses multiple layers of small-world graphs for fast approximate nearest neighbor search.
    - **Use Case**: It is Ideal for scenarios requiring high recall and accuracy, such as NLP tasks and semantic search.
    - **Advantages**: It has an excellent recall performance with a good balance between speed and accuracy.
    - **Drawback**: It is memory intensive and more computationally expensive than IVF for large datasets.
- **Flat (Brute Force)**:
    - **Concept**: Every vector in the dataset is compared with the query vector using exact distance calculations.
    - **Use Case**: It is suitable for smaller datasets where exact search results are required and computational cost is manageable.
    - **Advantages**: It provides exact results, with no approximation being involved.

- **Drawback**: It is computationally expensive for large datasets as every vector is compared.

- **Product Quantization (PQ)**:
  - **Concept**: It compresses high-dimensional vectors into smaller codes using vector quantization. It reduces memory usage while speeding up search operations.
  - **Use Case**: It is best for high-dimensional data, like image or video search, where memory efficiency is crucial.
  - **Advantages**: It is memory-efficient and fast search.
  - **Drawback**: There is some loss of accuracy due to quantization.

Sparse Indexes

Sparse indexing methods are tailored for vectors that are sparse, meaning that most of their elements are zeros or near-zero. Sparse vectors are common in applications such as NLP (word embeddings) and recommendation systems.

- **IVF_SQ (Inverted File with Scalar Quantization)**:
  - **Concept**: It is an extension of IVF that combines scalar quantization for sparse vectors, optimizing search within sparse data.
  - **Use Case**: It is used for sparse vectors where not all elements contribute meaningfully to the data.
  - **Advantages**: It has efficient storage and faster search times for sparse datasets.
  - **Drawback**: It is less efficient for dense vectors where quantization may introduce too much errors.

- **Binary Indexing**:
  - **Concept**: The targets binary vectors, where each vector is represented by binary values (0s and 1s). This index uses bitwise operations to perform fast searches.
  - **Use Case**: It is useful for datasets with binary vectors, such as hash embeddings or binary feature vectors.
  - **Advantages**: It is extremely memory-efficient and fast due to bit-level operations.
  - **Drawback**: It is limited to binary vectors, not suitable for general high-dimensional vectors.

- **Sparse Indexing**:
  - **Concept**: It is specifically optimized for vectors that have a large number of zero values, like in NLP applications (for example, word embeddings).
  - **Use Case**: It is efficient for large, sparse data representations common in text processing and recommender systems.
  - **Advantages**: It has a reduced memory usage and faster search by focusing only on non-zero elements.
  - **Drawback**: It is less effective for dense data or data that is not highly sparse.

GPU-Based Indexes

GPU-based indexing mechanisms leverage the parallel processing power of GPUs to accelerate both index construction and search. These indexes are ideal for large datasets and high-performance environments that require real-time processing.

- **GPU_CAGRA (Clustered Approximate Graph-based Random Access)**:
  - **Concept**: It accelerates graph-based approximate nearest neighbor search using the GPU, dividing the space into clusters and building a graph for efficient search.
  - **Use Case**: It is a large-scale, high-dimensional dataset where speed and scalability are critical.
  - **Advantages**: It has faster indexing and search than CPU-based methods, ideal for real-time applications.
  - **Drawback**: It requires GPU hardware.
- **GPU_IVF_FLAT (Inverted File Index with Flat Search)**:
  - **Concept**: It combines the IVF method with flat (brute-force) search, using GPU acceleration to speed up distance calculations for each cluster.
  - **Use Case**: It is suitable for large datasets where approximate search is acceptable but with good accuracy in each cluster.
  - **Advantages**: This can provide with fast search times on the GPU, thereby, reducing computational costs for large-scale datasets.
  - **Drawback**: It still relies on brute-force search within clusters, which may not be the most efficient for extremely large datasets.

- **GPU_IVF_PQ (Inverted File Index with Product Quantization)**:
  - **Concept**: It uses GPU to accelerate both the IVF and product quantization steps, reducing memory consumption while speeding up search.
  - **Use Case**: It is best for high-dimensional data where both memory efficiency and search speed are critical.
  - **Advantages**: It has efficient memory usage with fast search.
  - **Drawback**: It might cause approximate search with a potential loss of accuracy due to quantization.
- **GPU_BRUTE_FORCE (GPU-Accelerated Brute Force Search)**:
  - **Concept**: It utilizes GPU to speed up the brute-force search method, where every vector in the dataset is compared to the query vector.
  - **Use Case**: This is best for smaller datasets requiring exact search results and real-time performance.
  - **Advantages**: It provides exact search results with fast execution, leveraging GPU parallelism.
  - **Drawback**: It is not efficient for very large datasets, where brute-force comparisons are computationally expensive.

Binary Indexes

Milvus offers two main indexing mechanisms for **binary vectors**: **BIN_IVF** and **BIN_IVF_FLAT**. These are optimized for datasets where vectors are represented as binary values (0s and 1s), commonly used in hash-based embedding, recommendation systems, and other applications requiring efficient storage and search of binary data.

BIN_IVF (Binary Inverted File Index)

- **Concept**: **BIN_IVF** is a binary version of the **Inverted File Index (IVF)**, specifically designed for binary vectors. It partitions the vector space into multiple clusters (inverted lists) and performs a search within the most relevant clusters based on the query. The binary vectors are indexed to improve search efficiency by reducing the number of vectors to examine.
- **Use Case**: It is suitable for applications dealing with large-scale binary datasets, such as binary hash embeddings in machine learning, product recommendations, and binary feature search.
- **Advantages**:
  - **Efficient Search**: It reduces search space by narrowing down the search to a few clusters, providing faster results.

- **Scalability**: It is well-suited for large datasets where approximate search is acceptable, ensuring good performance with minimal computational overhead.

- **Drawback**:
  - Approximate search, which means that the results may not always be the exact nearest neighbors.

BIN_IVF_FLAT (Binary Inverted File Index with Flat Search)

- **Concept**: **BIN_IVF_FLAT** combines the **BIN_IVF** method with a **flat search** within the relevant inverted list. After determining which clusters are most relevant for the query, it performs a brute-force (flat) search within each cluster, using exact distance calculations to find the nearest neighbors.
- **Use Case**: Best for scenarios where **approximate search** within clusters is acceptable, but **exact search** is needed for fine-grained results within each cluster. It isideal for smaller datasets where speed is critical and exact matches are required within the reduced search space.
- **Advantages**:
  - **Exact Search within Clusters**: After narrowing down the search space to relevant clusters, it performs exact search, ensuring high accuracy within the chosen clusters.
  - **Scalable**: Faster than brute-force search across the entire dataset while maintaining high precision within clusters.
- **Drawback**:
  - Although it performs an exact search within clusters, it is still approximate in terms of the overall search, as it relies on clustering to reduce the dataset size.
  - **Memory Consumption**: While faster than full brute-force methods, the use of exact search within clusters might still consume more memory compared to pure approximate methods.

Summary of Binary Indexing Types in Milvus

- **BIN_IVF**:
  - **Description**: Binary version of the Inverted File Index (IVF), divides the dataset into clusters and performs approximate nearest neighbor search within the most relevant clusters.
  - **Use Case**: Suitable for large-scale binary datasets where approximate search is acceptable.

  - **Advantages**: Faster than brute-force, scalable for large datasets.
  - **Drawback**: Approximate search, leading to possible loss of exact matches.
- **BIN_IVF_FLAT**:
  - **Description**: Combines the IVF clustering method with a flat (brute-force) search within each cluster to find exact nearest neighbors.
  - **Use Case**: Ideal for scenarios where the search space can be reduced to specific clusters, and exact search within those clusters is required.
  - **Advantages**: Provides exact results within relevant clusters, faster than full brute-force search.
  - **Drawback**: Still relies on approximations at the clustering level, and memory consumption may be higher than other approximate methods.

Implementation of the IVF Indexing Scheme

The Inverted File (IVF) indexing scheme accelerates similarity search by organizing vectors into clusters. Each vector is assigned to the nearest centroid, creating partitions that reduce the search space during queries. During retrieval, only the most relevant clusters are scanned, improving efficiency and search performance.

IVF Implementation in FAISS - Key Code Snippets Summary

The `IndexIVF` class is a core part of the IVF index structure of FAISS. Here is a summary of key pieces of the code that define how the IVF index operates:

Class Definition and Members:

- **`IndexIVF` class** inherits from Index and `IndexIVFInterface` and manages inverted lists, clustering, and vector quantization.

```
struct IndexIVF : Index, IndexIVFInterface {
InvertedLists* invlists = nullptr;
    bool own_invlists = false;
size_tcode_size = 0;
    int parallel_mode = 0;
DirectMapdirect_map;
    bool by_residual = true;
};
```

The IVF index quantizes the indexes into a set of inverted lists with the quantization factor very similar to hashing on buckets.

- **Initialization**: The constructor initializes the IVF index, takes a quantizer, dimension d, number of clusters nlist, code size, and distance metric.

```
IndexIVF(Index* quantizer, size_t d, size_tnlist, size_tcode_
size, MetricType metric = METRIC_L2);
```

Training and Adding Vectors:

- **Training**: The `train()` function trains the quantizer and computes cluster centroids using k-means.

```
void train(idx_t n, const float* x) override;
```

- **Adding Vectors**: Vectors can be added via the `add()` function, either with or without predefined IDs.

```
void add(idx_t n, const float* x) override;
void add_with_ids(idx_t n, const float* x, constidx_t* xids)
override;
```

Vector Encoding and Indexing:

- **Encoding Vectors**: Vectors are encoded into quantized representations in the inverted list.

```
virtual void encode_vectors(
idx_t n,
const float* x,
constidx_t* list_nos,
    uint8_t* codes,
    bool include_listno = false) const = 0;
```

- **Adding Encoded Vectors**: The function `add_core()` handles the addition of preencoded vectors (using the `encode_vectors` function).

```
virtual void add_core(
idx_t n,
const float* x,
constidx_t* xids,
constidx_t* precomputed_idx);
```

Search Operations

- **Search**: The `search()` method retrieves the k nearest neighbors for a given query vector by first performing a coarse search over the centroids, followed by fine search within the selected clusters.

```
void search(
idx_t n,
```

```
const float* x,
idx_t k,
    float* distances,
idx_t* labels,
constSearchParameters* params = nullptr) const override;
```

- **Range Search**: A similar search operation where the range (radius) of neighbors is specified.

```
void range_search(
idx_t n,
const float* x,
    float radius,
RangeSearchResult* result,
constSearchParameters* params = nullptr) override;
```

Reconstruct and Update Vectors

- **Reconstruction**: The `reconstruct()` function reconstructs a vector from its ID or list offset.

```
void reconstruct(idx_t key, float* recons) const override;
void reconstruct_n(idx_t i0, idx_tni, float* recons) const override;
```

- **Updating Vectors**: Updates a subset of vectors indexed by IDs.

```
void update_vectors(int nv, constidx_t* idx, const float* v);
```

Additional Utility Functions

- **Direct Map**: Methods like `make_direct_map()` and `set_direct_map_type()` manage the direct mapping of IDs to vectors.

```
void make_direct_map(bool new_maintain_direct_map = true);
void set_direct_map_type(DirectMap::Type type);
```

- **Inverted List Replacement**: The function `replace_invlists()` allows replacing the current inverted lists with a new one.

```
void replace_invlists(InvertedLists* il, bool own = false);
```

- **Standalone Codec**: Functions like `sa_encode()` handle encoding vectors into standalone codes.

```
void sa_encode(idx_t n, const float* x, uint8_t* bytes) const
override;
```

- **Destructor:** The function ensures proper cleanup when the `IndexIVF` object is destroyed.

```
~IndexIVF() override;
```

Key Code Summary

- **Constructor**: Initializes the IVF index with quantizer, dimension, number of clusters, and metric.
- **Training**: `train()` partitions the data into clusters and trains the quantizer using k-means.
- **Adding Vectors**: Adds vectors to the inverted lists either with or without IDs (`add()`, `add_with_ids()`).
- **Vector Encoding**: `encode_vectors()` encodes vectors before adding them to inverted lists.
- **Search**: `search()` and `range_search()` retrieve nearest neighbors or perform range queries with fine and coarse search.
- **Reconstruction**: `reconstruct()` and `reconstruct_n()` reconstruct original vectors from IDs or list offsets.
- **Direct Map**: `make_direct_map()` and `set_direct_map_type()` handle ID-to-vector mapping.
- **Inverted List Replacement**: `replace_invlists()` replaces the current inverted list with a new one.
- **Standalone Codec**: `sa_encode()` encodes vectors for standalone use.
- **Destructor**: Cleans up resources when the object is destroyed.

Implementation of the Index IVF Addition and Search Functions

The `add_core()` function adds vectors to an IVF index in batches, processing them in parallel using OpenMP for efficiency. It encodes the vectors into a compressed form, then inserts them into the appropriate inverted lists based on their coarse quantization indices. It also manages vector-to-ID mappings and tracks the number of successfully added vectors and invalid ones.

```
Code Block Summary: IndexIVF::add_core()

void IndexIVF::add_core(
        idx_t n,
        const float* x,
        constidx_t* xids,
        constidx_t* coarse_idx) {
    // do some blocking to avoid excessive allocs
    idx_t bs = 65536;
```

```
    if (n > bs) {
        for (idx_t i0 = 0; i0 < n; i0 += bs) {
            idx_t i1 = std::min(n, i0 + bs);
            if (verbose) {
               printf("   IndexIVF::add_with_ids %" PRId64 ":%" PRId64 "\n",
                        i0,
                        i1);
            }
            add_core(
                    i1 - i0,
                    x + i0 * d,
                    xids ? xids + i0 : nullptr,
                    coarse_idx + i0);
        }
        return;
    }
    FAISS_THROW_IF_NOT(coarse_idx);
    FAISS_THROW_IF_NOT(is_trained);
    direct_map.check_can_add(xids);

    size_tnadd = 0, nminus1 = 0;

    for (size_ti = 0; i< n; i++) {
        if (coarse_idx[i] < 0)
            nminus1++;
    }

    std::unique_ptr<uint8_t[]>flat_codes(new uint8_t[n * code_size]);
    encode_vectors(n, x, coarse_idx, flat_codes.get());

    DirectMapAdddm_adder(direct_map, n, xids);

#pragma omp parallel reduction(+ : nadd)
    {
        int nt = omp_get_num_threads();
        int rank = omp_get_thread_num();

        // each thread takes care of a subset of lists
        for (size_ti = 0; i< n; i++) {
            idx_tlist_no = coarse_idx[i];
            if (list_no>= 0 &&list_no % nt == rank) {
                idx_t id = xids ? xids[i] : ntotal + i;
                size_tofs = invlists->add_entry(
                        list_no, id, flat_codes.get() + i * code_size);
a
                dm_adder.add(i, list_no, ofs);
```

```
                nadd++;
            } else if (rank == 0 &&list_no == -1) {
                dm_adder.add(i, -1, 0);
            }
        }
    }

    if (verbose) {
        printf("    added %zd / %" PRId64 " vectors (%zd -1s)\n",
               nadd,
               n,
               nminus1);
    }

    ntotal += n;
}
```

This function, `add_core()`, handles adding vectors to the IVF (Inverted File) index in a parallelized manner. It processes large batches of data efficiently, while also managing the inversion and encoding of vectors before inserting them into the corresponding inverted list.

Here is a summary of the steps:

- **Batch Processing**:
  - The function processes vectors in blocks (batch size of 65,536 by default). If the number of vectors (n) exceeds this batch size, the function splits the task into smaller batches to avoid excessive memory allocation and keep processing manageable.
- **Input Validations**:
  - The function checks if the `coarse_idx` (coarse quantization index) is valid and whether the index is trained (`is_trained`).
  - It also ensures that the `direct_map` can add the provided IDs (`xids`).
- **Counting Invalid Indices**:
  - The function counts how many vectors have a `coarse_idx` value of -1, indicating that they were not assigned to a valid cluster during quantization.
- **Vector Encoding**:
  - The function encodes the vectors into a compressed form using the `encode_vectors()` function. The encoded vectors are stored in `flat_codes`, which is a dynamically allocated array.

- **Parallel Processing (OpenMP)**:
  - The function leverages OpenMP for parallelization, allowing multiple threads to process different subsets of the inverted lists.
  - Each thread handles a specific subset of vectors, adding them to the appropriate inverted list based on their `coarse_idx`.
  - The `DirectMapAdd` object (`dm_adder`) manages adding entries to the `direct_map`.
- **Inserting into Inverted Lists**:
  - For each vector, if the `coarse_idx` is valid (not -1), it is added to the corresponding inverted list. The entry is added using `invlists->add_entry()`, which returns the offset within the list.
  - For vectors with `coarse_idx` == -1, a placeholder entry is added (only on the first thread).
- **Updating Counters**:
  - The number of successfully added vectors (`nadd`) and the number of invalid vectors (`nminus1`) are tracked.
  - The total count of vectors (`ntotal`) is updated after all vectors are processed.
- **Verbose Logging**:
  - If the verbose flag is enabled, it prints the progress, showing how many vectors were successfully added and how many had invalid indices.

Key Takeaways

- **Batch Processing**: Large numbers of vectors are processed in smaller chunks to avoid memory overload.
- **Parallelization**: OpenMP is used to parallelize the task, improving performance by distributing work across multiple threads.
- **Vector Encoding**: Vectors are encoded using `encode_vectors()` before being added to the inverted lists.
- **Efficient Insertion**: The vectors are inserted into inverted lists based on their assigned `coarse_idx`, and the process is optimized with the `DirectMapAdd` for managing vector-to-ID mappings.
- **Verbose Output**: The function provides optional logging for debugging and monitoring the progress of vector insertion.

This method efficiently adds vectors to the IVF index, handling large datasets while ensuring that the vectors are properly quantized, encoded, and added to the correct inverted lists in parallel.

`IndexIVF::search()`

The `search()` function performs the search operation on the IVF index, handling multiple queries in parallel if necessary. It executes the search by first quantizing the input vectors and fetching the corresponding inverted list entries, then performing the actual search in the lists and returning the closest vectors based on the k nearest neighbors. The function is optimized for parallel execution and collects relevant statistics for performance analysis.

The key steps in the function are:

- **Input Validation**:
  - It ensures that the number of nearest neighbors k is positive.
  - It verifies that the search parameters (`params_in`) are of the correct type (IVFSearchParameters).
- **Search Parameters**:
  - It determines the nprobe value (the number of lists to search in the inverted file). It uses either the provided `params_in` or a default value.
- **Sub-Search Function**:
  - It is a lambda function (`sub_search_func`) handles the search for a subset of queries by:
    - Performing quantization of the input vectors using the `quantizer->search()`.
    - `invlists->prefetch_lists()`.
    - Calling `search_preassigned()` to retrieve the top k closest vectors from the selected lists.
- **Parallelization**:
  - If the parallelization mode allows, the function runs the search in parallel using OpenMP, distributing the work across multiple threads.
  - For each thread, it processes a subset of queries (n), computes results for the respective range of queries, and accumulates search statistics.
- **Error Handling**:
  - It catches any exceptions during the search process, locking and storing the exception message if one occurs. It throws an error if any exception is encountered.

- **Statistics Collection**:
    - The function tracks statistics during the search, such as quantization time and search time, and aggregates these statistics from all parallel threads.
- **Fallback for Non-Parallel Search**:
    - If parallelization is disabled or cannot be used, the function runs the search on a single thread, calling `sub_search_func` directly.

Key Bullet Points:

- **Input Validation**: Ensures k > 0 and correct `params_in` type for search.
- **Search Parameters**: Uses nprobe to determine how many inverted lists to search.
- **Sub-Search Execution**: The main search logic is encapsulated in a lambda function that handles quantization and search in inverted lists.
- **Parallel Search**: If enabled, the search is run in parallel across multiple threads using OpenMP, with each thread handling a slice of the queries.
- **Exception Handling**: Catches and handles exceptions during the search, ensuring the program does not crash unexpectedly.
- **Performance Stats**: Collects and aggregates stats for quantization and search times, helpful for performance analysis.
- **Non-Parallel Fallback**: If parallelization is not possible, the search runs serially.

This method efficiently searches for the nearest neighbors across multiple queries, with options for parallel execution and performance tracking.

Implementation of the Index PQ Addition and SearchFunctions

The ProductQuantizer struct implements product quantization for vector compression, specifically for **L2 distance metric**. It divides the vectors into smaller subvectors (subquantizers), and each subvector is quantized independently, enabling efficient approximation of distances. This structure contains methods for training the quantizer, encoding and decoding vectors, computing distance tables, and performing search queries. The key features are as follows:

- **Initialization**:
    - It defines the number of subquantizers (M), bits per subquantizer (nbits), and dimensionality of the vectors.

- **Training**:
  - It can train the product quantizer using different initialization strategies (for example, hot start, shared dictionary, hypercube).
- **Quantization**:
  - It has methods for quantizing vectors into compressed codes and decoding them back to original vector approximations.
- **Distance Tables**:
  - It calculates distance tables between a vector and all centroids for each subquantizer, used for encoding and searching.
- **Search**:
  - It implements L2 distance-based search for finding closest vectors by comparing the query codes with precomputed database codes.
- **SDC (Symmetric Distance Coding)**:
  - It supports symmetric distance table computations and searches based on SDC.
- **Centroid Management**:
  - It stores and manages the centroids for each subquantizer and provides methods to synchronize or clear the transposed centroid table.

An overview of the methods is as follows:

- **Training**:
  - `train()`: It trains the quantizer on input vectors, adjusting centroids based on selected clustering parameters.
- **Quantization and Decoding**:
  - `compute_code()`, `compute_codes()`: It quantizes vectors into compressed codes.
  - `decode()`: It decodes compressed codes back into vectors.
- **Distance Computation**:
  - `compute_distance_table()`: It computes distances between a vector and each centroid of the subquantizers.
  - `compute_distance_tables()`: It compute distance tables for multiple input vectors.
- **Search**:
  - `search()`: It performs a search using L2 distance between query vectors and pre-quantized database vectors.

  - `search_ip()`: It performs a search based on inner product similarity.
  - `search_sdc()`: It performs a search using symmetric distance coding.

- **SDC Management**:
  - `compute_sdc_table()`: It computes symmetric distance computation table from centroids.

- **Centroid Synchronization**:
  - `sync_transposed_centroids()`, `clear_transposed_centroids()`: These syncs or clears the transposed centroid table when needed.

The ProductQuantizer struct is highly optimized for vector quantization and search operations, making it suitable for applications like large-scale similarity search and compression.

`pq_estimators_from_tables` Function Summary

The function `pq_estimators_from_tables` performs a search using a precomputed distance table and a set of quantized codes. It estimates the distances between code entries and the centroids of a Product Quantizer (PQ), and updates a heap to store the k closest entries. It uses different methods based on the number of subquantizers M in the PQ, optimizing for cases where M is a multiple of 4. The key points are:

- **Function Parameters**:
  - **pq:** The ProductQuantizer object containing the PQ structure, including subquantizers and their centroids.
  - **codes:** The quantized codes (indices of centroids) for the vectors.
  - **ncodes:** The number of codes to process.
  - **dis_table:** A precomputed distance table, which contains the squared distances between each code and its corresponding centroids.
  - **k:** The number of closest neighbors to retrieve.
  - **heap_dis:** An array to store the distances of the closest neighbors.
  - **heap_ids:** An array to store the indices of the closest neighbors.

- **Flow**:
  - For M == 4, a specialized function `pq_estimators_from_tables_M4` is used to efficiently estimate distances.
  - For M being a multiple of 4, another optimized function `pq_estimators_from_tables_Mmul4` is used.
  - If M is not a multiple of 4, the function falls back to a slower default method where it iterates through all codes and updates the heap with the closest distances.

- **Heap Update**:
    - The heap stores the closest k entries (vectors), where heap_dis contains the distances and heap_ids stores the corresponding indices.
    - The function checks if the current distance is smaller than the top distance in the heap. If so, it replaces the top element with the new entry.

Key Steps:

- It checks the number of subquantizers M and decides on the appropriate optimization technique.
- It iterates through the codes, computing the distance to each centroid and updating the heap with the k closest distances and their indices.

This function is primarily used for efficiently estimating the closest vectors in a product quantizer-based index using precomputed distance tables.

Implementation of the Index Flat Addition and Search Functions

An **index** in FAISS is a data structure used to **store vectors** and perform **nearest neighbor searches** on them. The core idea is to find the vectors in your database that are closest to a given query vector—typically using some similarity metric like **L2 distance** (Euclidean) or **inner product** (dot product).

Flat Index: The Foundation of FAISS (Facebook AI Similarity Search)

The **Flat index**, sometimes referred to as a **brute-force index**, is the **simplest and most accurate** index type in FAISS.

How It Works

- It stores all vectors **as-is**, in memory, without any quantization, clustering, or hashing.
- At query time, it **compares the query vector to every single stored vector** in the index.
- This ensures that the search is **exact**: the results are the true nearest neighbors according to the distance metric used.

Types of Flat Indexes

FAISS provides multiple types of indexes designed for different accuracy and speed requirements. Common types include **Flat Index** for exact search, **IVF (Inverted File Index)** for faster approximate search, and **HNSW (Hierarchical Navigable Small World)** for graph-based nearest neighbor search. Some indexes also combine **Product Quantization (PQ)** to compress vectors and reduce memory usage while maintaining efficient retrieval.

Index Type	Description
IndexFlatL2	Uses **L2 (Euclidean) distance**
IndexFlatIP	Uses **inner product**
IndexFlat1D	Optimized for scalars.

Table 5.1: *Types of Flat Indexes*

Search Operation in the Flat Index Scheme

FAISS Code: `IndexFlat::search` Method

```
void IndexFlat::search(
idx_t n,
const float* x,
idx_t k,
        float* distances,
idx_t* labels,
constSearchParameters* params) const {
IDSelector* sel = params ? params->sel : nullptr;
    FAISS_THROW_IF_NOT(k > 0);

    // we see the distances and labels as heaps
    if (metric_type == METRIC_INNER_PRODUCT) {
float_minheap_array_t res = {size_t(n), size_t(k), labels, distances};
knn_inner_product(x, get_xb(), d, n, ntotal, &res, sel);
    } else if (metric_type == METRIC_L2) {
float_maxheap_array_t res = {size_t(n), size_t(k), labels, distances};
        knn_L2sqr(x, get_xb(), d, n, ntotal, &res, nullptr, sel);
    } else if (is_similarity_metric(metric_type)) {
float_minheap_array_t res = {size_t(n), size_t(k), labels, distances};
knn_extra_metrics(
                x, get_xb(), d, n, ntotal, metric_type, metric_arg, &res);
    } else {
        FAISS_THROW_IF_NOT(!sel);
```

```
float_maxheap_array_t res = {size_t(n), size_t(k), labels, distances};
knn_extra_metrics(
                x, get_xb(), d, n, ntotal, metric_type, metric_arg, &res);
    }
}
```

Explanation

Function Purpose

This method performs **brute-force nearest neighbor search** over the database vectors stored in a **Flat index**. It calculates the distances (or similarities) between n query vectors and all database vectors, then returns the top k closest or most similar ones for each query.

Parameters

- **n:** Number of query vectors.
- **x:** Pointer to the array of query vectors (n × d).
- **k:** Number of nearest neighbors to return.
- **distances:** Output buffer to store the n × k distances.
- **labels:** Output buffer to store the n × k indices of the nearest database vectors.
- **params:** Optional parameters, including a possible IDSelector to filter candidate database vectors.

1. **Selector Setup:**

   ```
   IDSelector* sel = params ? params->sel : nullptr;
   ```

   - If search parameters include a selector (`sel`), it will be used to **filter the candidate vectors** from the database.
   - Otherwise, the search runs on **all stored vectors**.

2. **Sanity Check on k:**

   ```
   FAISS_THROW_IF_NOT(k > 0);
   ```

   - Ensures the number of neighbors to return is valid.

3. **Dispatch Based on Metric Type:**

   The actual search logic is dispatched based on the **metric type** specified for the index.

A. **Inner Product Metric:**

   ```
   float_minheap_array_t res = {size_t(n), size_t(k), labels, distances};
   knn_inner_product(x, get_xb(), d, n, ntotal, &res, sel);
   ```

- Uses **dot product** to measure similarity.
- Keeps track of the top-k **largest values** using a **min-heap**.
- `knn_inner_product()` computes all inner products between query and database vectors.

B. L2 (Euclidean) Distance:

```
float_maxheap_array_t res = {size_t(n), size_t(k), labels,
distances};
knn_L2sqr(x, get_xb(), d, n, ntotal, &res, nullptr, sel);
```

- Computes **squared Euclidean distances** between query and database vectors.
- Uses a **max-heap** to maintain the smallest k distances (closer means more similar).
- `knn_L2sqr()` does the brute-force distance computation.

Other Similarity Metrics

```
float_minheap_array_t res = {size_t(n), size_t(k), labels, distances};
knn_extra_metrics(x, get_xb(), d, n, ntotal, metric_type, metric_arg, &res);
```

- For similarity metrics beyond inner product (say cosine, JS-divergence).
- Uses **min-heap** since higher similarity means better match.

Other Distance Metrics

```
FAISS_THROW_IF_NOT(!sel);
float_maxheap_array_t res = {size_t(n), size_t(k), labels, distances};
knn_extra_metrics(x, get_xb(), d, n, ntotal, metric_type, metric_arg,
&res);
```

- For distance-based metrics that are not L2.
- Uses a **max-heap** for tracking top-k **smallest** distances.
- Rejects filtering (`sel`) in this case—throws if a selector is provided.

Heaps Recap

- **Min-heap**: Used for **similarity metrics** (larger is better).
- **Max-heap**: Used for **distance metrics** (smaller is better).

Helper Functions Called

- **`knn_inner_product()`**: Brute-force top-k inner product search.

- **`knn_L2sqr()`:** Brute-force top-k Euclidean distance search.
- **`knn_extra_metrics()`:** Handles all other metric types with a common interface.

In summary, this method is the **core of brute-force search** in IndexFlat. It:

- Prepares the search configuration (heaps and optional filtering).
- Selects the right algorithm based on the configured metric.
- Delegates to optimized Faiss routines to compute distances/similarities and fill the results.

It is accurate but linear in complexity — used when you need **exact results** or are working with **small datasets**.

Index Addition Operation in the Flat Index Scheme

Code: `IndexFlatCodes::add`

```
void IndexFlatCodes::add(idx_t n, const float* x) {
    FAISS_THROW_IF_NOT(is_trained);
    if (n == 0) {
        return;
    }
codes.resize((ntotal + n) * code_size);
sa_encode(n, x, codes.data() + (ntotal * code_size));
ntotal += n;
}
```

Detailed Explanation

This function adds n high-dimensional float vectors (x) to the `IndexFlatCodes` structure, which stores all vectors in **encoded** (compressed) form. It follows a simple pipeline: check if the index is ready, resize storage, encode vectors, and update metadata.

`is_trained` Check:

The method ensures the index is properly trained before accepting new data. In quantized or compressed vector indexes (like PQ-based ones), training involves learning codebooks or centroids. Attempting to encode vectors before this training would produce meaningless results, hence the check.

Zero-Vector Early Exit:

If the number of vectors to add (n) is zero, there is nothing to do. The method simply returns without allocating memory or performing encoding.

Resizing the Code Storage:

The internal codes vector is a flat buffer holding all the encoded vectors. Each vector is represented using code_size bytes. To accommodate the new n vectors, the buffer is resized to fit (ntotal + n) * code_size bytes. This is essentially appending n new slots for incoming encoded vectors.

Vector Encoding with `sa_encode`:

The core operation is calling `sa_encode`, which encodes the n input vectors starting from pointer x into compact representations. These representations are written into the codes array, starting from the byte offset that follows the current content.

The `sa_encode` function is short for "standalone encode." It is an abstraction over whatever encoding mechanism is used by the subclass (for instance, IndexPQ, IndexLSQ). Here is how it generally works:

- The input x is a matrix of shape (n × d) stored in row-major order.
- Each row (vector) is compressed using the encoding scheme defined by the index.
- In IndexPQ, for example, each vector is divided into M subspaces. Each subvector is quantized separately using its own codebook. The resulting subspace indices (quantization bins) are packed into a code of M bytes.
- The encoded output is a compact byte array (often using 8-bit unsigned integers), reducing the storage footprint dramatically.

This step is critical for performance, especially when storing millions or billions of vectors, since it enables fast approximate search with low memory use.

Updating the Metadata

After encoding and storing the new vectors, the `ntotal` variable is incremented to reflect the new total number of vectors in the index. This ensures that future search or addition operations account for the correct dataset size.

What Happens Internally

- For IndexPQ, `sa_encode`→ uses product quantization to encode each vector to a byte-code of sub-quantizer indices.
- For IndexLSQ, `sa_encode`→ applies linear least-squares projection followed by quantization.
- For other `IndexFlatCodes` variants, `sa_encode` may encode using other learned codebooks or transformation models.

The `IndexFlatCodes::add` method efficiently adds and encodes new vectors into the index. It ensures that the index is trained, resizes internal buffers, encodes the new data using `sa_encode`, and updates internal counters. The encoded form is compact, enabling efficient storage and fast approximate similarity search.

Implementation of the HNSW Flat Addition and SearchFunctions

HNSW is a graph-based Approximate Nearest Neighbor (ANN) indexing algorithm that enables **fast and accurate similarity search** in high-dimensional spaces.

Core Idea

HNSW builds a **multi-layer graph**, where:

- **Top layers** have fewer nodes with long-range connections (shortcuts).
- **Lower layers** are denser and capture local proximity.

Each node (vector) is connected to its **nearest neighbors** using a dynamic link selection strategy that balances graph connectivity and search efficiency.

Construction

- When a new point is added:
  - It is placed at the highest randomly chosen layer.
  - It connects to its closest neighbors in that layer and lower ones using a greedy search.
- This results in a **navigable small-world graph**.

Search

- Starts from an entry point in the top layer.
- Navigates greedily by following closer neighbors layer by layer down to the bottom.
- Returns the top-k closest points by distance.

Pros

- High recall and search accuracy
- Fast query times (sublinear in practice)
- Robust to high-dimensional data
- Supports incremental insertion

Cons

- Larger memory footprint
- Slower index construction compared to simpler methods

HNSW is used in Milvus, FAISS, and other modern vector databases due to its excellent balance of speed, accuracy, and scalability.

Structure Overview of `IndexHNSW`

`IndexHNSW` is a class that implements the Hierarchical Navigable Small World (HNSW) algorithm for approximate nearest neighbor (ANN) search. It is built on top of the Index base class in Faiss, enabling fast similarity search by combining a multi-layer graph structure (HNSW) with a vector storage backend (Index).

Components

HNSW hnsw: This member holds the actual HNSW graph structure, which contains:

- The nodes (each corresponding to a vector),
- Multi-layer connectivity (from sparse top layers to denser bottom layers),
- Neighbor links for each node per layer,
- Methods for inserting and searching the graph.

Index* storage:

This is a pointer to another Faiss index used to store the raw vectors (such as IndexFlatL2, IndexPQ, and the like.). It allows `IndexHNSW` to decouple the graph structure from the vector representation.

bool own_fields:

It indicates whether the `IndexHNSW` instance own the storage. If true, the storage is created and managed internally. If false, the user provides the storage, and `IndexHNSW` will not delete it upon destruction.

ReconstructFromNeighbors* reconstruct_from_neighbors:

It is an optional reconstruction helper used when the actual vector storage is compressed or not directly accessible. It allows the system to reconstruct approximate vectors from their graph neighbors.

Constructors

- `IndexHNSW(int d = 0, int M = 32, MetricType metric = METRIC_L2`
  Creates an index with internal vector storage (typically a flat index), where d

is dimensionality, M is the maximum number of connections per node, and metric is the distance measure.

- `IndexHNSW(Index* storage, int M = 32)`
  Allows the user to plug in a custom vector storage backend.

Key Methods

`void add(idx_t n, const float* x)`

It adds n new vectors to the index. For each vector:

- It is added to the storage backend.
- A new node is inserted into the HNSW graph, connected to its neighbors based on the HNSW linking strategy.

`void train(idx_t n, const float* x)`

It trains the storage backend if it requires training (for instance, a product quantization index). HNSW itself does not require training.

`void search(...) const`

It performs ANN search using the HNSW graph. It:

- Starts from entry points in the graph.
- Traverses through graph layers from top to bottom using greedy and beam search.
- Returns the top-k closest vectors based on the distance metric.

`void reconstruct(idx_t key, float* recons) const`

It reconstructs the vector corresponding to a specific key. It either reads directly from storage or uses `reconstruct_from_neighbors` if reconstruction from neighbors is configured.

`void reset()`

It clears both the graph and the stored vectors, resetting the index to an empty state.

Advanced Graph Functions

`void shrink_level_0_neighbors(int size)`

It reduces the number of neighbors each node has at level 0, which is useful for managing memory or improving runtime performance.

`void search_level_0(...) const`

It performs search only in the level 0 graph. This is useful in scenarios like hybrid search or reranking when the higher layers are bypassed.

`void init_level_0_from_knngraph(int k, const float* D, constidx_t* I)`

It initializes the level-0 graph using a precomputed k-NN graph, allowing for external graph construction or import.

`void init_level_0_from_entry_points(...)`

It allows graph construction from manually specified entry points and their nearest neighbors, giving users full control over topology.

void reorder_links()

It sorts neighbor lists in each node to improve search speed, ensuring that closer neighbors are accessed first.

void link_singletons()

It adds connections for isolated nodes that have no neighbors, ensuring that they are reachable during search.

void permute_entries(constidx_t* perm)

It reorders internal entries to match a user-defined permutation, and is typically used during post-processing or when aligning with external data layouts.

`IndexHNSW` encapsulates an HNSW-based ANN index by:

- Managing both a navigable graph and the vector storage,
- Providing fast approximate search with high accuracy,
- Offering customization of graph topology, memory trade-offs, and storage format,
- Supporting various distance metrics (like L2, inner product).

It is widely used in high-performance vector search applications due to its balance of search speed and accuracy, especially when dealing with millions of high-dimensional vectors.

Addition of Vectors to the HNSW Index

Here is the **line-by-line explanation** of the `hnsw_add_vertices` function, followed by the code for reference:

```
void hnsw_add_vertices(
IndexHNSW&index_hnsw,
size_t n0,
size_t n,
const float* x,
        bool verbose,
        bool preset_levels = false) {
```

- Function to add n new vectors to the `IndexHNSW` starting from an existing base of n0 vectors.
- x points to the vector data (flattened array).
- verbose controls logging.
- `preset_levels` indicates whether levels for new nodes are preset or to be randomly assigned.

```
size_t d = index_hnsw.d;
    HNSW&hnsw = index_hnsw.hnsw;
size_tntotal = n0 + n;
    double t0 = getmillisecs();
```

- d: dimension of each vector.
- Reference hnsw graph inside the index.
- `ntotal`: total number of vectors after adding new ones.
- `t0`: records start time for measuring duration.

```
  if (verbose) {
printf("hnsw_add_vertices: adding %zd elements on top of %zd "
               "(preset_levels=%d)\n",
               n,
               n0,
               int(preset_levels));
    }
```

- Print info about how many vectors are being added and whether levels are preset.

```
  if (n == 0) {
        return;
    }
```

- Nothing to do if no new vectors are added.

```
  int max_level = hnsw.prepare_level_tab(n, preset_levels);
```

- Assign hierarchical levels to each new vector. If `preset_levels` is false, assign random levels following the probabilistic model of HNSW.
- Returns the maximum level assigned in this batch.

```
std::vector<omp_lock_t> locks(ntotal);
    for (int i = 0; i<ntotal; i++)
omp_init_lock(&locks[i]);
```

- Create and initialize a vector of OpenMP locks, one for each vector in the index (old + new).

- Locks will be used to synchronize graph updates during parallel insertions.

```
std::vector<int> hist;
std::vector<int> order(n);
```

- hist will hold counts of how many vectors are assigned to each level.
- order will hold vector IDs sorted by level for insertion order.

```
    { // make buckets with vectors of the same level

        // build histogram
        for (int i = 0; i< n; i++) {
storage_idx_tpt_id = i + n0;
            int pt_level = hnsw.levels[pt_id] - 1;
            while (pt_level>= hist.size())
hist.push_back(0);
            hist[pt_level]++;
        }
```

- For each new vector:
    - Calculate the assigned level (`pt_level`).
    - Extend the histogram vector if needed.
    - Increment the count for that level.

```
        // accumulate
std::vector<int> offsets(hist.size() + 1, 0);
        for (int i = 0; i<hist.size() - 1; i++) {
            offsets[i + 1] = offsets[i] + hist[i];
        }
```

- Create a prefix sum array offsets from the histogram, used to determine insertion points for each bucket during sorting.

```
    // bucket sort
        for (int i = 0; i< n; i++) {
storage_idx_tpt_id = i + n0;
            int pt_level = hnsw.levels[pt_id] - 1;
            order[offsets[pt_level]++] = pt_id;
        }
    }
```

- Distribute vector IDs into the order array sorted by their levels, using the offsets as write pointers.

```
idx_tcheck_period = InterruptCallback::get_period_hint(
max_level * index_hnsw.d * hnsw.efConstruction);
```

- Determine how often to check for interrupts during computation to allow graceful cancellation.

```
    { // perform add
RandomGenerator rng2(789);
```

- Begin adding vectors with a random generator initialized to a fixed seed (for reproducibility).

```
int i1 = n;

for (int pt_level = hist.size() - 1; pt_level>= 0; pt_level--) {
    int i0 = i1 - hist[pt_level];
```

- Iterate over levels from the highest to the lowest.
- i0 and i1 define the range of vectors in order belonging to the current level.

```
      if (verbose) {
printf("Adding %d elements at level %d\n", i1 - i0, pt_level);
            }
```

- Print progress info.

```
      // random permutation to get rid of dataset order bias
            for (int j = i0; j < i1; j++)
std::swap(order[j], order[j + rng2.rand_int(i1 - j)]);
```

- Shuffle vectors within the level to avoid insertion bias caused by ordered data.

```
            bool interrupt = false;
#pragma omp parallel if (i1 > i0 + 100)
            {
VisitedTablevt(ntotal);
```

- Parallel region begins if there are enough vectors to benefit from parallelism.
- Each thread creates a `VisitedTable` to track nodes visited during the search insertion.

```
DistanceComputer* dis =
storage_distance_computer(index_hnsw.storage);
                ScopeDeleter1<DistanceComputer> del(dis);
```

- Create a `DistanceComputer` instance to compute distances between vectors.
- It is automatically deleted at the end of the scope.

```
        int prev_display =
                        verbose &&omp_get_thread_num() == 0 ? 0 : -1;
size_t counter = 0;
```

- Variables to control verbose progress display and interrupt checking.

```
#pragma omp for schedule(static)
```

```
            for (int i = i0; i< i1; i++) {
storage_idx_tpt_id = order[i];
                dis->set_query(x + (pt_id - n0) * d);
```

- Each thread loops over assigned vectors.
- Set the current query vector for distance calculation.

```
        if (interrupt) {
                continue;
            }
```

- Skip insertion if an interrupt was requested.

```
hnsw.add_with_locks(*dis, pt_level, pt_id, locks, vt);
```

- Insert the vector `pt_id` at `pt_level` into the HNSW graph.
- Uses locks to avoid concurrent modification of neighbor lists.
- Uses `VisitedTable` to prevent revisiting nodes during insertion.

```
            if (prev_display>= 0 &&i - i0 >prev_display + 10000) {
prev_display = i - i0;
printf("  %d / %d\r", i - i0, i1 - i0);
fflush(stdout);
                }
```

- Periodically print progress updates (every 10,000 insertions) if verbose and on main thread.

```
            if (counter % check_period == 0) {
                    if (InterruptCallback::is_interrupted()) {
                        interrupt = true;
                    }
                }
                counter++;
            }
        }
```

- Check for interrupts periodically to allow graceful termination.

```
        if (interrupt) {
            FAISS_THROW_MSG("computation interrupted");
        }
        i1 = i0;
    }
    FAISS_ASSERT(i1 == 0);
}
```

- If interrupted, throw an exception.
- After processing all the levels, ensure that all vectors have been inserted.

```
    if (verbose) {
printf("Done in %.3f ms\n", getmillisecs() - t0);
    }
```

- Print total elapsed time.

```
  for (int i = 0; i<ntotal; i++) {
omp_destroy_lock(&locks[i]);
    }
}
```

- Clean up locks to avoid resource leaks.

Search Nearest Vectors Using the HNSW Index

The HNSW index performs approximate nearest neighbor search using a hierarchical graph structure. Vectors are organized in multiple layers, allowing the search algorithm to quickly navigate toward the closest nodes. This approach provides high recall and fast query performance even for large-scale vector datasets.

Explanation of the Function

```
void IndexHNSW::search(
idx_t n,
const float* x,
idx_t k,
        float* distances,
idx_t* labels,
constSearchParameters* params_in) const {
```

- Main search function for n query vectors (x).
- k is the number of nearest neighbors to return.
- Outputs are distances and labels arrays.
- Optional params_in can customize search behavior (say efSearch).

```
  FAISS_THROW_IF_NOT(k > 0);
    FAISS_THROW_IF_NOT_MSG(
            storage,
            "Please use IndexHNSWFlat (or variants) instead of IndexHNSW
directly");
```

- Checks that k is positive.
- Ensures that this base `IndexHNSW` has a valid underlying storage index, recommending use of `IndexHNSWFlat` for direct use.

```
constSearchParametersHNSW* params = nullptr;
    int efSearch = hnsw.efSearch;
    if (params_in) {
        params = dynamic_cast<constSearchParametersHNSW*>(params_in);
        FAISS_THROW_IF_NOT_MSG(params, "params type invalid");
efSearch = params->efSearch;
    }
```

- Parses and validates the optional HNSW-specific search parameters.
- Uses efSearch either from parameters or default from the index.

```
size_t n1 = 0, n2 = 0, n3 = 0, ndis = 0, nreorder = 0;
```

- Variables to accumulate statistics about the search process (e.g., number of nodes visited).

```
idx_tcheck_period =
InterruptCallback::get_period_hint(hnsw.max_level * d * efSearch);
```

- Defines how often to check for external interrupts during long-running search operations.

```
   for (idx_t i0 = 0; i0 < n; i0 += check_period) {
idx_t i1 = std::min(i0 + check_period, n);
```

- Splits the queries into chunks to limit interrupt checking overhead.

```
#pragma omp parallel
        {
VisitedTablevt(ntotal);

DistanceComputer* dis = storage_distance_computer(storage);
            ScopeDeleter1<DistanceComputer> del(dis);
```

- Parallel region for batch processing queries.
- Each thread creates a fresh VisitedTable to track visited nodes during search.
- Creates a DistanceComputer for distance computations with the underlying storage.

```
#pragma omp for reduction(+ : n1, n2, n3, ndis, nreorder) schedule(guided)
            for (idx_ti = i0; i< i1; i++) {
idx_t* idxi = labels + i * k;
                float* simi = distances + i * k;
                dis->set_query(x + i * d);

maxheap_heapify(k, simi, idxi);
HNSWStats stats = hnsw.search(*dis, k, idxi, simi, vt, params);
n1 += stats.n1;
                n2 += stats.n2;
```

```
                n3 += stats.n3;
                ndis += stats.ndis;
                nreorder += stats.nreorder;
maxheap_reorder(k, simi, idxi);
```

- For each query vector:
  - Prepare heaps for top-k nearest neighbors.
  - Perform the actual HNSW graph search to find the nearest neighbors.
  - Accumulate search stats.
  - Reorder heap to get sorted neighbors.

```
        if (reconstruct_from_neighbors&&
reconstruct_from_neighbors->k_reorder != 0) {
                    int k_reorder = reconstruct_from_neighbors->k_reorder;
if (k_reorder == -1 || k_reorder > k)
                         k_reorder = k;

nreorder += reconstruct_from_neighbors->compute_distances(
k_reorder, idxi, x + i * d, simi);

                    // sort top k_reorder
maxheap_heapify(
k_reorder, simi, idxi, simi, idxi, k_reorder);
maxheap_reorder(k_reorder, simi, idxi);
                }
            }
        }
InterruptCallback::check();
    }
```

- Optional step: if configured, refine distances for top results by reconstructing vectors from neighbors and recomputing distances.
- Perform sorting again after refinement.
- Check for external interrupts between batches.

```
  if (is_similarity_metric(metric_type)) {
        // we need to revert the negated distances
        for (size_ti = 0; i< k * n; i++) {
            distances[i] = -distances[i];
        }
    }
```

- For similarity metrics (where higher is better), the distances were negated internally, so revert to positive values for the user.

```
hnsw_stats.combine({n1, n2, n3, ndis, nreorder});
}
```

- Update the index-wide statistics object with the results from this search batch.

Conclusion

In this chapter, we have explored the various indexing mechanisms available in **Milvus** to enhance the performance of vector search operations. These indexing methods are essential for optimizing the search and retrieval of high-dimensional data across a wide range of use cases, from machine learning and image recognition to recommendation systems and Natural Language Processing.

We categorized the indexing schemes into **floating-type indexes**, **sparse indexes**, **GPU-based indexes**, and **binary indexes**, each tailored to specific data types and performance requirements. **Floating-type indexes** like IVF, HNSW, and Flat are designed for dense, high-dimensional vectors, offering different trade-offs between search speed and accuracy. These methods are ideal for large datasets where approximate nearest neighbor search is acceptable.

Sparse indexes are optimized for sparse data, where most vector elements are zero or near-zero. These indexes improve search efficiency and reduce memory consumption for applications dealing with sparse representations.

GPU-based indexes take advantage of the computational power of GPUs to accelerate both indexing and search. These indexes, including GPU_IVF_FLAT and GPU_IVF_PQ, provide significant performance improvements for large-scale and real-time applications, ensuring faster search times and reduced latency.

Binary indexes, specifically **BIN_IVF** and **BIN_IVF_FLAT**, are tailored for binary vectors, commonly used in hash-based systems. These indexing methods provide efficient search capabilities for binary datasets, offering a balance between speed and search accuracy.

Each indexing type in Milvus offers distinct advantages depending on the nature of the data and the specific requirements of the application. Thus, by understanding the strengths and trade-offs of each method, you can choose the most appropriate indexing scheme for your use case, ensuring optimal performance in vector search tasks.

As the field of vector search continues to evolve, Milvus remains at the forefront, providing flexible, scalable, and high-performance solutions to meet the growing demands of modern data processing and retrieval.

The upcoming chapter plays an important role on how Milvus leverages the indexing capability from FAISS and acts as an architectural orchestrator while FAISS performs the heavy lifting on management of data and indexes.

CHAPTER 6
Indexing Schemes Binary, Sparse, and GPU

Introduction

In the rapidly evolving field of Artificial Intelligence (AI) and Machine Learning (ML), efficient data retrieval and processing are fundamental to the success of search and recommendation systems. Milvus, an open-source vector database, plays a key role in addressing the growing demands of similarity search, particularly for high-dimensional vector data. One of the core strengths of Milvus lies in its ability to support various types of indexes that optimize search performance based on the unique characteristics of the data. Among these, sparse, binary, and GPU indexes stand out as essential components, offering significant advantages depending on the nature of the data and the hardware used.

Sparse Indexes are particularly relevant in scenarios where the data is sparse in nature, meaning that only a small subset of values in the dataset are non-zero or relevant. For example, in Natural Language Processing (NLP) applications, such as word embeddings or document vectors, sparse vectors often represent high-dimensional data with many zero values. Sparse indexing allows for efficient storage and retrieval of such data, minimizing the computational overhead associated with storing and processing unnecessary zeros. By leveraging sparse representations, Milvus ensures that similarity searches involving sparse vectors are both memory-efficient and faster.

On the other hand, Binary Indexes have become increasingly important in the realm of data that can be represented in binary form, such as binary embeddings or hash-based representations. Binary vectors offer significant storage savings and performance improvements, particularly when dealing with large-scale datasets. Binary indexing techniques in Milvus enable efficient search and comparison of binary vectors by employing specialized algorithms that optimize the distance calculation, such as the Hamming distance. This type of index is especially useful in applications like image retrieval, document matching, and real-time recommendation systems, where speed and low memory footprint are critical.

The GPU Indexes in Milvus are designed to take full advantage of the parallel processing power of Graphics Processing Units (GPUs), which can significantly accelerate vector search tasks. By offloading the computationally intensive operations to the GPU, Milvus ensures that even the most complex similarity searches can be performed at lightning speed. GPU indexing is particularly beneficial for large-scale datasets and high-dimensional vector spaces, which would otherwise be computationally prohibitive when processed solely by the CPU. For applications that require real-time responses, such as video analytics or online recommendation engines, GPU-powered indexes provide the performance necessary to meet these demands.

This chapter delves deeper into the mechanisms behind these three types of indexes—sparse, binary, and GPU—exploring their respective use cases, implementation details, and performance considerations within Milvus. By understanding the strengths and limitations of each index type, developers can make informed decisions about the most appropriate indexing strategy for their specific application, ultimately achieving optimal search performance and resource efficiency.

Structure

In this chapter, we will discuss the following topics:

- Implementation of the Hierarchial Navigable Small World (HNSW) Indexing Scheme for Sparse Indexes
- Implementation of the Binary IVF Flat Binary Index
- Implementation of the GPU_CABRA Index

Implementation of the Hierarchial Navigable Small World (HNSW) Indexing Scheme

The provided code defines the **HNSW (Hierarchical Navigable Small World)** structure, which is used for efficient nearest neighbor search in high-dimensional spaces. In the following subsection, is a concise summary of the HNSW implementation structure in FAISS as explained in the following paragraph.

Overview

- The HNSW struct implements an **HNSW graph** for **fast Approximate Nearest Neighbor (ANN) search**.
- It supports multiple levels of neighbors and uses a **multi-level graph structure** where each level holds a different number of neighbors for a set of vectors.

- **Random levels** are assigned to vectors and **hierarchical layers** help guide the search efficiently.

Key Components

- `MinimaxHeap`:

  It is a heap structure designed for fast insertion and extraction of nodes based on their distance values, maintaining either a max or min heap order.

- `NodeDistCloser` / `NodeDistFarther`:

  These are structures used to compare nodes by distance, with different ordering (closer or farther).

- **Attributes**:
  - `assign_probas`: Assignment probabilities for each level.
  - `cum_nneighbor_per_level`: Cumulative number of neighbors per level.
  - `levels`: Levels for each vector.
  - `offsets`: Index offsets for the neighbor list of each vector.
  - `neighbors`: The actual neighbor lists for vectors at all levels.
  - `entry_point`: The entry point in the search structure.
  - `efConstruction` and `efSearch`: Expansion factors during construction and search.
  - `max_level`: The maximum number of levels.
  - `upper_beam`: Number of entry points at higher levels.
  - `search_bounded_queue`: Flag to use a bounded queue during search.

- **Methods**:
  - `set_default_probas()`: Initializes probabilities and neighbor counts.
  - `random_level()`: Picks a random level for a new point.
  - `add_with_locks()`: Adds a new point to the graph and builds link structure with locks.
  - `search()`: Main search function for finding the nearest neighbors.
  - `reset()`: Resets the data structure.
  - `clear_neighbor_tables()`: Clears the neighbor lists for a specified level.
  - `shrink_neighbor_list()`: Shrinks a list of neighbors based on a maximum size constraint.

- **Neighbor Management**:

  These are methods for managing neighbors across different levels and layers, including adding, clearing, and printing neighbor statistics.

Purpose

- **HNSW** provides an efficient way to perform approximate nearest neighbor search with hierarchical indexing, allowing fast retrieval of vectors based on distance metrics. It is commonly used in high-dimensional data scenarios where brute force search would be too slow. The use of **multiple levels** in the HNSW structure enables quick navigation and reduces the search space, making it highly efficient for large-scale datasets.

Applications

- High-dimensional vector search (for example for image retrieval, natural language processing, recommendation systems).
- **Approximate nearest neighbor search** in large datasets where speed is crucial but exact accuracy is not required.

Implementation of the Hierarchical Navigable Small World (HNSW) Search

The function `search_from_candidates` performs a **nearest neighbor search** using the **HNSW (Hierarchical Navigable Small World)** algorithm, specifically working with a set of **candidate neighbors** at a given **level**. It iterates through these candidates, exploring their neighbors in the HNSW graph, and attempts to find the **k nearest neighbors** to a query point. A step-by-step explanation is covered in the following subsection.

Input Parameters

- `hnsw`: The HNSW index, which holds the structure of the graph.
- `qdis`: A `DistanceComputer` that computes the distance between vectors.
- `k`: The number of nearest neighbors to find.
- `I`: An array to store the indices of the k nearest neighbors found.
- `D`: An array to store the distances corresponding to the k nearest neighbors.
- `candidates`: A **`MinimaxHeap`** that holds the candidate neighbors to consider during the search.
- `vt`: A **`VisitedTable`** that tracks which vectors have been visited.

- **`stats`**: The **`HNSWStats`** structure used to accumulate search statistics.
- **`level`**: The current level in the HNSW graph that we are searching at.
- **`nres_in`**: The number of results found so far (defaults to 0).
- **`params`**: Additional search parameters (like `efSearch` or `check_relative_distance`), if provided.

Key Operations

- **Initial Setup**:
  - **`nres`** is initialized to `nres_in` (number of results found so far), and **`ndis`** tracks the number of distances calculated.
  - Search parameters like `do_dis_check`, `efSearch`, `and` `sel` (a selector for filtering valid vectors) are configured based on the params or default values from HNSW.
- **Push Candidates to Max Heap**:
  - The **candidates** heap contains potential nearest neighbors. For each candidate (a vector with a specific distance), the function either pushes it to the result heap (if the result heap has space) or replaces the top of the heap with the current candidate if its distance is smaller than the current closest neighbor.
- **Main Search Loop**:
  - The algorithm processes the candidates in the heap until either the heap is empty or the stopping conditions are met:
    - **`do_dis_check`**: If enabled, the search can stop early if the distances of the remaining candidates are larger than a threshold.
    - **Neighbor Exploration**: For each candidate, the algorithm fetches its neighbors (from the HNSW structure), marking them as visited and adding them to the candidate heap.
    - **4-Neighbour Processing**: Instead of checking each neighbor one by one, the function batches the processing of 4 neighbors at a time for efficiency. For each batch of 4 neighbors, it computes their distances and adds them to the heap.
- **Stopping Condition**:

  The search will stop early if the number of candidates processed exceeds the expansion factor `efSearch` (or if the stopping condition based on distance checks is met).

- **Statistics Update**:

  During the search at level 0, statistics are updated based on the number of candidates processed (n1, n2, n3), which can help in analyzing search performance.

- **Return**:

  The function returns the total number of results found (`nres`), which is the number of nearest neighbors.

Detailed Steps in the Function

1. **Initial Search Setup**:
   - The first loop pushes candidates from the `MinimaxHeap` into the result heap if they are valid, keeping track of the closest k neighbors.
2. **Candidate Exploration Loop**:
   - The main loop extracts the nearest candidate (`pop_min`), explores its neighbors, and adds those neighbors back to the `MinimaxHeap` if they are closer than the current farthest neighbors.
3. **Efficient Neighbor Processing**:
   - The loop batches the neighbor processing in chunks of 4, improving efficiency by computing the distances for multiple neighbors at once and pushing the results back to the heap.
4. **Stopping Condition**:
   - The search halts early if the number of candidates processed exceeds the `efSearch` parameter or the distance checks suggest no further progress can be made.

Key Structures Involved

- **`MinimaxHeap`**:

  It is a heap that stores candidate neighbors along with their distances. It allows for efficiently retrieving the closest (or farthest) neighbors, as well as adding and removing neighbors as new candidates are processed.

- **`VisitedTable` (vt)**:

  It keeps track of which vectors have been visited during the search to avoid redundant work and loops.

- **`HNSWStats`**:

  It is a structure used to collect statistics during the search, such as the number of processed candidates, the number of neighbors found, and the like.

Optimization Techniques

- **Prefetching**:

  The code uses `prefetch_L2` to prefetch memory for the next set of candidates, optimizing for cache locality when processing large numbers of neighbors.

- **Batch Processing**:

  By processing 4 neighbors at a time, the function avoids calling the distance computation function individually for each neighbor, which speeds up the process.

- **Early Termination**:

  The search can stop early under certain conditions, such as when the distances of the remaining candidates are unlikely to improve the current results.

Implementation of the Binary IVF Index

The `IndexBinaryIVF` class is a specialized index structure for binary data, specifically designed for efficient **vector search** using the **Inverted File (IVF)** method with **binary vectors**. This class inherits from IndexBinary and is used to organize and search a large collection of binary vectors by first mapping them to **inverted lists** (IVF), which makes querying more efficient.

Key Components of the `IndexBinaryIVF` Class

- **Inverted Lists**:
  - **`invlists`:** A pointer to the `InvertedLists` object, which holds the actual data. This structure organizes the vectors into lists based on quantization. Each list corresponds to a quantization cluster of vectors.
  - **`own_invlists`:** A boolean flag indicating whether the index owns the `invlists` object or not.
- **Search Parameters**:
  - **`nprobe`:** The number of probes to use during query time, that is , how many lists to search through when performing a query.
  - **`max_codes`:** The maximum number of codes to visit while performing a query. It acts as a stopping condition for the search.
- **Search Strategy**:
  - **`use_heap`:** A flag indicating whether to use a heap-based method or a counting method to select the k smallest values when scanning the inverted lists.

- **per_invlist_search:** A boolean that specifies whether to collect computations per batch for each inverted list during the search.

- **Direct Mapping**:
  - **direct_map:** A map for direct access to the elements, enabling efficient reconstruction of vectors. This helps with retrieving original vectors after they have been quantized.

- **Quantizer**:
  - **quantizer:** A pointer to another `IndexBinary` object that maps vectors to inverted list identifiers (usually for coarse quantization). The quantizer helps in the initial classification of vectors into clusters or lists.

- **Quantization Details**:
  - **nlist:** The number of possible lists (clusters) that the quantizer can assign vectors to.
  - **own_fields:** A boolean that indicates whether the `IndexBinaryIVF` class owns the quantizer and other related fields.

- **Clustering Parameters**:
  - **cp:** A structure holding the clustering parameters to override the default settings during clustering.
  - **clustering_index:** An optional index used during the clustering process, overriding the default one.

- **Constructor and Destructor:**
  - ***IndexBinaryIVF(IndexBinary quantizer, size_t d, size_tnlist)**:** This constructor initializes the IVF index with the given quantizer, vector dimension d, and number of lists nlist.

- **IndexBinaryIVF():** A default constructor.
  - **~IndexBinaryIVF():** The destructor that handles cleanup when the object is destroyed.

Main Functions

- **Training**:
  - **train(idx_t n, const uint8_t* x):** This function trains the quantizer by providing it with n binary vectors. The training process is based on clustering and partitioning the dataset into clusters.

- **Adding Vectors**:
  - **add(idx_t n, const uint8_t* x):** Adds n binary vectors to the index.

  - **add_with_ids(idx_t n, const uint8_t* x, constidx_t* xids)**: Adds n binary vectors with specific IDs.
- **Core Add Function**:
  - **add_core(idx_t n, const uint8_t* x, constidx_t* xids, constidx_t* precomputed_idx)**: This function adds vectors where the quantization indices are pre-computed, and the vector assignments are predefined.
- **Searching**:
  - **search_preassigned(...)**: A search function that assumes the vectors are pre-quantized by the IVF quantizer. It uses the coarse quantization assignments (assign) to find the nearest neighbors.
  - **search(...)**: Performs a search by first quantizing the vectors, and then finding the k nearest neighbors. It fills in the results (distances and labels) based on the query vectors.
  - **range_search(...)**: A range search where you find all vectors within a certain radius of the query.
  - **range_search_preassigned(...)**: A range search where the vectors are pre-quantized, similar to `search_preassigned()` but for range search.
  - **search_and_reconstruct(...)**:Performs a search and also reconstructs the vectors corresponding to the search results.
- **Reconstruction**:
  - **reconstruct(idx_t key, uint8_t* recons)**: Reconstructs a vector given its key. This is used for retrieving the actual binary vector after the search.
  - **reconstruct_n(idx_t i0, idx_tni, uint8_t* recons)**: Reconstructs a batch of vectors.
- **Direct Map**:
  - **make_direct_map(bool new_maintain_direct_map)**: Creates or clears a direct map depending on the provided flag.
  - **set_direct_map_type(DirectMap::Type type)**: Sets the type of direct map (for instance whether to map directly to vector IDs or something else).
- **Inverted List Management**:
  - **replace_invlists(InvertedLists* il, bool own)**: Replaces the current inverted lists with new ones. It can also take ownership of the new inverted lists.

- **Merge and Compatibility Checks**:
  - `remove_ids(constIDSelector&sel)`: Removes vectors identified by a selector (say for deleting vectors).
  - `merge_from(IndexBinary& other, idx_tadd_id)`: Merges data from another index into this one.
  - `check_compatible_for_merge(constIndexBinary&otherIndex)`: Checks whether the current index is compatible with another index for merging.
- **Accessing Inverted Lists**:
  - `get_list_size(size_tlist_no)`: Returns the size of a specific inverted list (that is, how many vectors are in that list).

Summary:

- The `IndexBinaryIVF` class is an implementation of the **Inverted File (IVF)** index for **binary data**. It provides a highly efficient way to search large datasets of binary vectors, using clustering-based quantization and organizing data into inverted lists. The class allows for adding vectors, searching, range querying, and reconstructing vectors, all while supporting efficient batch processing and memory optimizations.
- This index structure is widely used for applications like **image retrieval**, **recommendation systems**, and **large-scale binary vector searches**, where the dataset is too large to store or query all at once efficiently.

Searching within the Binary IVF Index

The function `search_knn_hamming_heap` performs a **k-nearest neighbor (k-NN) search** using **binary data** and the **Inverted File (IVF)** index. It leverages multi-threading (using OpenMP) to speed up the search process. Here is a detailed breakdown of the code:

Function Parameters

- `ivf`: A pointer to an `IndexBinaryIVF` object, representing the inverted file index used for searching.
- `n`: The number of query vectors to search for.
- `x`: The query vectors (binary).
- `k`: The number of nearest neighbors to find for each query vector.
- `keys`: The coarse quantization keys for each query vector, indicating which lists in the inverted file to search.

- **`coarse_dis`:** The distances to the coarse centroids (used in multi-probe searching).
- **`distances`:** The output distances of the nearest neighbors found.
- **`labels`:** The output labels (IDs) of the nearest neighbors found.
- **`store_pairs`:** A boolean flag indicating whether to store pairs of list indices and offsets in the results.
- **`params`:** Optional search parameters to override the default settings (for instance, **`nprobe`**, **`max_codes`**).

Code Overview

- **Initialization**:
    - **`nprobe`:** The number of probes (lists) to search for each query. It is either taken from params or the default value in `ivf`.
    - **`max_codes`:** The maximum number of codes (list entries) to visit during the search. This is either from params or the default in `ivf`.
    - **`metric_type`:** The type of metric used for distance computation (say Inner Product or L2 distance).
- **Parallel Search (OpenMP)**:

  The search process is parallelized using OpenMP with a reduction operation on variables (`nlistv`, `ndis`, `nheap`), which accumulate the number of lists visited, the number of distances calculated, and the number of heap updates.
- **Heap Initialization**:

  Depending on the `metric_type` (Inner Product or L2), it initializes a heap to store the k nearest neighbors for each query vector. This heap keeps track of the top k closest neighbors and their corresponding distances and labels.
- **Query Processing Loop**:

  For each query vector (loop over n queries):
    - The query vector is extracted (xi), and the list of quantization keys (`keysi`) for this query is accessed.
    - The heap of the query is initialized for distance calculations depending on the `metric_type` (either Inner Product or L2).
    - The list of coarse quantization keys (`keysi`) is used to determine which inverted lists to probe.
    - For each key (list) in `keysi`, the function checks if the key is valid (not negative) and retrieves the corresponding inverted list.

- The `BinaryInvertedListScanner` is used to scan the entries of the inverted list, comparing the query vector with the entries in the list and updating the heap with the k nearest neighbors.
- The search stops early if the maximum number of codes (`max_codes`) is reached.

- **Heap Reordering**:

  After scanning the lists, the heap is reordered to ensure that the k nearest neighbors are correctly sorted by their distances (depending on the metric type).

- **Statistics Update**:

  The function tracks various statistics during the search, such as the number of queries processed (`nq`), the number of lists visited (`nlist`), the number of distances calculated (`ndis`), and the number of heap updates (`nheap_updates`).

Summary:

- The `search_knn_hamming_heap` function performs **parallel k-NN searches** using an **Inverted File Index** for binary data.
- The search is efficient due to the use of **multi-threading**, **coarse quantization keys**, and the **heap-based approach** for selecting the nearest neighbors.
- The function processes multiple queries in parallel, scans multiple inverted lists (using `nprobe`), and keeps track of the closest neighbors using a heap-based data structure.
- After the search, the function updates statistics for the number of queries, lists, distances, and heap updates.

Implementation of the GPU IVF Index

The class `GpuIndexIVF` is a specialized **GPU-based** version of the **Inverted File (IVF)** index used for efficient vector search. This class is part of the **Faiss** library, which is designed for fast similarity search, particularly in high-dimensional spaces. Here is a detailed breakdown of the code:

Class Overview

`GpuIndexIVF` inherits from two base classes:

- **`GpuIndex`**: Base class for GPU-based indexing.
- **`IndexIVFInterface`**: Interface class for IVF indexing, which is designed for searching vectors using inverted files.

Constructor(s)

- **Auto-Constructs a Flat Coarse Quantizer**:

  This constructor takes in parameters like the dimension of vectors (dims), the **metric** (similarity measure), nlist (number of inverted lists), and a configuration object (`GpuIndexIVFConfig`). It auto-constructs a **flat coarse quantizer** based on the provided metric.

- **Uses an Existing Coarse Quantizer**:

  This constructor allows you to pass an **existing coarse quantizer** (an Index object). The `GpuIndexIVF` does **not own** this quantizer, meaning it will not delete it when the index is destroyed.

Destructor

- **`~GpuIndexIVF()`**: Destructor to clean up resources.

Private Initialization Method

- **`init_()`**: A shared function for initializing the index, likely called in the constructors to set up the index.

Public Methods

- **`*copyFrom(constfaiss::IndexIVF index)**:`** Copies relevant data from a **CPU-based IVF index** to the GPU-based index.

- **`copyTo(faiss::IndexIVF index) const*`**: Copies data from the GPU index to a **CPU-based IVF index**.

- **`updateQuantizer()`**: This function should be called if the **coarse quantizer** is changed manually (for example a new instance is substituted or the vectors are modified externally).

- **`getNumLists()`**: It returns the number of inverted lists managed by the index.

- **`getListLength(idx_tlistId)`**: It returns the number of vectors in a specific inverted list.

- **`getListVectorData(idx_tlistId, bool gpuFormat = false) const`**: It returns the encoded vector data of a list. If `gpuFormat` is true, the data is returned in the GPU format; otherwise, it is converted to the CPU format.

- **`getListIndices(idx_tlistId) const`**: It returns the indices of vectors contained in a specific inverted list.

- `search_preassigned()`: This method is used for **pre-assigned search**. It performs a search using vectors that have already been assigned to inverted lists (that is the coarse quantization step is precomputed).
- `range_search_preassigned()`: This method performs a **range search** but is not yet implemented for the GPU.
- `getCurrentNProbe_()`: It determines the number of probes (`nprobe`) for the current search, either from the set `nprobe` or from the `SearchParameters`.
- `verifyIVFSettings_()`: It is a utility function to verify the settings of the IVF index.
- `addImplRequiresIDs_()`: It checks if adding vectors requires IDs (a requirement for certain operations in IVF indexing).
- `trainQuantizer_()`: It is a function to train the **quantizer** for the coarse quantization step, using the given vectors.
- `addImpl_()`: It adds vectors to the index, either with or without associated IDs.
- `searchImpl_()`: It performs a search on the index, returning the closest vectors and their distances.

Protected Members

- `ivfConfig_`: The configuration for the GPU IVF index.
- `baseIndex_`: A reference to the base IVF index (possibly a shared pointer to an `IVFBase` object) that holds the core IVF index structure.

Summary:

The `GpuIndexIVF` class provides a **GPU-accelerated version of the IVF index** in Faiss, enabling faster nearest neighbor searches on GPUs. It includes functionality for:

- Constructing or using a custom coarse quantizer.
- Adding vectors to the index.
- Searching for nearest neighbors using pre-assigned quantization keys.
- Copying between CPU and GPU versions of the index.
- Debugging and inspecting individual inverted lists.

This class abstracts the complexity of handling large-scale vector indexing on GPUs and ensures efficient computation for high-dimensional data. The methods also offer a flexible interface for customization, such as manually updating the quantizer or adjusting the number of probes (`nprobe`) during the search process.

Searching the GPU IVF Index

The function `GpuIndexIVF::search_preassigned` is designed to perform a **pre-assigned search** on a GPU-based IVF (Inverted File) index. A breakdown of what the function does is elaborated in the following subsection.

Function Overview

This function handles the search operation when the vectors are already **pre-assigned** to inverted lists, which means the coarse quantization step has already been performed.

Steps and Explanation

1. **Initial Checks**:
    - **`FAISS_THROW_IF_NOT_MSG(stats == nullptr, "IVF stats not supported");`**: The function ensures that the stats parameter is `nullptr` because IVF statistics are not supported in this function.
    - **DeviceScope and stream setup**: The function initializes the device context and the stream for GPU operations using `resources_` and `config_` (likely representing GPU resources and configuration).
    - **Pre-assigned search validation**: It checks whether the `store_pairs` parameter is false (since storing pairs is not currently supported), and it ensures that the index has been trained (`this->is_trained`).
    - **Validates k**: The function validates that k (number of nearest neighbors) is valid using `validateKSelect(k)`.
2. **Edge Case Handling**:
    - If either n (number of queries) or k (number of neighbors to retrieve) is 0, the function returns early because there is nothing to search.
3. **Handling Search Parameters**:
    - It retrieves the **number of probes** (`nprobe`) from the search parameters (params) or defaults to `this->nprobe`.
    - The function validates the **number of probes** (`nprobe`) using `validateNProbe(use_nprobe)`.
    - It checks the `max_codes` parameter from params and raises an error if it is not zero, as this is not supported for GPU IVF.

4. **Prepare Data on GPU**:
   - The query vectors (x), centroid distances (`centroid_dis`), and assignment indices (assign) are moved to the GPU using `toDeviceTemporary` (likely a helper function to transfer data to GPU memory).
   - Output buffers for the **distances** and **indices** (distances and labels) are also allocated on the GPU.
5. **Search Execution**:
   - The function calls `baseIndex_->searchPreassigned`, which performs the actual search on the GPU. It passes the pre-assigned quantizer, the query vectors, the centroid distances, the assignment indices, the number of neighbors (k), and the output buffers for distances and indices. The `store_pairs` parameter is also passed.
6. **Copy Results Back to CPU**:
   - If the search results were computed on the GPU, they are copied back to the CPU memory using `fromDevice` for both **distances** and **indices**.

Summary:

This function executes a pre-assigned search on a **GPU-based IVF index** by:

- Validating input parameters and configurations.
- Moving data to the GPU (query vectors, centroid distances, and assignments).
- Calling the GPU-based search function.
- Returning the search results (distances and indices) from GPU to CPU.

It optimizes the search for cases where the coarse quantization has already been computed, reducing the overhead of recomputing it. The GPU accelerates both the search process and data movement, providing a high-speed solution for large-scale similarity searches.

Conclusion

In conclusion, the exploration of advanced indexing techniques, particularly those using Inverted File (IVF), GPU-based IVF, binary, and sparse indexes, reveals the significant potential for optimizing large-scale nearest neighbor searches in high-dimensional spaces. The IVF index, both in its CPU and GPU implementations, serves as a powerful tool by reducing the search space through coarse quantization, making it efficient for managing large datasets. The IVF architecture allows for fast retrieval by grouping vectors into inverted lists, significantly reducing the computational cost of finding approximate nearest neighbors.

The `GPUIndexIVF` class demonstrates the strength of leveraging GPU acceleration for IVF indexing. By transferring data processing to the GPU, it not only speeds up the search process but also scales efficiently with the growing volume of data.

Binary indexes, such as `IndexBinaryIVF`, offer a unique advantage in cases where data is stored in binary format. These indexes are optimized for tasks where memory storage and retrieval speed are critical. By employing binary encoding for vectors, these indexes drastically reduce memory requirements and enable faster searches. The use of inverted lists, similar to their floating-point counterparts, further streamlines the search process by organizing binary data into manageable chunks, facilitating efficient lookups for approximate nearest neighbors.

Sparse indexing methods, on the other hand, cater to scenarios where data is inherently sparse, such as high-dimensional sparse vectors found in many natural language processing (NLP) and recommendation system applications. Sparse indexes efficiently handle such data by focusing on non-zero elements, minimizing storage overhead and computation. By utilizing structures that map sparse vectors to compressed forms, these indexes can quickly retrieve relevant information while maintaining a low computational cost.

Overall, these indexing mechanisms—IVF, GPU-enhanced IVF, binary, and sparse indexes—are crucial for real-time applications that require fast and efficient similarity search, such as image retrieval, recommendation systems, and large-scale machine learning tasks. With the GPU-enhanced IVF implementation and the unique advantages of binary and sparse indexing, the ability to handle massive datasets while maintaining high performance makes these tools invaluable in modern data-driven research and industry applications.

CHAPTER 7
Distributed Data Management

Introduction

In the current data-driven world, the ability to efficiently manage, store, and retrieve large volumes of high-dimensional data is paramount. Milvus, an open-source vector database, offers an innovative solution for handling such complex data, especially for applications involving machine learning, AI, and data science. One of the core strengths of Milvus lies in its distributed architecture, which allows it to scale horizontally, ensuring high availability, fault tolerance, and the ability to process large-scale data sets seamlessly.

Distributed data management in Milvus is designed to address the challenges of growing data sizes and the demands of real-time performance. By leveraging a distributed system, Milvus can partition and replicate data across multiple nodes, enabling parallel processing and reducing bottlenecks that often occur in monolithic databases. This architecture is crucial for maintaining the speed, consistency, and availability of the system when faced with extensive queries or massive data operations.

In this chapter, we will explore the distributed data management features of Milvus in detail, including its storage, indexing, and querying mechanisms. We will cover how Milvus handles data partitioning and replication, ensuring scalability and fault tolerance. Additionally, we will dive into the processes involved in setting up and managing a distributed Milvus deployment, examining the key components that work together to deliver high-performance results in production environments.

Therefore, by understanding Milvus' approach to distributed data management, readers will gain insight into how this powerful platform enables the handling of vast amounts of vector data in real-world applications, from image search to recommendation systems, and beyond.

Structure

In this chapter, we will discuss the following topics:

- Implementation of the Data Coordinator
- Implementation of the Data Nodes

Implementation of the Data Coordinator

In Milvus, the Data Coordinator plays a critical role in managing and orchestrating the data operations across the distributed architecture. As a key component of the system, the Data Coordinator is responsible for ensuring that data is efficiently handled, synchronized, and distributed across the various nodes in a Milvus cluster. It serves as the intermediary between the data storage layer and the higher-level application logic, ensuring that operations such as data insertion, retrieval, and indexing are executed correctly and efficiently.

The Data Coordinator manages tasks such as data partitioning, data placement, and coordination of data access across multiple nodes, ensuring fault tolerance and consistency in a distributed environment. It also plays a vital role in load balancing, helping to optimize the performance of queries by distributing workloads evenly. By effectively coordinating the data flow, it ensures that Milvus can handle large-scale, high-dimensional vector data with minimal latency, making it an essential component for supporting real-time applications like recommendation systems, similarity search, and AI-driven analytics.

In this section, we will explore the functionality of the Data Coordinator in Milvus, how it interacts with other components in the system, and the role it plays in enabling scalable, efficient, and high-performance data management in distributed environments.

Operations of the Root Data Coordinator: The `DataNodeManager` Interface

Introduction

In a distributed vector database system like Milvus, efficient coordination and management of data nodes are critical for maintaining system reliability, data consistency, and high performance. The `DataNodeManager` interface plays a pivotal role as the operational backbone of the root data coordinator, orchestrating numerous tasks involving data nodes, which handle storage, indexing, querying, and maintenance of vector data segments.

Data nodes form the backbone of a scalable distributed storage system by managing segments of data across clusters. The `DataNodeManager` interface abstracts the operations needed to maintain sessions, data flows, compaction processes, health monitoring, and shutdown procedures. This interface acts as a gateway for controlling and communicating with data nodes, ensuring that data operations are performed seamlessly and the system remains robust under varying workloads.

Session Management

Sessions represent active connections or registrations of data nodes within the system. Proper session management is essential for tracking node availability, managing load, and ensuring reliable communication.

- **Key Methods:**
    - `AddSession`:

      It registers a new session for a specific data node. This process involves establishing a live connection and initializing necessary metadata, allowing the coordinator to recognize and interact with the node.
    - `DeleteSession`:

      It removes or terminates an existing session. This is crucial for gracefully handling node disconnections, failures, or maintenance windows to avoid dangling or stale session references.
    - `GetSessionIDs`:

      It provides a list of all active session identifiers, which enables monitoring and administration tools to display or process node connectivity status.
    - `GetSessions`:

      It returns detailed information about all current sessions, facilitating auditing, diagnostics, and load balancing decisions.
    - `GetSession`:

      It fetches information about a specific session by its ID, allowing targeted queries and operations on a particular node.
- **Significance:**

  Effective session management ensures that the system is aware of all active nodes and can react dynamically to changes in node status. It helps maintain high availability by allowing fast detection of node failures and supports load distribution for balanced resource utilization.

Data Operations

Data operations are the core activities that manipulate, maintain, and move data segments across nodes. These operations are crucial for ensuring data durability, accessibility, and freshness.

- **Key Methods:**
  - `Flush`:

    It triggers a flush of data segments on a specific node, forcing in-memory data or buffered changes to be persisted to stable storage. Flushing is often necessary before querying or after a bulk data insertion.
  - `FlushChannels`:

    It is similar to flush but targets specific data channels. This granular control allows selective persistence based on workload or query patterns.
  - `Compaction`:

    It initiates compaction processes to merge fragmented or outdated data segments. Compaction reduces storage overhead and improves query efficiency by optimizing segment layouts.
  - `SyncSegments`:

    It ensures that segment data is synchronized across nodes. This is vital for data consistency in distributed systems, especially during replication or recovery operations.
  - `PreImport` and `ImportV2`:

    It prepares and executes data import processes, allowing bulk data ingestion. `PreImport` stages the data, validating and transforming it as needed, while ImportV2 carries out the actual import.
  - `QueryPreImport` and `QueryImport`:

    It provides status information about pre-imported or imported data, enabling monitoring and error handling during bulk ingestion.
  - `DropImport`:

    It removes import data, either due to errors, cancellation requests, or cleanup after successful import.
- **Significance:**

  These operations enable the system to handle large-scale data efficiently, ensuring durability through flushing, improving storage efficiency through compaction, and facilitating smooth data ingestion workflows. The ability to query import status provides transparency and control over batch operations, improving system reliability and user experience.

Compaction and Health Management

Data compaction and health checks maintain the operational integrity of the system and optimize data storage.

- **Key Methods:**
    - `GetCompactionPlanResult` and `GetCompactionPlansResults`:

      It retrieves results from individual or multiple compaction plans. These methods allow tracking of compaction progress and results, facilitating diagnostics and decision-making on subsequent maintenance.
    - `DropCompactionPlan`:

      It cancels or removes specific compaction plans, which is necessary if the plan is outdated, erroneous, or superseded.
    - `CheckHealth`:

      It performs system health checks, verifying that nodes and data segments are functioning correctly. This method can detect node failures, segment corruption, or performance degradation early.
- **Significance:**

  Regular compaction ensures efficient use of storage and better query performance by minimizing fragmentation. Health checks maintain system stability and help avoid catastrophic failures by proactive detection and mitigation of issues.

Channel Operations

- **Overview:**

  Channels represent data streams or partitions for segment management and real-time updates. Managing channel operations ensures synchronized data flow and consistency.
- **Key Methods:**
    - `NotifyChannelOperation`:

      It informs nodes about operations on data channels, such as adding, removing, or modifying channels. This notification mechanism keeps nodes updated on structural changes.
    - `CheckChannelOperationProgress`:

      It queries the status of ongoing channel operations to monitor progress and detect bottlenecks or failures.
- **Significance:**

  Channel operations management supports real-time data streaming scenarios and ensures that nodes handle channel changes gracefully, maintaining data consistency and low latency.

Query and Slot Management

- **Overview:**

  Efficient query execution and slot management are critical in balancing workloads and routing queries to the appropriate data partitions.

- **Key Method:**

  - `QuerySlot`:

    It provides information about slot statuses, which are logical partitions of data used for distributing queries and updates. This helps to coordinate distributed query execution and load balancing.

- **Significance:**

  Proper slot management improves query performance by ensuring queries are sent to the nodes responsible for relevant data partitions, reducing latency and avoiding hotspots.

System Shutdown

- **Overview:**

  A clean shutdown process is necessary to prevent data loss and ensure graceful termination of services.

- **Key Method:**

  - `Close`:

    Shuts down the `DataNodeManager`, closing all active sessions and releasing resources. This method is critical during system upgrades, maintenance, or complete shutdowns.

- **Significance:**

  Graceful shutdown ensures data integrity and avoids corruption, allowing the system to resume operations smoothly when restarted.

The `DataNodeManager` interface is a cornerstone of the root data coordinator in distributed vector database systems. By managing node sessions, orchestrating complex data operations like flushing, compaction, and import, monitoring health, coordinating channel updates, managing queries, and supporting graceful shutdowns, it ensures that the system operates reliably, efficiently, and at scale.

This interface abstracts the complexity of managing distributed data nodes and provides a consistent API for higher-level components to interact with the data layer, making it indispensable for scalable, high-performance vector search infrastructures like Milvus.

Data Management by the Cluster

The `Flush` function of the data co-ordinator of the cluster manager is responsible for flushing segments of data to a specific node within a cluster.

```
func (c *ClusterImpl) Flush(ctxcontext.Context, nodeID int64, channel
string, segments []*datapb.SegmentInfo) error {
    // Retrieve the channel associated with the node
ch, founded := c.channelManager.GetChannel(nodeID, channel)
    if !founded {
log.Warn("node is not matched with channel",
zap.String("channel", channel),
            zap.Int64("nodeID", nodeID),
        )
        return fmt.Errorf("channel %s is not watched on node %d",
channel, nodeID)
    }

    // Helper function to extract segment ID
getSegmentID := func(segment *datapb.SegmentInfo, _ int) int64 {
        return segment.GetID()
    }

    // Create a FlushSegmentsRequest
req := &datapb.FlushSegmentsRequest{
        Base: commonpbutil.NewMsgBase(
commonpbutil.WithMsgType(commonpb.MsgType_Flush),
commonpbutil.WithSourceID(paramtable.GetNodeID()),
commonpbutil.WithTargetID(nodeID),
        ),
CollectionID: ch.GetCollectionID(),
SegmentIDs:   lo.Map(segments, getSegmentID),
ChannelName:  channel,
    }

    // Trigger the flush operation via session manager
c.sessionManager.Flush(ctx, nodeID, req)

    return nil
}
```

Function Overview

- **Purpose**: The function flushes data segments for a specific channel to a particular node in the cluster.

Detailed Steps

1. **Channel Validation**:
    a. It first attempts to retrieve the channel information for the given nodeID and channel by calling `c.channelManager.GetChannel(nodeID, channel)`.
    b. If the channel is not found (founded is false), it logs a warning and returns an error indicating the channel is not watched on the given node.
2. **Segment ID Extraction**:
    a. A helper function `getSegmentID` is defined to extract the segment ID from each segment in the segments array using `segment.GetID()`.
3. **Creating a Flush Request**:
    a. A `FlushSegmentsRequest` is constructed. This request contains:
        - Metadata (base message information) like message type, source ID, and target node ID.
        - The collection ID associated with the channel.
        - A list of segment IDs, which are obtained by mapping over the segments array using the `getSegmentID` function.
        - The channel name where the segments belong.
4. **Session Management**:
    a. Finally, the function calls `c.sessionManager.Flush(ctx, nodeID, req)` to trigger the flush operation, passing the request along with the context and node ID.

The `Flush` function is used to flush data segments for a specific channel to a node. It validates that the node is watching the channel, prepares a flush request, and then triggers the flush operation using the session manager. If the channel is not found for the given node, it logs a warning and returns an error.

Implementation of the Data Nodes

In a modern distributed vector database system, Data Nodes are fundamental components responsible for storing, managing, and serving vector data segments. The `DataNode` struct represents an instance of such a node. It encapsulates complex functionality related to data management, synchronization, lifecycle handling, resource allocation, and interaction with other system components like coordinators and external services.

The `DataNode` is designed with fault tolerance, concurrency, and scalability in mind, supporting the demands of large-scale vector search applications with real-time updates and bulk ingestion.

Core Structure and Context Management

- **Context and Lifecycle:**
  - `ctx` (Context):

    The `DataNode` maintains a context object that governs the lifecycle of asynchronous operations. This context ensures that all long-running or cancellable operations within the node can be cleanly aborted or timed out as needed.
  - `cancel`:

    A `cancel` function paired with the context allows the `DataNode` to trigger a graceful shutdown by cancelling all ongoing processes and cleaning up resources.
- **Significance:**

  The use of context is a standard idiom in distributed systems programming, facilitating robust lifecycle management and preventing resource leaks during shutdown or failure recovery.

Node Role and State Management

- **Role:**
  - It defines the operational role of the node, such as a data storage node or a coordinator. This role determines the responsibilities of the node and the types of operations it must support.

  `stateCode`: It tracks the current state of the node (say, initializing, active, stopping). This state machine prevents illegal operations and aids in status reporting and troubleshooting.
- **Significance:**

  Explicit role and state tracking enable the system to handle nodes differently based on their lifecycle phases and responsibilities, improving stability and clarity in distributed workflows.

Managers for Data Operations

The `DataNode` orchestrates various managers to modularize complex data workflows:

- **`flowgraphManager`:**

  It manages data flow graphs which represent pipelines of data processing tasks. This includes segment data ingestion, filtering, indexing, and transformation.

- **`channelManager`:**

  It handles the management of data channels, which correspond to data streams or partitions. It manages their lifecycle, including subscription, checkpointing, and data delivery.

- **`syncMgr`:**

  It is responsible for synchronizing segment metadata and data states between DataNodes and coordinating components to ensure consistency.

- **`writeBufferManager`:**

  It manages to write buffers that temporarily hold incoming data before flushing to persistent storage, optimizing throughput and reducing latency.

- **`importTaskMgr`:**

  It oversees import tasks for bulk data ingestion, coordinating task scheduling, execution, retries, and status tracking.

- **`importScheduler`:**

  It is a dedicated scheduler that queues and schedules import operations, ensuring efficient resource utilization and orderly execution. These managers decouple concerns, enabling the DataNode to scale complex data operations independently and maintain high performance in diverse workloads.

Data Structures for Caching and Execution

- **`segmentCache`:**

  It acts as an in-memory cache for frequently accessed data segments, thereby, dramatically improving read performance by reducing disk I/O.

- **`compactionExecutor`:**

  It executes compaction tasks that merge fragmented or small data segments to optimize storage layout and improve query efficiency.

- **`timeTickSender`:**

  It sends periodic time ticks used for synchronization purposes, such as coordinating snapshot creation, TTL management, or distributed transactions.

- **`channelCheckpointUpdater`:**

  It updates checkpoints for data channels, tracking the progress of data consumption or processing to guarantee exactly-once or at-least-once semantics.

Significance:

Caching and execution structures allow the `DataNode` to balance speed and resource usage, ensuring low-latency reads and efficient background maintenance.

External System Interfaces

- `etcdCli`:

  Client to interact with etcd, a distributed key-value store that acts as the backbone for service discovery, metadata storage, and distributed locking.

- `address`:

  The network address of the DataNode, used for communication and registration with the cluster.

- `rootCoord`:

  Client interface to the Root Coordinator, which manages system-wide metadata and orchestrates cluster operations.

- `dataCoord`:

  Client interface to the Data Coordinator, handling data placement, segment management, and replication coordination.

- `broker`:

  Messaging or event broker client used for publishing and subscribing to internal system events or distributed task notifications.

Significance:

Interfacing with external distributed services enables the DataNode to participate in cluster-wide coordination, ensuring consistency and scalability across nodes.

Initialization and Lifecycle Control

- `initOnce`, `startOnce`, `stopOnce`:

  These synchronization primitives guarantee that initialization, startup, and shutdown logic execute exactly once, preventing race conditions and undefined states.

- `sessionMu`:

  A mutex protecting session-related operations to ensure thread safety when sessions are modified concurrently.

- `session`:

  Represents the active session of the `DataNode` within the cluster, encapsulating node identity and connectivity information.

- `watchKv`:

  Watches for changes in system key-value pairs, such as configuration updates or leadership changes, enabling dynamic response to cluster events.

- **`chunkManager`:**

  Manages storage chunks for data persistence and retrieval, abstracting the underlying storage medium.

- **`allocator`:**

  Allocates resources such as memory and storage segments dynamically according to workload needs.

Significance:

Robust lifecycle and session management prevent concurrency bugs and ensure that nodes can join, leave, or recover cleanly from faults.

Additional Components and Metrics

- **`closer`:**

  It is a cleanup resource that ensures all allocated resources are released upon shutdown.

- **`dispClient`:**

  It is Dispatcher client facilitating communication between different components within the node or across nodes.

- **`factory`:**

  It is the Dependency injection factory that creates components such as managers or clients, enabling flexible configuration and testing.

- **`reportImportRetryTimes`:**

  It tracks retry attempts for import operations, aiding fault tolerance and error recovery.

- **`pool`:**

  It is a concurrency pool managing goroutines or threads, balancing resource usage.

- **`metricsRequest`:**

  It contains monitoring data such as throughput, latency, and error counts for observability and alerting.

MultiSegmentWriter Struct

Overview:

The `MultiSegmentWriter` is a critical component in managing data writes during processes such as compaction, bulk ingestion, and index building. It abstracts writing operations over multiple data segments, enabling dynamic segment size control, metadata management, and support for advanced search features like BM25 ranking.

IO and Resource Allocation

- `binlogIO`:

  It is an interface responsible for reading and writing binlogs – append-only binary logs that record all changes or data entries. Binlogs enable durable writes and incremental replay.

- `allocator`:

  It manages resource allocation related to compaction, such as memory or persistent storage blocks, ensuring efficient usage and preventing overflow.

Significance:

Efficient IO and resource management are crucial for maintaining high throughput during write-heavy operations and enabling fault-tolerant recovery.

Writer and Segment Tracking

- `writer`:

  The primary writer object that handles the actual serialization of records to binlogs.

- `currentSegmentID`:

  It identifies the segment currently receiving data. This tracking allows dynamic switching or rotation of segments as they reach capacity or require sealing.

Significance:

Segment tracking facilitates fine-grained control over data partitioning, ensuring that segments remain within size limits and are easily manageable.

Segment Size Management

- `maxRows`:

  The maximum number of rows allowed per segment. This limit prevents segments from growing too large, which could degrade query performance or increase compaction overhead.

- `segmentSize`:

  The size in bytes of the current segment. Although it can be dynamically adjusted, the target size is defined during compaction plan creation to balance write performance and resource usage.

Significance:

Dynamically managing segment size optimizes storage utilization and query efficiency while avoiding resource exhaustion.

Schema and Metadata

- `schema`:

  It encapsulates the schema of the collection, including data types, fields, and indexing rules. The schema ensures data consistency and validation during writes.

- `partitionID`:

  It is the identifier of the partition to which the current segment belongs. Partitioning allows horizontal data distribution and parallel query execution.

- `collectionID`:

  It identifies the collection (or table) that contains the segment, enabling namespace isolation and multi-tenancy support.

- `channel`:

  It represents the communication channel, often related to streaming data or replication pathways.

Significance:

Metadata ensures that the data is written and managed according to system rules, enabling consistent, multi-tenant, and partitioned data management.

Compaction Data and BM25 Support

- `res`:

  It is a slice of compaction segments involved in the current compaction operation. These segments are merged, reorganized, or optimized.

- `bm25Fields`:

  It is a list of field IDs relevant for BM25 ranking, a popular probabilistic model used in search to rank documents by relevance. Supporting BM25 indicates that the `MultiSegmentWriter` plays a role not only in data storage but also in preparing data for search and retrieval.

Significance:

Integration of BM25 support highlights the dual role of the writer in both storage and search-related processes, enabling seamless end-to-end indexing.

Summary and Final Remarks

The `DataNode` struct and `MultiSegmentWriter` represent foundational elements in a distributed vector database system. The `DataNode` encapsulates a wide range of responsibilities from lifecycle management, data operation orchestration, external coordination, and system health monitoring. Meanwhile, the `MultiSegmentWriter` specializes in efficient data writing, segment management, and compaction with search indexing support.

Together, they form a highly modular, fault-tolerant architecture designed to handle the complexity of large-scale vector data storage and retrieval with high throughput, low latency, and robust fault tolerance.

Conclusion

In this chapter, we have explored the core principles and mechanisms that power distributed data management in Milvus, a high-performance vector database designed to handle large-scale machine learning and AI applications. We have also examined how Milvus efficiently manages and organizes vast amounts of vector data across multiple nodes in a distributed environment, ensuring scalability, fault tolerance, and high availability.

By understanding the roles of key components such as **DataNodes**, **Root Data Coordinators**, and **Compaction Executors**, we have gained insights into how Milvus handles data partitioning, synchronization, and optimization. The chapter has also highlighted how processes like data insertion, indexing, and compaction, are orchestrated to maintain high performance, low latency, and optimal storage usage in a distributed setting.

Additionally, we have explored critical concepts such as **session management**, **segment handling**, and **compaction**, which are essential for maintaining data integrity, improving query performance, and ensuring system efficiency. Hence, by applying a distributed approach to data management, Milvus not only supports massive amounts of data but also enables users to perform similarity searches with speed and accuracy.

Ultimately, the distributed data management architecture of Milvus empowers it to deliver reliable, scalable, and efficient services, making it an ideal choice for modern AI and machine learning applications that require managing and querying massive datasets. As we continue to scale data systems in increasingly complex environments, understanding these distributed data management strategies will remain crucial for optimizing performance and achieving data-driven success.

CHAPTER 8
Distributed Index and Query Management

Introduction

Milvus is an open-source vector database designed for efficient similarity search and retrieval of high-dimensional data. As the demand for real-time processing and querying of large-scale machine learning and artificial intelligence models increases, Milvus has emerged as a leading solution for managing and indexing vector data. A key feature of Milvus is its ability to perform distributed index management, which enables it to handle massive volumes of data, provide high-performance search capabilities, and scale dynamically across multiple nodes.

As data grows exponentially, a single machine may no longer be able to efficiently manage the index due to memory and computational limitations. This is where distributed index management comes into play. Distributed index management involves splitting the index, across multiple machines or nodes in a distributed system. This enables the system to handle vast amounts of data and perform faster searches by leveraging parallelism, load balancing, and fault tolerance. This is achieved by utilizing distributed computing resources for building and managing indices that can scale.

Structure

In this chapter, we will discuss the following topics:

- Implementation of the Index Coordinator
- Implementation of the Index Nodes
- Implementation of the Query Coordinator
- Implementation of the Query Management

Implementation of the Index Co-ordinator

The **Index Coordinator** in Milvus is a key component responsible for managing the lifecycle of indexes within the system. In vector databases like Milvus, indexes play a critical role in accelerating search and retrieval operations, particularly for high-dimensional vector data. The Index Coordinator oversees the creation, maintenance, and synchronization of these indexes across various nodes in the cluster, ensuring that they are efficiently built and updated as data changes. The key responsibilities are:

- **Index Creation**: The Index Coordinator is responsible for initiating and managing the process of index creation on the data stored in the database. This involves selecting the appropriate index type based on the query needs of the user (for example, IVF, HNSW, or other index structures for vector data).
- **Index Synchronization**: After an index is created on one node, the Index Coordinator ensures that it is properly synchronized across all relevant nodes, ensuring consistency and high availability of indexed data across the cluster.
- **Index Optimization**: The Index Coordinator may trigger optimizations and updates to indexes when there are changes to the underlying data, such as when new vectors are added or old vectors are deleted. This helps to maintain the accuracy and efficiency of search queries.
- **Resource Management**: The Index Coordinator also manages resources required for indexing, such as CPU, memory, and storage. It ensures that indexing tasks are distributed efficiently to avoid overloading any single node.
- **Monitoring and Error Handling**: It monitors the status of index creation and updates, handling any errors or failures that may occur during the indexing process and ensuring that the system can recover gracefully from issues.

Implementation of the Index Nodes

Here is a detailed breakdown of the methods and functionality present in the `service.go` file of the **IndexNode service** in Milvus:

1. `Prepare()`
    - **Purpose**: The `Prepare()` method is responsible for initializing the necessary components of the IndexNode service before it starts running.
    - **Functionality**:
        - It initializes the gRPC server using the context and listener for the the service of the IndexNode.

   - It sets up the connection to etcd (a distributed key-value store) to store configuration data and manage the distributed state of the system.
   - It ensures that components such as IndexCoord (which manages index coordination) and DataCoord (which handles data coordination) are ready for use.

- **Outcome**: At the end of Prepare(), the IndexNode is set up and ready for communication over gRPC and interaction with other Milvus components.

2. `Run()`

- **Purpose**: The `Run()` method starts the actual operation of the IndexNode service after its preparation.
- **Functionality**:
   - It runs the gRPC service, which listens for incoming requests and interacts with the rest of the Milvus cluster.
   - The method calls startGrpcLoop(), which actually sets up the network connections for the service and listens to incoming requests.
   - It ensures that any necessary configurations are applied and prepares the system for interactions with clients.
- **Outcome**: The service starts, allowing the IndexNode to serve indexing requests, manage indexes, and maintain synchronization across the Milvus cluster.

3. `Stop()`

- **Purpose**: The `Stop()` method is used to gracefully shut down the IndexNode service.
- **Functionality**:
   - It handles the cleanup process, ensuring that open network connections (such as gRPC connections) and resources (say memory or files) are properly closed or released.
   - It shuts down the underlying gRPC server, ensuring that no new requests are accepted and ongoing operations are completed.
   - It provides a safe and controlled way of stopping the service without leaving resources in an inconsistent state.
- **Outcome**: The IndexNode service is properly stopped, and resources are cleaned up.

4. **`startGrpcLoop()`**
    - **Purpose**: This method is responsible for setting up the gRPC server loop to listen for incoming requests and handle client interactions.
    - **Functionality**:
        - It initializes a network listener (using TCP/IP) on a specified address and port, waiting for connections from clients.
        - It configures the gRPC server with appropriate settings, such as **keep-alive** configurations to ensure continuous communication and prevent connection timeouts.
        - It sets up middleware components like interceptors for logging, metrics collection, tracing, and handling authorization (if necessary).
        - The loop allows the server to continue running, handling incoming client requests until the server is stopped.
    - **Outcome**: The gRPC server continuously listens for incoming requests and processes them using the defined methods for index management, such as index creation, deletion, and retrieval.
5. **`init()`**
    - **Purpose**: The init() method is used for initializing the core components and configurations of the IndexNode service.
    - **Functionality**:
        - It sets up **etcd** connection for distributed state management, allowing the IndexNode to communicate with other services (such as the RootCoord or DataCoord).
        - It ensures that the configuration system of Milvus is initialized and synchronized with the state of the system, such as retrieving configuration values like the address of other services.
        - It initializes key Milvus components like **IndexCoord**, which is responsible for handling index-related tasks, and **DataCoord**, which coordinates data distribution across nodes.
    - **Outcome**: This method prepares the service for running and allows the server to interact with other Milvus components like the root and data coordinators.
6. **`newGrpcServer()`**
    - **Purpose**: This method is a helper for creating a new gRPC server.

- **Functionality**:
    - It creates and configures a new gRPC server to handle requests.
    - It sets up the server to use custom interceptors for logging, metrics, and other middleware, ensuring that the server behaves correctly in a distributed and monitored environment.
    - The server is also configured with a connection to the specific **etcd** instance, facilitating coordination between distributed nodes.
- **Outcome**: It returns a new gRPC server, ready to handle requests and respond with the appropriate results.

7. **`setupGrpcServer()`**
    - **Purpose**: This method configures the gRPC server and registers the services.
    - **Functionality**:
        - Registers various services, including the **IndexService** that handles specific indexing tasks such as creation, deletion, and retrieval of indexes.
        - It also registers handlers for managing the **IndexCoord** service, which is essential for coordinating index operations across the cluster.
    - **Outcome**: The gRPC server is fully set up to handle the required services, ensuring that the IndexNode can process indexing tasks and interact with clients and other Milvus services.

Summary of the Roles of Methods in the `service.go` File:

- The **`Prepare()`** method initializes the environment for the IndexNode to run, setting up necessary services and configurations.
- The **`Run()`** method starts the operation of the service, allowing the IndexNode to handle indexing requests via gRPC.
- The **`Stop()`** method ensures a graceful shutdown of the service, cleaning up resources.
- The **`startGrpcLoop()`** method starts and listens for incoming gRPC connections, ensuring that the service can process requests.
- The **`init()`** method prepares and synchronizes core components, such as the connection to **`etcd`** and other necessary services for coordination.
- The **`newGrpcServer()`** and **`setupGrpcServer()`** methods help create and configure the gRPC server for managing client communications and service registrations.

In conclusion, the methods in the `service.go` file work together to set up, manage, and shut down the lifecycle of the `IndexNode` service in Milvus, ensuring that indexing operations in the distributed system are performed efficiently and reliably.

Implementation of the Query Coordinator

The Server struct is a central component in Milvus that manages the coordination and execution of various system tasks in a distributed environment. It integrates multiple services, clients, and managers necessary to run and control the different functionalities of Milvus. The key components of the Server Struct are:

- **Context and Lifecycle Management**:
    - **`ctx` and `cancel`:** It is used to manage the lifecycle of the server, ensuring that the server can gracefully handle context cancellation and shutdown.
    - **`wg`:** It is a `sync.WaitGroup` for managing concurrent operations and ensuring that all background tasks are completed before shutdown.
- **Status and Configuration**:
    - **`status`:** It is an atomic integer tracking the status of the server.
    - **`etcdCli`:** Client for interacting with etcd, used for distributed coordination.
    - **`tikvCli`:** Client for TiKV (distributed storage system) for transactional operations.
    - **`address`:** It is the network address of the server.
    - **`session`:** It represents a session interface for managing cluster sessions.
- **Meta and Catalog**:
    - **`kv` and `meta`:** It represents the key-value store and metadata management for the system.
    - **`store`:** It is the catalog for querying information about collections and their configurations.
    - **`dist`:** It manages distribution across the cluster.
    - **`broker`:** It handles data distribution and resource management.
    - **`targetMgr`:** It manages targets for data processing.
- **Coordinators and Clients**:
    - **`dataCoord` and `rootCoord`:** Clients for communicating with the Data and Root Coordinators in the Milvus system.

- **Session Management**:
    - **`cluster`**: It represents the cluster configuration.
    - **`nodeMgr`**: It manages nodes in the cluster.
    - **`queryNodeCreator`**: It is responsible for creating query nodes for processing.
- **Schedulers**:
    - **`jobScheduler`**: It schedules various system jobs, such as maintenance tasks.
    - **`taskScheduler`**: It manages the scheduling of tasks in the cluster.
- **HeartBeat and Monitoring**:
    - **`distController`**: It manages distributed coordination for heartbeats and node health checks.
    - **`checkerController`**: It oversees system checks for health and resource availability.
- **Observers**:
    - **`collectionObserver`, `targetObserver`, `replicaObserver`, `resourceObserver`, and `leaderCacheObserver`**: These observers monitor different aspects of the Milvus system, such as collections, resources, and the leader election process.
- **Balancer and Active-Standby**:
    - **`getBalancerFunc`**: It is a function for retrieving the balancer, which distributes load across the system.
    - **`balancerMap` and `balancerLock`**: It stores and manages the balancers used for load balancing in the system.
    - **`enableActiveStandBy`**: It is a flag for enabling active-standby mode, ensuring high availability.
    - **`activateFunc`**: It is a function that activates standby nodes when needed.
- **Node and Proxy Management**:
    - **`nodeUpEventChan` and `notifyNodeUp`**: These are channels for handling events when nodes are brought up or go down.
    - **`proxyCreator`, `proxyWatcher`, and `proxyClientManager`**: These are components for managing proxy clients that interact with Milvus.

- **Metrics**:
  - `metricsCacheManager`: It manages caching and retrieval of metrics data.
  - `metricsRequest`: It holds metrics-related requests to be processed.

The Server struct is central to the operation of a Milvus instance, handling communication with other Milvus components (like `RootCoord`, `DataCoord` and `querycoord`), managing resources, balancing loads, and ensuring system health. It integrates distributed coordination mechanisms (via etcd), session management, job/task scheduling, heartbeats, and system monitoring. The struct also handles advanced features like active-standby node management, proxy client management, and metrics collection, ensuring the scalability, reliability, and performance of Milvus in a distributed environment.

Implementation of the Query Management

The provided code includes methods for the **QueryNode** in Milvus, handling operations like loading indexes and querying data. Here is a summary of the methods:

1. `loadIndex()`
   - **Purpose**: This method loads the index for the given segments.
   - **Functionality**:
     - It starts by logging the collection ID and segment IDs being processed.
     - It iterates over the segment load information (`SegmentLoadInfo`) from the request.
     - For each segment, it checks if the segment is found and if it is local.
     - If the segment is marked for **lazy loading**, it sets the load info and marks the segment for reloading.
     - Otherwise, it uses the loader to load the index. If the index load fails, it logs a warning and sets an error status.
   - **Outcome**: The method either loads the index for the segments or logs an error if it fails.
2. `queryChannel()`
   - **Purpose**: This method executes a query on a specified channel.
   - **Functionality**:
     - It starts by logging the request details, including the collection ID, channel, and query scope.

    - It increments a metric counter for query requests.
    - A **delegator** is fetched for the specified channel, and if not found, it logs an error.
    - It performs the query via the delegator and processes the results.
    - After obtaining results, the method uses a **reducer** to aggregate the results from all shards.
    - The method logs the latency for the query and increments success or failure counters for the query metrics.
  - **Outcome**: Returns the reduced results if successful or logs and returns an error, if something goes wrong.

3. `queryChannelStream()`
  - **Purpose**: This method handles streaming queries for a specific channel.
  - **Functionality**:
    - Similar to `queryChannel()`, it logs the request and increments the query metrics.
    - A **delegator** is fetched for the specified channel to handle the query stream.
    - It executes the query in a streaming manner by calling the `QueryStream` method of the delegator, allowing the results to be sent back continuously.
    - It tracks the time taken for the query and logs the total latency.
  - **Outcome**: Handles streaming queries, returning the streamed results or an error, if the query fails.

Key Concepts and Flow

- **Delegators**: Each channel has a corresponding delegator that is responsible for handling query operations for that channel. If a delegator is not found, an error is logged.
- **Reducers**: After querying the delegator, the results are reduced (aggregated) to form the final query response.
- **Metrics**: The methods track various query metrics, including success/failure counts and latency, to monitor system performance.
- **Lazy Loading**: The `loadIndex` method supports lazy loading for segments, which delays the index loading until necessary.

Summary

The methods in this code enable the **QueryNode** to load indexes for specific segments and handle queries both in standard and streaming modes. The **delegator** pattern is used for distributed query processing, ensuring that queries are routed to the appropriate segments for processing. The methods also incorporate detailed logging and metric tracking to monitor query performance and diagnose issues.

Conclusion

In this chapter, we have delved into the **distributed index and query management** systems of **Milvus**, a powerful open-source vector database designed to handle large-scale high-dimensional data. The ability to efficiently manage indexes and queries across distributed environments is fundamental to the performance and scalability of Milvus, especially in scenarios involving billions of vectors and high-concurrency workloads.

The distributed index and query management system in Milvus represents a **state-of-the-art approach** to handling high-dimensional data at scale. By leveraging advanced indexing techniques, distributed query execution, and dynamic resource management, Milvus ensures efficient data retrieval even in the most demanding environments. Its architecture, which integrates robust fault tolerance, high availability, and performance optimization strategies, positions Milvus as a leader in the field of vector databases.

As the need for **real-time analytics**, **AI-driven applications**, and **massive data retrieval** continues to grow, the distributed system of Milvus will play a crucial role in enabling faster and more accurate results for similarity search, recommendation systems, and machine learning tasks. Moreover, the ability of Milvus to scale seamlessly in cloud and multi-cloud environments ensures its relevance and adaptability in an increasingly distributed world.

Looking ahead, ongoing enhancements in **indexing algorithms**, **query optimization**, and **cloud-native features** will further empower Milvus to handle even larger datasets, more complex queries, and more demanding workloads, keeping it at the forefront of next-generation data management systems.

CHAPTER 9
Design of the Proxy Server

Introduction

Milvus is a highly scalable, open-source vector database designed for similarity search, serving use cases in machine learning, AI, and data analytics where large volumes of unstructured data (like images, text, or videos) needs to be processed and queried efficiently. One of the core components of Milvus is the Proxy, which acts as the gateway for clients to interact with the system and serves as an intermediary between the client requests and the backend components of Milvus. The Proxy handles everything from query routing, load balancing, session management, fault tolerance, and response aggregation, making it a critical part of the Milvus architecture.

In this chapter, we will delve into the various aspects of the Proxy in Milvus, examining its architecture, responsibilities, and how it enables the system to scale and perform efficiently in a distributed environment. We will also explore how the Proxy ensures fault tolerance, high availability, and load balancing, crucial for distributed vector search applications.Anomaly Detection: Milvus is also used in fraud detection and cybersecurity, where outlier or anomaly vectors are indexed and queried to identify unusual patterns or behaviors.

Structure

In this chapter, we will cover the following topics:

- The Role of Proxy in Milvus
- Architectural Design of the Proxy
- Responsibilities of the Proxy
- Proxy and Scalability

- Proxy and Query Execution
- Proxy for Multi-Tenancy

The Role of Proxy in Milvus

In a distributed system like Milvus, multiple components handle different aspects of data storage, query execution, indexing, and more. The Proxy serves as a middleware layer that communicates between the client and these backend components. The Proxy ensures that requests are routed to the appropriate services, and it manages the flow of data and information through the system, from receiving client queries to returning the results. The key functions of Proxy are as follows:

- **Request Routing:** Every client request must be routed to the correct backend service. The Proxy performs this routing based on the type of request (for example, search, insert, update, delete) and the data involved.
- **Load Balancing:** The Proxy ensures that the backend nodes (for instance, Query Nodes, Data Nodes) handle requests evenly by distributing them appropriately based on their capacity and load.
- **Client Connection Management:** The Proxy ensures that client sessions are managed efficiently. It handles client authentication, tracks session states, and supports multiple concurrent requests from clients.
- **Query Delegation:** Queries are often directed to different backend nodes depending on the distribution of data. The Proxy is responsible for delegating queries to the right nodes, ensuring minimal latency and optimal resource usage.
- **Failover Handling:** In the event of a node failure, the Proxy ensures that requests are rerouted to healthy nodes, preventing disruptions in service.

Architectural Design of the Proxy

The Proxy in Milvus is designed to handle multiple responsibilities that span request management, load balancing, session handling, and query execution. It acts as a single entry point into the system, connecting clients with the various service nodes in the distributed infrastructure.

Proxy Components

To better understand the role of Proxy, we will break down its internal components and their responsibilities:

- **Client Interface:** The Client Interface layer handles incoming client requests. It is the first point of interaction between the client and the system, ensuring that requests are formatted correctly and routed to the appropriate internal services.
    - **Session Management:** Each client request is associated with a session that contains state information about the operations of the client. The Proxy keeps track of these sessions for a smoother experience, allowing clients to reconnect or issue multiple requests without losing their context.
- **Request Router:** The Request Router is the core component responsible for analyzing client requests and determining which backend service should handle each request. The routing logic uses system state information, metadata, and internal rules (such as data partitions, query types, and the like) to make these decisions.
    - **Routing Rules:** The routing logic ensures that operations are sent to the correct nodes, for instance, directing a vector search query to the Query Node or an insert operation to the Data Node. This helps optimize the overall system performance and avoids unnecessary overhead.
- **Load Balancer:** The Load Balancer is responsible for ensuring that no single node in the system becomes a bottleneck. It dynamically assigns requests to available service nodes based on current load conditions, minimizing the risk of overloading any particular node.
    - **Dynamic Load Balancing:** The Proxy continuously monitors the load on each node and adapts the routing decisions accordingly. If a node is under heavy load, the Proxy can redirect new requests to less busy nodes.
- **Session Manager:** The Session Manager ensures that each client interaction is properly tracked.
- **Request Delegation:** Request Delegation is about dispatching client requests to the correct backend services (for example, Query Node, Data Node). This step is crucial because Milvus is a distributed system, and different types of requests (insertions, deletions, queries) are handled by different nodes.
    - **Delegation Logic:** Based on the data distribution and the specific request type, the Proxy uses metadata and partitioning information to determine the correct service node to handle the request.
- **Response Aggregator:** Once the backend service processes the request, the Response Aggregator ensures that all results from multiple backend nodes are collected, unified, and presented as a single coherent response to the client.

- **Query Aggregation:** For distributed queries that span multiple nodes, the Proxy aggregates results from all relevant nodes, ensuring consistency and coherence in the final response.

Communication between Components

The role of the Proxy as an intermediary means it must efficiently coordinate with the backend components, including Query Nodes, Data Nodes, Index Nodes, and the Root Coordinator.

- **Query Node:** The Proxy routes queries to Query Nodes for retrieval and search operations. Query Nodes perform the heavy lifting of vector searches and return search results to the Proxy.
- **Data Node:** Data Nodes store and manage vector data, and they handle insertions, deletions, and updates. When an insertion request is sent, the Proxy directs it to the relevant Data Node.
- **Index Node:** Indexing tasks, such as building and managing search indexes, are handled by Index Nodes. The Proxy ensures that indexing requests are sent to the right node.
- **Root Coordinator:** The Proxy works with the Root Coordinator to ensure metadata consistency and to retrieve necessary operational data (like, partition mappings, data availability).

The communication between these components typically follows gRPC, a high-performance remote procedure call (RPC) framework, ensuring low-latency and efficient data transmission.

Responsibilities of the Proxy

The **Milvus Proxy** acts as the entry point that receives client requests such as vector insertions, searches, and collection operations. It validates the requests and routes them to the appropriate internal components like QueryNodes, DataNodes, or coordinators. It also manages request timestamps, load balancing, and aggregates distributed query results before returning them to the client.

Request Handling and Routing

When a request arrives at the Proxy, it is the job of the Proxy to determine where and how the request should be routed. Whether it is an insert, search, or delete operation, the Proxy examines the request and uses the following information to route the request:

- **Request Type:** It determines whether the request is related to data manipulation (insertions, deletions) or querying.

- **Data Location:** The Proxy checks metadata to decide which nodes hold the necessary data. For example, if a search query is requesting data from a specific segment, the Proxy ensures that the query is sent to the node holding that segment.

The key elements of Request Routing are:

- **Query Requests:** For queries, the Proxy sends requests to Query Nodes.
- **Data Manipulation:** Insertions, updates, and deletions are routed to Data Nodes.

Session Management

Managing sessions ensures that clients can interact with the system without interruptions. The Proxy manages client connections, stores session data, and ensures that multiple requests from the same client are handled in the correct order.

- **Stateful Requests:** Each request from a client may depend on the state of the previous request. The Proxy tracks session data to handle such dependencies correctly.

Load Balancing

Load balancing is essential to prevent bottlenecks. The Proxy uses a dynamic load balancing mechanism to distribute client requests across different backend services. The balancing process considers various factors:

- **Current Load:** The Proxy checks the current load of each backend service (for example, CPU usage, memory usage, request processing time).
- **Data Partitioning:** The Proxy also considers how data is partitioned across nodes. If a query is partitioned, the Proxy will route it accordingly to all necessary partitions.

The types of Load Balancing are as follows:

- **Request-Based Load Balancing:** The Proxy balances requests based on demand, ensuring that no node is overwhelmed.
- **Data-Based Load Balancing:** For partitioned data, the Proxy balances requests across nodes to ensure that data is accessed efficiently.

Query Aggregation

When a query involves multiple data segments or partitions, the Proxy needs to aggregate results from different nodes. The aggregation logic ensures that the client receives a unified response even if the data is distributed across multiple nodes.

- **Result Reduction:** The Proxy performs result reduction, filtering, or post-processing to combine data from different query nodes and return a final response.

Fault Tolerance and High Availability

The Proxy is designed to handle failures gracefully:

- **Health Checks:** The Proxy continuously monitors the health of the backend nodes. If a node becomes unresponsive or fails, the Proxy automatically reroutes the request to a healthy node.
- **Replication:** In case of failure, the Proxy leverages replicated nodes to ensure that client requests are still served.

Proxy and Scalability

As the Milvus system grows, so does the need for horizontal scaling. The Proxy ensures that the system can scale without disrupting operations by:

- **Efficient Load Distribution:** As more nodes are added, the Proxy dynamically balances load and adapts to the growing infrastructure.
- **Session Handling:** Even as new nodes join the system, the Proxy maintains session persistence and ensures that requests are routed correctly.

Proxy and Query Execution

Milvus is built for high-performance vector search, and the Proxy plays a crucial role in optimizing query execution:

- **Parallel Execution:** The Proxy routes queries to multiple Query Nodes in parallel to ensure faster query execution.
- **Caching:** The Proxy uses query caching to speed up repeated queries, reducing load on the system and improving response time for frequently executed queries.

Proxy for Multi-Tenancy

Milvus supports multi-tenancy, allowing multiple clients to use the system simultaneously. The Proxy ensures data isolation by routing requests to the correct namespaces or collections, ensuring that clients do not access data from other clients.

- **Isolation:** Requests are routed according to the namespace or collection to which the client belongs.

Conclusion

The Proxy in Milvus is an essential component that orchestrates the interactions between clients and the backend services in a distributed environment. It performs crucial tasks such as request routing, session management, load balancing, fault tolerance, and query aggregation. Through efficient management of these tasks, the Proxy ensures that Milvus can handle large-scale, high-performance vector searches in a distributed and fault-tolerant manner. With the Proxy in place, Milvus provides a reliable, scalable, and efficient solution for managing and querying large volumes of vector data.

The upcoming chapter discusses about the role of sparse indexes as well as optimizations on such cases. GPU based indexes provide an overview of the performance gains achievable using such schemes, and these are also discussed in the next chapter.

CHAPTER 10

GPU Based Indexes and Optimizations

Introduction

In the age of big data, Artificial Intelligence (AI), and Machine Learning (ML), the need for faster data processing has become critical. Vector-based search engines, such as Milvus, are at the forefront of this transformation, offering high-performance solutions for similarity search, recommendation systems, and various AI applications. Milvus, an open-source vector database, has made significant strides in scaling performance through hardware accelerations, and one of the key enablers of this performance boost is the use of Graphics Processing Units (GPUs).

GPUs, originally designed for rendering graphics in video games, have proven to be exceptionally efficient at handling parallelized computations required for modern AI workloads. Milvus leverages this capability to accelerate vector search, feature extraction, and data indexing, offering a substantial reduction in query latency and an increase in throughput, especially when dealing with large-scale datasets.

In this chapter, we will explore how Milvus harnesses the power of GPUs to optimize vector searches. We will also delve into the architecture of GPU acceleration within Milvus, the different types of optimizations applied, and how these optimizations enhance the performance of common operations such as similarity searches, indexing, and retrieval in a variety of use cases. Whether you are working with high-dimensional vectors or large-scale databases, understanding these GPU optimizations will provide valuable insights into maximizing the potential of Milvus for your AI-driven applications.

By the end of this chapter, you will have a clear understanding of how Milvus integrates GPU capabilities to deliver faster, more efficient vector search performance and how you can leverage these optimizations in your own projects to meet the demands of modern data processing.

Structure

In this chapter, we will discuss the following topics:

- Implementation of the GPU Based Index GPU IVF Flat
- Implementation of the GPU Based Index GPU_PQ
- Implementation of the GPU Based Index GPU Scalar Quantizer

Implementation of the GPU Based Index GPU IVF Flat

In recent years, the explosion of high-dimensional data in domains like image search, Natural Language Processing, and recommendation systems has driven the need for efficient and scalable nearest neighbor search algorithms. Traditional exact search methods, which scan the entire dataset, become infeasible as data size grows. To address this, Approximate Nearest Neighbor (ANN) search algorithms have gained popularity for their ability to offer a balance between search speed and accuracy.

One particularly effective approach combines **Inverted File (IVF) indexing** with **flat (exact) search** inside clusters, further accelerated by **GPU computing**. This approach is implemented as **GPU Index IVF Flat** in the FAISS library developed by Facebook AI Research. This section expands on the principles, workings, and benefits of this indexing technique, which has become a cornerstone for large-scale similarity search.

Key Concepts

Inverted File (IVF) Indexing

The core idea of IVF indexing is to reduce the search space dramatically by partitioning the dataset into multiple, disjoint subsets, called **clusters** or **cells**. This is commonly done by applying clustering algorithms like **k-means** to the dataset, where each cluster center represents a "cell."

- **Partitioning the data:** The dataset vectors are assigned to their closest cluster centers. This assignment creates an inverted file structure where each cluster points to the vectors it contains.
- **Querying efficiency:** Instead of searching the entire dataset, the ANN algorithm first identifies the cluster(s) closest to the query vector, and then searches **only within these clusters**.
- **Reduction in complexity:** By limiting the search to a few clusters, the computational cost is reduced from **O(N)** (entire dataset) to **O(N / num_clusters)** or less.

Flat Indexing within Clusters

Inside each cluster, the **flat** approach means storing all vectors in their original form without further compression or quantization. When searching, the exact distance between the query and every vector in the cluster is computed. The number of probes provided improves both the quality and granularity of the search.

- **Exact search in clusters:** No approximations are used at this level, ensuring high accuracy.
- **Trade-off:** Flat indexing can be more computationally intensive within large clusters, but because the search is limited to a few clusters, the overall performance remains efficient.

GPU Acceleration

GPUs are highly parallel devices, capable of executing thousands of threads concurrently. This makes them ideal for accelerating ANN searches, especially when:

- Computing distances between query vectors and candidate vectors,
- Performing sorting and selection for top-k nearest neighbors.

In GPU IVF Flat, the workload of searching and distance computations is offloaded to the GPU, resulting in significant speed-ups over CPU-only implementations.

How GPU Index IVF Flat Works

Step 1: Clustering and Building the Inverted Index

Before querying, the dataset is clustered into a predefined number of cells (say, 1024, 4096, or more) using a clustering algorithm such as **k-means**. Each data vector is assigned to the nearest cluster center.

- The inverted file structure is built such that each cluster stores pointers (or indices) to the vectors it contains.
- The cluster centers themselves are stored and used during querying to find the closest clusters to a query vector.

Step 2: Query Processing and Cluster Selection

When a query vector arrives, the system:

- Computes the distance between the query and all cluster centers.
- Selects the top nprobe clusters that are closest to the query (where nprobe is a tunable parameter controlling the trade-off between speed and recall).
- Limits subsequent search to vectors in these selected clusters.

Step 3: Flat Search within Selected Clusters on GPU

For each selected cluster:

- The query vector is compared to every vector in the cluster using an exact distance metric, such as Euclidean (L2) or inner product.
- The distance computations and selection of the top-k nearest neighbors happen **on the GPU** for fast parallel processing.
- The flat nature ensures that the nearest neighbors are exact within those clusters.

Step 4: Results Aggregation and Return

After processing all selected clusters:

- The results from each cluster are merged and the global top-k nearest neighbors are identified.
- These neighbors, along with their distances and indices, are returned to the user.

Benefits of GPU IVF Flat

Scalability

- **Large datasets:** By partitioning the dataset, the search complexity is drastically reduced, allowing handling of datasets with millions or even billions of vectors.
- **Adjustable trade-offs:** The number of clusters and probes can be adjusted for a balance between recall and speed.

Speed

- **GPU acceleration:** Parallel computations of distances on GPUs yield orders of magnitude speed improvements.
- **Parallel cluster search:** Multiple clusters can be searched simultaneously on the GPU, making this approach suitable for real-time applications.

Accuracy

- **Exact search inside clusters:** Unlike other approximate methods that quantize vectors within clusters, the flat approach guarantees exact nearest neighbor search within selected clusters.

This yields better accuracy compared to methods with approximate vector representations.

Limitations and Considerations

- **Memory footprint:** Storing raw vectors in flat form for each cluster consumes more memory compared to compressed or quantized approaches.
- **Search speed depends on parameters:** Increasing nprobe improves recall but also increases search latency.
- **GPU memory limits:** Very large datasets might exceed GPU memory, requiring careful management or multiple GPUs.

Applications

GPU IVF Flat indexing is widely used in domains where fast and accurate similarity search is critical, such as:

- **Image retrieval:** Searching for visually similar images in large databases.
- **Recommendation systems:** Finding users or products with similar features or embeddings.
- **Natural language processing:** Fast semantic search in word or sentence embedding spaces.
- **Biometric identification:** Matching fingerprints, faces, or voice embeddings against large databases.

Summary

GPU-based IVF Flat is a powerful indexing technique combining:

- **Inverted File clustering** to prune search space,
- **Exact flat search within clusters** for accuracy,
- **GPU acceleration** for speed.

This approach balances the need for scalability, speed, and precision in high-dimensional nearest neighbor searches. It is widely adopted in industrial and research settings, particularly when real-time search over large vector datasets is required.

Structure of the GPU Index IVF Flat

The `GpuIndexIVFFlat` in FAISS class is a GPU-accelerated version of the `faiss::IndexIVFFlat`, which is an inverted file index for vector search with flat quantization. This class allows users to perform efficient similarity searches on large datasets by utilizing GPU resources for faster computation.

Here is a breakdown of its key features and functionalities:

- **Constructors:**
    - From an existing `faiss::IndexIVFFlat` instance: Copies the data from a pre-existing index, transferring it to the GPU if the index is trained.
    - With an empty flat quantizer: Initializes a new index, where the user provides the number of inverted file (IVF) lists desired, the dimensionality of the vectors, and the metric to be used (say, L2 distance).
    - With a provided coarse quantizer: Initializes the index with a user-provided coarse quantizer (either CPU or GPU-based) and the necessary IVF lists.
- **Destructor:** It cleans up resources when the index is destroyed.
- **Memory Management:**
    - `reserveMemory(size_tnumVecs)`: It reserves GPU memory for a specified number of vectors.
    - `reclaimMemory()`: It reclaims GPU memory used by the index, returning the space freed in bytes.
    - `copyFrom()`: It copies data from a CPU `faiss::IndexIVFFlat` to the GPU index.
    - `copyTo()`: It copies data from the GPU index to a CPU `faiss::IndexIVFFlat`.
- **Index Management:**
    - `reset()`: It clears out the inverted lists but retains coarse centroid information.
    - `updateQuantizer()`: It updates the coarse quantizer if it has been modified manually.
    - `train()`: It trains the coarse quantizer using vector data.
- **Private Method** (`set_index_`)**:** It initializes the index with various configuration options, such as dimension, number of lists, metric type, and memory space.
- **Configuration Options:** The class has a `GpuIndexIVFFlatConfig` object that holds the configuration settings for the GPU-based IVF flat index.
- **Inverted Lists:** The class uses a shared pointer to an IVFFlat instance, which holds the inverted lists for vector search.

Overall, `GpuIndexIVFFlat` extends the functionality of the original CPU-based `IndexIVFFlat` by enabling GPU-based processing, allowing for faster training, searching, and memory management for large-scale vector data. The method train helps recreate the quantizers on the basis of the presence of GPU.

GPU Based Quantization

The function `trainQuantizer_` in FAISS is responsible for training the quantizer used in the IVF (Inverted File) index for vector search. The quantizer is a key component in grouping vectors into clusters (lists) for efficient retrieval. Here is a summary of the steps and logic of the function:

Function Overview

- **Input:** It takes two parameters:
    - n: The number of vectors to train the quantizer on.
    - x: A pointer to the vector data (of dimension d and count n).
- **Objective:** The function trains the quantizer (coarse quantizer for IVF) using the provided vector data x and updates the quantizer, if necessary.

Steps

1. **Device Scope:** The function starts by setting the device context for the GPU (via DeviceScope scope(config_.device)), ensuring that the operations are executed on the correct device (GPU or CPU).
2. **Check for No Training Needed:**
    - If n (the number of vectors) is zero, the function returns immediately as there is no data to train on.
    - If the quantizer is already trained and the number of total entries in the quantizer (quantizer->ntotal) matches the number of IVF lists (nlist), it prints a message (if verbose) and skips the training process.
3. **Training Message:** If training is needed, it prints a message indicating the number of vectors and their dimensionality (if verbose).
4. **Reset the Quantizer:** The quantizer is reset to prepare for new training.
5. **Use RAFT for Training (GPU):**
    - If RAFT (RAPIDS AI's library) is enabled (config_.use_raft), it uses the efficient implementation of RAFT for training the IVF quantizer on the GPU.
    - The RAFT index parameters are set, including the number of lists, metric type (L2 or Inner Product), and K-means training parameters.
    - RAFT builds an IVF index and retrieves the trained centers (quantizer centroids).
    - The quantizer is trained using the centers computed by RAFT.

6. **Fallback to CPU-side K-means (if RAFT is not available):**
    - If RAFT is not used, the function falls back to using the CPU-side K-means clustering method (via Clustering clus).
    - This method also works for GPU-based indices and trains the quantizer using the provided vector data.
7. **Finalization:**
    - After training, the quantizer is marked as trained (quantizer->is_trained = true).
    - The function asserts that the number of total entries in the quantizer matches the number of IVF lists (nlist).

Key Logic

- The function first checks if training is necessary and skips if it is already trained.
- It uses RAFT for GPU-based training (if available), otherwise falls back to the CPU-side K-means algorithm.
- It updates the quantizer with the centroids from the training process and ensures that the quantizer is properly trained by verifying the number of entries.

This function is crucial for efficiently training the quantizer in the IVF index, which is a foundational part of fast vector search operations in Milvus.

Implementation of the GPU Based Index GPU_IVF_PQ

Product Quantization (PQ) is a compression technique that reduces memory usage and computational overhead by representing high-dimensional vectors as compact codes. When implemented on Graphics Processing Units (GPUs), it exploits massive parallelism to speed up both the training and query processes. As a result, the GPU-based Index GPU_PQ becomes an efficient approach for performing large-scale approximate nearest neighbor (ANN) search.

GPU-Based Index GPU_PQ: An In-depth Overview

With the exponential growth of high-dimensional data in fields such as multimedia retrieval, Natural Language Processing, and recommendation systems, efficiently searching through such data has become a critical challenge. Nearest neighbor search in high-dimensional spaces is computationally expensive, especially when datasets scale to millions or billions of vectors.

Product Quantization (PQ) is a powerful compression-based technique that reduces the memory footprint and computational cost by encoding vectors into compact codes. When this technique is implemented on Graphics Processing Units (GPUs), it leverages the parallel computing power to accelerate both the training and querying phases, making GPU-based Index GPU_PQ an essential tool in large-scale approximate nearest neighbor (ANN) search.

This document elaborates on the principles, implementation details, benefits, and use cases of GPU PQ.

Core Concepts of Product Quantization

Understanding Product Quantization

Product Quantization is a vector compression technique designed to represent high-dimensional vectors by combining quantizations of multiple smaller subvectors. Instead of quantizing the entire vector as a whole, PQ splits each vector into several disjoint subvectors, and then quantizes each subvector independently.

- **Vector splitting:** A vector of dimension D is divided into m smaller subvectors of dimension D/m.
- **Independent quantization:** Each subvector is assigned to the closest centroid from a codebook built for that subvector space.
- **Compact code:** The original vector is then approximated by concatenating the indices of the closest centroids of its subvectors, and accordingly producing a compact code representing the original vector.

Compression and Memory Efficiency

Because each subvector is quantized independently and stored as a small integer index referring to a centroid, the original vector—which might be hundreds or thousands of floating-point numbers—is replaced by a much smaller code, often just a few bytes.

- For example, a 128-dimensional vector split into 8 subvectors (each 16-dimensional) with 256 centroids per subvector can be encoded with just 8 bytes.
- This drastically reduces storage requirements, enabling the handling of massive datasets that otherwise would be impractical to store or process fully.

How GPU Index GPU_IVF_PQ Works

Training Phase on GPU

Training PQ involves learning the codebooks (sets of centroids) for each subvector partition. This typically requires running a clustering algorithm like k-means on each subvector dimension:

1. **Data Preparation:** Input vectors are split into subvectors.
2. **Parallel Clustering:** GPU parallelism enables simultaneous k-means clustering on each subvector space.
3. **Codebook Creation:** For each subvector, a set of centroids (codebook) is created.
4. **Vector Encoding:** Each vector is then quantized by mapping its subvectors to the closest centroid in the corresponding codebook, producing compressed codes.

The ability of the GPU to perform thousands of operations concurrently greatly accelerates this process compared to CPU implementations.

Query and Search Phase

Once the vectors are compressed into PQ codes, the search phase involves finding the nearest neighbors to a query vector efficiently:

- **Asymmetric Distance Computation (ADC):** The query vector remains uncompressed. Its subvectors are compared directly against the centroids in the codebooks to calculate approximate distances to database vectors without decompressing them.
- **Parallel GPU Execution:** Thousands of compressed vectors are processed in parallel to compute approximate distances and retrieve the nearest neighbors.
- **Approximate Nearest Neighbor Search:** Using the ADC method, GPU PQ approximates distances with high accuracy and high throughput.

This process drastically reduces computation since distance calculations involve only lookups in the precomputed distance tables between query subvectors and centroids.

Advantages of GPU IVF PQ

Memory Efficiency and Compression

- The compact codes reduce memory consumption, making it feasible to store extremely large datasets in GPU memory.

- Smaller memory footprint also reduces data transfer overhead between CPU and GPU.

High Speed and Throughput

- GPU acceleration enables the system to handle massive parallelism, performing quantization and distance calculations concurrently.
- This results in significantly lower latency and higher query throughput compared to CPU-based implementations.

Accuracy versus Speed Trade-off

- Product Quantization provides a tunable trade-off, thereby increasing the number of subvectors or codebook size improves accuracy but increases memory and computational load.
- The GPU implementation helps mitigate this trade-off by enabling efficient scaling to higher precision parameters without prohibitive speed loss.

Limitations and Considerations

- **Approximate Results:** PQ is inherently an approximate method and may sometimes miss exact nearest neighbors, especially if the compression is aggressive.
- **Codebook Training Complexity:** Training codebooks efficiently for very large datasets may still require careful engineering.
- **Fixed Quantization:** The subvector partitioning and codebooks are fixed after training; adapting to new data distributions requires retraining.

Use Cases

Large-scale Multimedia Search:

Image and video search engines often embed multimedia content into high-dimensional vectors. GPU PQ enables fast, approximate nearest neighbor search across millions of such embeddings with low latency.

Recommendation Systems:

Matching user profiles or item vectors for personalized recommendations is accelerated by GPU PQ's ability to quickly retrieve closest matches from large databases.

Natural Language Processing:

Semantic search and information retrieval applications use embedding vectors of words, sentences, or documents. GPU PQ enables scalable search in these high-dimensional spaces.

GPU-based Index GPU_IVF_PQ is a powerful technique that combines the compression capabilities of the Product Quantization with the massive parallelism of GPUs. It compresses high-dimensional vectors into compact codes that allow fast, approximate nearest neighbor search while drastically reducing memory usage.

The GPU implementation accelerates both training and querying, enabling practical, large-scale applications such as image retrieval, recommendation systems, and semantic search. Although approximate, GPU PQ balances efficiency and accuracy, making it a preferred choice for real-world large dataset vector searches.

Structure of the Index GPU_IVF_PQ

The `GpuIndexIVFPQ` class is a GPU-accelerated version of the `faiss::IndexIVFPQ` that combines Inverted File (IVF) indexing with Product Quantization (PQ) for efficient similarity search on large-scale, high-dimensional datasets. It uses the GPU to accelerate both the training and search phases, making it highly suitable for large-scale vector search applications.

The key features are:

- **Constructors**:
  - **From a pre-existing `faiss::IndexIVFPQ` instance**: It copies data from an existing index (CPU or GPU) to the GPU, if the index is already trained.
  - **With a new empty flat quantizer**: It initializes a new instance with user-defined settings such as dimensions, number of lists, sub-quantizers, and bits per code.
  - **With a provided coarse quantizer**: It allows the use of a user-defined coarse quantizer (either CPU or GPU) and initializes the index with the necessary IVF lists.
- **Destructor**: It cleans up resources when the object is destroyed.
- **Memory Management**:
  - **`reserveMemory(size_tnumVecs)`**: It reserves GPU memory for storing inverted lists.
  - **`reclaimMemory()`**: It reclaims GPU memory used by the index, returning the freed space in bytes.

- **Pre-computed Codes**:
    - `setPrecomputedCodes(bool enable)`: It enables or disables the use of pre-computed codes for faster search.
    - `getPrecomputedCodes()`: It returns whether pre-computed codes are enabled.
- **Quantization Parameters**:
    - `getNumSubQuantizers()`: It returns the number of sub-quantizers used.
    - `getBitsPerCode()`: It returns the number of bits per product quantization code.
    - `getCentroidsPerSubQuantizer()`: It returns the number of centroids per PQ code (2^bits per code).
- **Training**:
    - `train(idx_t n, const float* x)`: It trains both the coarse quantizer and the product quantizer based on the input vectors.
    - `trainResidualQuantizer_(idx_t n, const float* x)`: It specifically trains the product quantizer using the residuals from the coarse quantizer.
- **Quantizer Access**:
    - The class exposes a public `ProductQuantizerpq`, which can be manipulated for fine-tuning the quantization process.
- **Reset and Update**:
    - `reset()`: It clears the inverted lists but retains coarse and product centroid information.
    - `updateQuantizer()`: It updates the coarse quantizer if its state changes outside of the training scope.
- **Verification**:
    - `verifyPQSettings_()`: It checks if the configuration settings for product quantization are valid.

Internal Data:

- `ivfpqConfig_`: It stores the configuration settings for the GPU-based IVF-PQ index.
- `usePrecomputedTables_`: It determines whether pre-computed tables are used for acceleration.
- `subQuantizers_ and bitsPerCode_`: It defines the number of sub-quantizers and the bits per sub-quantizer code for the PQ.

- **`index_`**: It is a shared pointer to the underlying IVFPQ instance, which contains the inverted lists and handles the indexing.

The `GpuIndexIVFPQ` class provides an efficient, GPU-accelerated implementation of the IVF-PQ index, combining both coarse quantization (IVF) and product quantization (PQ) for high-performance, large-scale similarity search. It offers powerful features for memory management, quantizer training, and search acceleration, making it ideal for vector search applications dealing with high-dimensional data.

Implementation of the GPU Based Index GPU Scalar Quantization

The `GpuIndexIVFScalarQuantizer` class is a GPU-accelerated version of the `faiss::IndexIVFScalarQuantizer` index, which combines **Inverted File (IVF)** indexing with **Scalar Quantization (SQ)**. This class is designed to enable fast, efficient similarity searches on high-dimensional datasets by leveraging GPU hardware for both training and querying phases.

The key features are:

- **Constructors**:
  - **From an existing `faiss::IndexIVFScalarQuantizer` instance**: It copies data from a pre-trained index (either on the CPU or GPU) to the GPU.
  - **With an empty flat quantizer**: It initializes a new instance with user-defined parameters such as dimensions, the number of IVF lists, and the quantizer type.
  - **With a provided coarse quantizer**: It allows the use of a user-defined coarse quantizer (either CPU or GPU) and initializes the index with the necessary IVF lists.
- **Destructor**: It cleans up GPU resources when the object is destroyed.
- **Memory Management**:
  - **`reserveMemory(size_tnumVecs)`**: It reserves GPU memory for storing inverted lists for a specified number of vectors.
  - **`reclaimMemory()`**: It frees up GPU memory used by the index, returning the reclaimed memory in bytes.
- **Copying**:
  - **`copyFrom()`**: It copies data from a given CPU IndexIVFScalarQuantizer instance to the GPU.
  - **`copyTo()`**: It copies data from the GPU back to a given CPU IndexIVFScalarQuantizer instance.

- **Training**:
  - `train(idx_t n, const float* x)`: It trains both the coarse quantizer and the scalar quantizer based on the provided vectors.
  - `trainResiduals_()`: A helper function which is called from train() to handle training of the residuals after coarse quantization.
- **Scalar Quantizer**:
  - `sq`: It exposes the ScalarQuantizer instance, which contains the logic for scalar quantization.
  - `by_residual`: A flag indicating whether the quantization should be done by residuals (that is, using the residuals from the coarse quantizer for further refinement).
- **Quantization Configuration**:
  - `verifySQSettings_()`: It validates the Scalar Quantizer parameters to ensure they are correct and usable.
- **Reset and Update**:
  - `reset()`: It clears the inverted lists while retaining the coarse quantizer and scalar quantizer information.
  - `updateQuantizer()`: It updates the coarse quantizer if its state has changed outside the scope of the training process.
- **Configuration**:
  - `ivfSQConfig_`: It stores the configuration options for the `GpuIndexIVFScalarQuantizer`.
  - `reserveMemoryVecs_`: It defines the number of vectors to reserve memory for in the inverted lists.

Internal Data:

- `sq`: The **Scalar Quantizer** used for the quantization of residuals, which helps reduce memory usage while maintaining high retrieval accuracy.
- `by_residual`: Indicates if the scalar quantization is performed by first calculating residuals after coarse quantization.
- `index_`: A shared pointer to the underlying IVFFlat instance that contains the inverted lists and manages the index.

The `GpuIndexIVFScalarQuantizer` class is designed to accelerate vector search on the GPU using both **Inverted File (IVF)** indexing and **Scalar Quantization (SQ)**. It provides efficient memory management, training, and querying capabilities for high-dimensional vector data. The class supports copying data from CPU to GPU, training the coarse and scalar quantizers, and managing memory resources effectively for large-scale search applications. By utilizing GPU resources, it significantly speeds up both the indexing and querying processes.

Implementation of Scalar Quantization

The train() function handles the complete training process of the **GPU-based IVF-Scalar Quantizer index**. It first ensures the necessary configurations are correct, trains the coarse quantizer (IVF), trains the scalar quantizer (SQ) using either the raw vectors or their residuals, and finally constructs the IVF index. This process allows for efficient nearest-neighbor search and vector quantization on high-dimensional data using GPU acceleration.

- `trainResiduals_()`:

  This function is responsible for training the **scalar quantizer (SQ)** using the residuals after coarse quantization. The function checks whether **residual encoding** is enabled (`by_residual flag`).

  - If residuals are not enabled, the scalar quantizer (sq) is trained directly using the input vectors x.
  - If residuals are enabled, the function performs the following steps:
    - **Assigns vectors to IVF lists**: Using the coarse quantizer, each vector in x is assigned to its nearest centroid.
    - **Computes residuals**: The residual vectors (the difference between the input vectors and their assigned centroids) are computed.
    - **Trains the scalar quantizer**: The scalar quantizer (sq) is then trained using the residuals.

- `train()`:

  This function is responsible for the **overall training** of the IVF-Scalar Quantizer (IVF-SQ) index.

  - **Verification**: The function begins by verifying the configuration settings for both the IVF index and the scalar quantizer.
  - **Training Conditions**: If the index is already trained (`is_trained`), it skips the training process.
  - **Data Preparation**: The input data x is moved to the **CPU** (if not already resident there), since parts of the training process rely on CPU-based operations.

- **Training Steps**:
  - **Train the Coarse Quantizer**: The `trainQuantizer_()` function is called to train the coarse quantizer on the input data.
  - **Train the Residual Quantizer**: The `trainResiduals_()` function is called to train the scalar quantizer, either directly on the data or on the residuals (depending on `by_residual`).
- **Index Construction**: After training the quantizers, the IVF index is constructed (IVFFlat), incorporating the trained quantizers and other configuration parameters.
- **Memory Reservation**: If a specific memory reservation is set (`reserveMemoryVecs_`), the index reserves memory for storing vectors.
- **Mark as Trained**: The index is marked as trained (`is_trained = true`), signaling that the training process is complete.

Detailed Explanation

- **Training the Quantizer**:
  - **Coarse Quantizer**: The IVF (Inverted File) index is trained on the vectors, and coarse quantization is performed. This quantization groups vectors into lists (clusters).
  - **Residual Quantizer**: The residuals (differences between the vectors and the assigned centroids) are computed and used to train the scalar quantizer. The residuals help further compress the vector data for efficient storage and retrieval.
- **Data Movement**:
  - The data is moved from the GPU to the CPU for certain operations (e.g., assigning vectors to centroids and computing residuals). This may be a limitation due to reliance on CPU-based algorithms.
- **IVF Index Construction**:
  - Once the quantizers are trained, an IVF index (IVFFlat) is constructed on the GPU, which incorporates the trained coarse and scalar quantizers.
- **Memory Management**:
  - The function ensures that enough memory is reserved for the inverted lists, allowing efficient search during the querying phase.

Key Functions

- **`trainQuantizer_()`**: It is responsible for training the coarse quantizer (IVF) part of the index.
- **`trainResiduals_()`**: It handles the training of the scalar quantizer (SQ), with or without residuals.
- **`verifySQSettings_()`** and **`verifyIVFSettings_()`**: It ensures that the configuration settings are valid.
- **`updateQuantizer()`**: It ensures that the quantizer state is up-to-date.

Conclusion

In this chapter, we have explored the powerful integration of GPU-based indexes in **Milvus**, a vector database designed for efficient similarity search in high-dimensional spaces. Milvus leverages GPU acceleration to significantly speed up both the training and querying of vector indices, providing a substantial performance improvement over CPU-based solutions. The integration of GPU-based indexes in Milvus significantly boosts the performance and scalability of vector search operations. By leveraging the computational power of GPUs, Milvus provides a fast, efficient, and scalable solution for handling large-scale, high-dimensional data. This chapter illustrated how different GPU-based indexing methods, such as IVF, IVF-PQ, and IVF-Scalar Quantizer, are optimized for real-time, low-latency applications across various industries, from AI to recommendation systems. The combination of these optimizations makes Milvus a powerful tool for managing complex vector search tasks.

CHAPTER 11
Auxiliary Components

Introduction

As the demand for real-time, high-performance vector search and AI-driven data analytics grows, distributed systems have become the backbone of modern data infrastructure. Milvus, a leading open-source vector database, is designed to handle the massive scale and complexity of vector-based similarity search. In order to deliver high availability, consistency, scalability, and fault tolerance across its distributed architecture, Milvus relies on several critical technologies that provide the necessary coordination, messaging, and data storage capabilities.

In this chapter, we will explore the crucial roles of Etcd, Kafka, and Pulsar in enabling Milvus to scale, ensure consistency, and efficiently manage metadata, configuration, and inter-node communication. These technologies work in concert to support the distributed operations of Milvus; simultaneously ensuring that it can handle large-scale data ingestion, search, and real-time analytics while maintaining high performance and reliability.

Etcd, a distributed key-value store, plays a central role in configuration management, service discovery, and coordination within Milvus. By ensuring the consistency of metadata and system state across the entire cluster, Etcd helps Milvus achieve synchronization and fault tolerance in a distributed environment.

Kafka and Pulsar, both distributed messaging systems, enable Milvus to handle the large volumes of data generated during vector indexing, querying, and updating operations. These message queues ensure that data is ingested and processed efficiently across different Milvus nodes while enabling asynchronous communication and event-driven architecture.

This chapter will dive deep into each of these technologies and examine how they contribute to Milvus' architecture, ensuring that it is scalable, resilient, and able to deliver real-time performance for demanding vector search workloads. By the end of this chapter, you will have a solid understanding of how these critical components integrate within Milvus and the roles they play in ensuring its robust operation in large-scale environments.

Structure

In this chapter, we will discuss the following topics:

- Role of Etcd in Milvus
- Role of Pulsar
- Role of Kafka

The Role of Etcd in Milvus

Etcd is a distributed key-value store that provides reliable, consistent, and fault-tolerant storage for configuration and metadata in a distributed system. It is designed to be simple, highly available, and used as the central source of truth for configuration management, service discovery, and coordination tasks. Etcd is often utilized in cloud-native architectures, container orchestration platforms like Kubernetes, and large-scale distributed systems to ensure that different components can operate in a consistent and synchronized manner.

In the case of Milvus, which is a high-performance vector database designed for large-scale similarity search, Etcd plays a crucial role in managing the state and coordination of the distributed system. Milvus, by nature, involves multiple nodes working together to process and query vector data. Managing these nodes efficiently requires a reliable mechanism for state management, coordination, and consistency—exactly what Etcd provides. The key roles of Etcd are as follows.

Cluster Coordination and Node Discovery

Milvus typically operates as a distributed system with different types of nodes, such as query nodes, storage nodes, and index nodes, each of which plays a different role in the overall system. These nodes need to discover each other and maintain consistent communication. This is where Etcd plays a vital role.

- **Service Discovery:** As new nodes join or leave the Milvus cluster, Etcd acts as the central registry for all the active nodes in the system. When a new node starts up, it can register itself with Etcd, allowing other nodes to discover it. This allows the system to adapt to dynamic changes, such as scaling the cluster or adding new resources, without manual intervention.
- **Leader Election:** In a distributed system, there are often tasks that require a single authoritative leader, such as managing the global state of indexing,

handling critical metadata, or overseeing the health of the system. Etcd facilitates leader election by using its built-in consensus mechanism (Raft algorithm). Only one node is elected as the leader at any given time, ensuring that there are no conflicting operations.

- **Health Checks and Failover:** With Milvus running across multiple nodes, it is critical to monitor the health and availability of the nodes in the cluster. Etcd provides mechanisms to check the health of nodes and ensures that if any node becomes unavailable, the system can gracefully handle failover and elect a new leader.

Configuration Management

One of the most significant challenges in managing a distributed system like Milvus is ensuring that all the nodes share a consistent configuration. Configuration data might include settings such as the number of partitions, indexing parameters, memory limits, and other system-wide options. If each node in a distributed system has its own configuration, inconsistencies may lead to unexpected behaviors or errors in operation.

- **Centralized Configuration Store:** Etcd stores the configuration data centrally, allowing all nodes in the Milvus cluster to retrieve the same set of configuration values. This ensures that all components of the system are using the same configuration, reducing the risk of discrepancies between nodes.
- **Dynamic Configuration Updates:** Since distributed systems are often subject to change, Milvus can dynamically update configurations without needing to restart or re-deploy all nodes. By storing configuration settings in Etcd, Milvus nodes can poll Etcd for updates and apply configuration changes in real-time.
- **Consistency:** Etcd uses a strong consistency model backed by the Raft consensus algorithm. This guarantees that the configuration data stored in Etcd is consistent across all nodes, even in the event of failures or network partitions.

Metadata Storage and Synchronization

Milvus often requires managing large amounts of metadata, such as the state of indexed data, segment information, or partition information. This metadata is essential for ensuring the correct execution of search queries and indexing operations.

- **Persistent Metadata:** Etcd is used to store critical metadata such as the state of indexing processes, vector metadata, partition details, and more. The metadata stored in Etcd is critical for the functioning of Milvus. If the metadata were lost or inconsistent, it could lead to data corruption or failure of search queries.

- **Synchronization Across Nodes:** In a distributed environment, each Milvus node might have its local memory to store temporary metadata or indexing information. However, for operations to be consistent and synchronized across the cluster, all nodes need to access the same up-to-date metadata. Etcd ensures this by maintaining a consistent view of the metadata across all Milvus nodes. When a node performs any operation (such as adding vectors or creating partitions), the metadata in etcd is updated and can be propagated across the entire cluster.

Fault Tolerance and Recovery

Distributed systems are susceptible to node failures, network partitions, and other faults. Ensuring fault tolerance and recovery is critical to maintaining the availability and consistency of Milvus. Etcd is designed to handle failures in a distributed environment.

- **Data Integrity and Consistency:** With the use of the Raft consensus protocol of Etcd, Milvus can ensure that critical configuration and metadata are durable and consistent even in the face of node failures. If a node fails or becomes unreachable, the replication mechanism of Etcd ensures that another replica of the data is available, and the system can continue to operate normally.
- **Failure Detection and Recovery:** In the event of a failure, Milvus relies on Etcd to detect the failure and trigger failover mechanisms, such as electing a new leader or reassigning tasks to healthy nodes. This ensures that the system can recover quickly and resume normal operation without significant disruption.
- **Data Replication:** Etcd provides replication of the stored data across multiple nodes, ensuring high availability. If one Etcd instance becomes unavailable, other replicas can continue to serve the data, preventing service interruptions.

Global State Management

Maintaining a global view of the state of the system is essential for distributed systems like Milvus, which may span multiple regions, data centers, or availability zones.

- **Distributed Global State:** Milvus uses Etcd to store and manage the global state of the system, such as the number of partitions, the availability of indexing nodes, and the progress of indexing operations. This allows Milvus to coordinate tasks like query routing, indexing updates, and data replication efficiently.
- **Cross-Node Synchronization:** Etcd ensures that all nodes in the system can synchronize their state by accessing the global state data. This is essential for large-scale distributed operations, where changes to the global state must be immediately reflected across all Milvus nodes to ensure consistency.

How Etcd Integrates with Other Components in Milvus

Milvus is built using multiple components, and Etcd interacts with these components to ensure that they function as a cohesive whole:

- **Indexing and Query Nodes:** The indexing nodes rely on Etcd for configuration and metadata storage. When new data is ingested, or indexes are created, these nodes need to synchronize with the global system state stored in Etcd. Similarly, query nodes can use Etcd to locate the most up-to-date index and routing information for search queries.
- **Load Balancing and Task Distribution:** Etcd helps with load balancing by tracking the state of each node and ensuring that tasks are evenly distributed across available resources. For instance, when performing indexing tasks, Milvus can assign portions of the data to different nodes by querying the configuration and task assignment details stored in Etcd.

In summary, Etcd plays a pivotal role in Milvus by providing:

- **Cluster Coordination:** Ensures nodes can discover each other, synchronize, and elect a leader.
- **Configuration Management:** Manages configuration data consistently across all nodes.
- **Metadata Storage and Synchronization:** Stores critical indexing and partition metadata.
- **Fault Tolerance:** Ensures system availability and consistency, even in the event of node failures.
- **Global State Management:** Maintains a consistent global view of the distributed system state of Milvus.

By leveraging Etcd, Milvus ensures that its distributed components are consistent, coordinated, and resilient, enabling high performance, reliability, and scalability for vector-based similarity search across large datasets.

The Role of Kafka in Milvus

Apache Kafka is a distributed event streaming platform capable of handling large-scale, real-time data streams. It is widely used for building data pipelines and streaming applications, offering high throughput, low latency, and fault tolerance. In the context of Milvus, Kafka plays an essential role in ensuring efficient data ingestion, event-driven communication, and fault-tolerant stream processing across distributed nodes.

Milvus, as a high-performance vector database, handles vast amounts of data, often in real time, making it crucial to have a messaging system that can support efficient data flow while maintaining high availability. Kafka integrates seamlessly into the architecture of Milvus, providing the necessary tools for coordinating indexing and query operations across multiple nodes in a scalable and fault-tolerant manner.

Here is a deeper dive into the role of Kafka in Milvus:

Efficient Data Ingestion and Asynchronous Processing

Milvus relies on Kafka to handle the ingestion of large volumes of vector data into the system. As new vectors or data points arrive, Kafka streams these messages (or events) to various processing components in the system. This allows Milvus to process data asynchronously, preventing blocking or delays in operations. Here is how Kafka fits into the data flow of Milvus:

- **Data Streaming:** When new data, such as vector embeddings or metadata, is generated by the user or external systems, it is immediately sent to Kafka topics. These topics act as message channels that enable different components of Milvus to subscribe and process data in parallel, facilitating real-time data ingestion and indexing.
- **Asynchronous Indexing:** Once the data is ingested, Milvus can asynchronously process the data in multiple stages, such as indexing or searching. Kafka ensures that the system can handle high throughput by decoupling the data ingestion layer from the data processing layer. This reduces system bottlenecks and improves overall performance by allowing different services to operate independently.
- **Decoupled Services:** Kafka enables Milvus to decouple data ingestion, indexing, and querying services. For example, the ingestion service can feed data into Kafka topics, while the indexing and query services can process that data independently without being tightly coupled. This decoupling allows each service to scale independently, contributing to the high scalability of Milvus.

Event-Driven Architecture

Milvus uses Kafka to build an event-driven architecture, allowing different components of the system to respond to events or changes in real time. For example, when a new batch of vectors is indexed, an event can be triggered, notifying other components to update their state, perform searches, or update the data. Kafka acts as the intermediary that ensures events are communicated reliably and in real time across different Milvus components.

Some examples of event-driven tasks include:

- **Metadata Updates:** When a new batch of vectors is added to the database, Kafka can trigger updates to metadata stores or query components that rely on this data for their operations.
- **Replication and Synchronization:** Kafka enables data replication across multiple Milvus nodes. If one node updates the index or processes data, Kafka can broadcast this change across the cluster, ensuring that all nodes are synchronized and up-to-date.
- **Fault Tolerance:** Kafka maintains a log of all messages sent through its system, allowing Milvus to replay events and restore the system state in case of failure. If a component fails or crashes, it can recover its state by replaying messages from the Kafka logs, ensuring minimal data loss.

Real-Time Query Processing and Parallelization

Kafka also plays an important role in the real-time query processing of Milvus. As users send queries to Milvus, Kafka helps handle these queries efficiently by distributing them across multiple worker nodes for parallel processing. This allows Milvus to scale to handle high query throughput, ensuring low latency for vector searches.

Here is how Kafka supports query processing:

- **Load Balancing:** Kafka can act as a load balancer for incoming queries by distributing them across different worker nodes. Each node consumes messages from Kafka topics, processes the queries, and sends back the results to the user. This distribution mechanism ensures that the workload is evenly spread across available resources, preventing any one node from becoming a bottleneck.
- **Scalable Query Execution:** Since Kafka decouples the producer (client) from the consumer (worker nodes), queries can be handled concurrently by multiple nodes. As the data size and query traffic increase, Kafka facilitates scaling the number of worker nodes to handle the growing demand.

Ensuring Consistency and Reliability

Kafka plays a key role in maintaining consistency and reliability within the distributed architecture of Milvus. By acting as a message broker, it ensures that all operations are completed reliably and in the correct sequence, even in the event of system failures.

Key features of Kafka that Milvus leverages for consistency include:

- **Message Durability:** Kafka stores messages in a durable log that is replicated across different brokers. This ensures that messages are not lost, and they can be replayed in case of system failure, ensuring data integrity.
- **Message Acknowledgment:** Kafka provides the ability to acknowledge the receipt of messages, allowing Milvus to track the progress of data processing. This helps in confirming that operations (such as data ingestion and indexing) are completed successfully.
- **Consistency across Nodes:** The partitioning and replication model of Kafka helps ensure that even if one node or broker fails, the data is still available, and the system can recover with minimal downtime. This guarantees that Milvus remains consistent and resilient, even in large-scale deployments.

Handling Large-Scale Indexing and Distributed Computation

Milvus often deals with very large datasets and performs intensive computational tasks like indexing vectors and executing similarity searches. Kafka helps Milvus handle these tasks efficiently by:

- **Enabling Distributed Computation:** Kafka allows Milvus to distribute tasks like indexing or clustering across multiple nodes, each consuming different parts of the data. This allows parallel processing, improving indexing performance, especially when dealing with large-scale vector data.
- **Flow Control:** Kafka can manage the flow of data between different components, ensuring that the system does not become overwhelmed by excessive data or requests. It acts as a buffer, ensuring that data is processed at the appropriate rate and that no node gets overloaded.

In summary, Kafka is a powerful tool in the distributed architecture of Milvus, enabling efficient data ingestion, event-driven communication, real-time query processing, and high scalability. By decoupling various components of the system, Kafka provides the flexibility and reliability necessary for Milvus to handle massive volumes of vector data in real time. Through its robust message processing and event handling capabilities, Kafka ensures that Milvus remains highly available, fault-tolerant, and able to scale with growing data demands, making it an indispensable part of the system.

In the next section, we will explore how Pulsar complements the functionality of Kafka within Milvus, further enhancing its messaging and event-driven capabilities.

The Role of Pulsar in Milvus

Apache Pulsar is a highly scalable, distributed messaging and event streaming platform designed for real-time processing of high-throughput data streams. Unlike traditional message brokers, Pulsar supports multi-tenancy, seamless scalability, and low-latency message delivery, making it well-suited for complex data processing tasks. In the context of **Milvus**, Pulsar plays a crucial role in enabling real-time streaming, event-driven communication, and message queuing across the distributed architecture.

Milvus, as a high-performance vector database, relies heavily on efficient and scalable messaging systems to ensure smooth data ingestion, indexing, and querying. Pulsar complements **Apache Kafka** by providing a more flexible, real-time data processing pipeline that enhances the ability of the system to handle large-scale, distributed, and real-time operations. While Kafka is used for general-purpose messaging, Pulsar brings additional capabilities for scalability, persistence, and messaging in large-scale distributed systems.

An in-depth look at how **Pulsar** contributes to **Milvus** is taken into consideration in the following sub-section.

Real-Time Stream Processing and Data Ingestion

Pulsar is primarily used in Milvus for its ability to handle high-throughput data ingestion. Milvus needs to process vast amounts of vector data in real time, which is typically generated from applications like machine learning, search engines, and recommendation systems. The low-latency streaming capabilities of Pulsar allow Milvus to efficiently handle the flow of real-time data from multiple sources, ensuring that incoming data is quickly ingested and made available for further processing.

Key functions Pulsar performs in the data ingestion pipeline of Milvus include:

- **Stream-based Data Ingestion**: Pulsar streams incoming vector data in real time. When vectors are generated or uploaded by users, they are ingested into Pulsar topics, allowing the data to be immediately available for processing by Milvus services. This ensures that data is not held up and can be processed asynchronously.
- **Event-Driven Communication**: Pulsar is used to trigger events in the Milvus pipeline. For example, when new vectors are ingested, Pulsar can notify other services to begin indexing or performing similarity searches. This event-driven architecture is crucial for maintaining real-time updates in Milvus.
- **High Throughput**: Milvus often deals with large-scale vector data that needs to be ingested and processed continuously. The high throughput capabilities

of Pulsar ensure that Milvus can handle massive volumes of data without bottlenecks, making it ideal for data-heavy applications.

Distributed Messaging and Scalability

Milvus is a distributed system, which means it must be able to coordinate and synchronize operations across multiple nodes. Pulsar facilitates this by acting as a message broker between different Milvus components. This distributed messaging ensures that data flows smoothly across the system without overwhelming any single node or component.

The scalability of Pulsar benefits Milvus in several ways, such as:

- **Horizontal Scalability**: Pulsar can easily scale horizontally by adding more brokers or nodes to the cluster. Milvus can take advantage of this scalability to handle increasing workloads, especially when managing large datasets or handling high-frequency query and ingestion requests.
- **Multi-Tenant Architecture**: The multi-tenant capabilities of Pulsar allow Milvus to serve multiple clients or applications simultaneously, without the need for separate messaging systems. This is important in environments where Milvus needs to serve multiple applications or services that require independent streams of data.
- **Decoupling of Services**: Pulsar helps decouple the ingestion, indexing, and querying layers of Milvus. These components can operate independently, allowing for asynchronous communication. For instance, the ingestion service can continuously feed data to Pulsar, while the query service can independently consume data from Pulsar topics to perform similarity searches.

Data Persistence and Durability

One of the critical aspects of the distributed architecture of Milvus is to ensure that data is persistent and resilient to failures. Pulsar provides strong durability guarantees that ensure data is not lost, even in the event of node failures or network issues.

Key persistence features in Pulsar that Milvus leverages include:

- **Message Durability**: Pulsar stores messages in persistent storage across multiple nodes. This ensures that data remains available even if the system undergoes failures or restarts. For Milvus, this is crucial for ensuring that vectors and index data are safely stored and retrievable.
- **Message Acknowledgment**: Pulsar allows Milvus to track message acknowledgments to confirm that data has been successfully processed. This ensures that data is not lost and that the system remains in a consistent state, even in case of errors or retries.

- **At-least-once Delivery**: Pulsar guarantees at-least-once delivery of messages, ensuring that messages are delivered to consumers even if a message broker fails. This reliability is vital for Milvus to maintain data integrity and consistency across distributed nodes.

Fault Tolerance and Recovery

The distributed architecture of Milvus requires fault tolerance to maintain uptime and ensure uninterrupted services. Pulsar enhances the fault tolerance of Milvus by providing several mechanisms for data recovery and failover:

- **Replication**: Pulsar replicates messages across multiple brokers in the cluster, ensuring that if a broker fails, the messages can be retrieved from other brokers. This ensures that Milvus can continue processing data without loss.
- **Automatic Failover**: In the event of a broker failure, Pulsar automatically redirects traffic to healthy brokers. This ensures that Milvus does not experience downtime, even if a part of the system goes down.
- **Message Retention**: The message retention policies of Pulsar allow Milvus to retain messages for a configured period, ensuring that data is not lost due to temporary network failures or crashes.

Event-Driven Architecture and Task Management

Milvus relies heavily on **event-driven processing**, where different tasks or services are triggered based on incoming events. Pulsar enables this architecture by providing an efficient, real-time messaging system for event propagation. This is especially important in a distributed system like Milvus, where different nodes or components need to react to specific events in real time.

Examples of event-driven tasks facilitated by Pulsar include:

- **Indexing and Updates**: When new vector data arrives in Milvus, Pulsar can trigger indexing processes to update the index. Additionally, when vectors are updated or removed, Pulsar helps propagate these changes throughout the system in real time.
- **Query Handling**: When a user query is made, Pulsar can help distribute the query processing tasks across multiple worker nodes. This enables parallel query execution, reducing latency and improving throughput.
- **Real-Time Notifications**: Pulsar can be used to notify external systems or services when certain operations in Milvus are completed. For example, once

an indexing process is complete, Pulsar can send a notification to the user or trigger further actions in downstream systems.

Seamless Integration with Other Components

Milvus uses Pulsar alongside other technologies such as Kafka and **Etcd**. Pulsar complements Kafka in scenarios where message durability and real-time stream processing are essential. Kafka might handle high-throughput, stream-based data pipelines, while Pulsar is used for fine-grained, event-driven communication and coordination across services.

Pulsar also integrates well with the distributed query and indexing services of Milvus. By acting as a reliable, low-latency communication layer between Milvus components, Pulsar ensures that data flows smoothly, even when operations scale across large distributed systems.

Apache Pulsar is an integral part of the architecture of Milvus, that enables high-performance, real-time data streaming and fault-tolerant messaging between the various components of the system. By leveraging the features of Pulsar such as high throughput, message durability, and event-driven communication, Milvus can efficiently handle large-scale vector data operations, ensure data consistency, and scale seamlessly in real-time environments.

Pulsar complements Kafka by offering additional capabilities for message persistence, fault tolerance, and distributed task management, which are critical in a large-scale distributed vector database like Milvus. Together with **Kafka** and **Etcd**, Pulsar forms a robust messaging ecosystem that supports the ability of Milvus to process vast amounts of vector data in real time, making it an essential technology for building scalable, event-driven applications.

Conclusion

In this chapter, we explored the vital roles of **Etcd**, **Kafka**, and **Pulsar** in the Milvus ecosystem, each contributing uniquely to the overall functionality, scalability, and performance of the vector database. These tools work in tandem to ensure that Milvus can efficiently manage high-throughput data, maintain consistency across distributed nodes, and provide real-time, fault-tolerant data processing capabilities.

Etcd plays a foundational role in maintaining consistency and coordination across the distributed components of Milvus. By providing a reliable, distributed key-value store, Etcd ensures that Milvus can manage configuration settings, store metadata, and synchronize system states effectively across the entire cluster. It helps Milvus maintain high availability and fault tolerance, ensuring that the system can recover gracefully from failures while preserving critical metadata.

Kafka is leveraged by Milvus primarily for stream-based data ingestion, message brokering, and real-time communication between services. Its ability to handle high-throughput data streams makes it an ideal choice for Milvus, where vast amounts of vector data need to be ingested, indexed, and queried in real time. The durability and fault tolerance of Milvus ensure that messages are safely transmitted and processed, supporting Milvus' real-time vector processing and query execution workflows.

Pulsar, on the other hand, excels in handling event-driven communication and stream processing in Milvus. It provides low-latency messaging and real-time task management, facilitating the ingestion of new data, triggering indexing operations, and handling queries in a distributed and scalable manner. The ability of Pulsar to handle large-scale data streams, its message durability, and its multi-tenancy features make it an essential tool for Milvus in supporting large-scale, real-time data processing pipelines.

Together, these tools form a powerful infrastructure for managing the complexity of distributed vector databases like Milvus. **Etcd** ensures coordination and consistency, **Kafka** drives high-throughput data ingestion and message queuing, and **Pulsar** enables real-time processing, event-driven tasks, and scalability. Their integration within Milvus enables efficient management of massive amounts of vector data while ensuring system reliability, scalability, and performance.

In conclusion, the roles of **Etcd**, **Kafka**, and **Pulsar** within Milvus are indispensable for building a robust, high-performance, and scalable vector database. These tools work together to handle the challenges posed by large-scale, distributed environments, ensuring that Milvus can meet the demands of modern data-driven applications requiring real-time analytics, seamless scaling, and fault-tolerant operations.

CHAPTER 12
Network Management

Introduction

In a world where large-scale data retrieval and machine learning are paramount, Milvus has emerged as a leading vector database designed to store, manage, and perform similarity searches on massive volumes of vector data. As an open-source, high-performance system, Milvus is built for low-latency, high-throughput operations, making it essential for applications that require real-time search capabilities across billions of data points. However, the success of any such system depends not just on its internal structure but also on how clients interact with it.

Connecting to Milvus efficiently and reliably is crucial to ensuring optimal performance, particularly in high-demand environments. Milvus supports a wide variety of client connections, providing developers with different methods to interact with the system, ranging from SDKs in multiple programming languages to communication protocols like gRPC and RESTful APIs. These connections enable users to perform essential operations such as data insertion, vector searches, and real-time updates.

In this chapter, we will explore the mechanisms through which clients connect to Milvus. We will discuss how these connections are established, what protocols are involved, and how different client SDKs and tools integrate with the Milvus platform. Furthermore, we will explore the best practices for managing client connections, ensuring both performance and reliability for your vector-based search applications.

Whether you arebuilding machine learning models, recommendation systems, or search engines, understanding client connections to Milvus is fundamental to unlocking its full potential in your applications. This chapter will serve as a guide to help you navigate these client interaction strategies, from initial connection setup to efficient query processing and system maintenance.

Structure

In this chapter, we will discuss the following topics:

- Client Management
- gRPC in Milvus: A Comprehensive Overview

Client Management

In a distributed system like Milvus, which is designed to handle large-scale vector data and perform real-time similarity searches, the way clients connect and interact with the system is crucial for performance, reliability, and scalability. Whether it is integrating Milvus into an existing application, accessing the vector database via a user interface, or processing machine learning models, understanding the mechanisms of client connections is the key to efficiently leverage Milvus.

In this section, we will explore the different methods and protocols through which clients connect to Milvus, including the Milvus client SDK, communication protocols, and connection strategies. We will discuss how client connections are established, how communication occurs, the types of clients supported by Milvus, and best practices for optimal performance when interacting with Milvus in a production environment.

Milvus Client SDK Overview

Milvus offers client SDKs in several programming languages, including Python, Go, Java, and others. These SDKs serve as the primary interface for developers to interact with Milvus, allowing them to issue vector search queries, insert data, perform updates, and manage the system. Through these SDKs, clients can easily connect to Milvus, send requests, and receive responses. We will examine the primary components of the Milvus client SDK, which are as follows:

- **Python SDK:**

  The **Milvus Python SDK** is one of the most widely used and well-documented SDKs. It allows users to perform a range of operations including creating, managing, and querying collections of vector data. The Python SDK provides a simple interface to interact with Milvus through its Python API, making it a popular choice for data scientists and machine learning engineers.

- **Java SDK:**

  The **Milvus Java SDK** provides the Java community with the necessary tools to interface with Milvus. Similar to the Python SDK, it provides support for creating collections, inserting vectors, and querying data. The Java SDK is often used in large-scale enterprise applications that rely on Java-based ecosystems.

- **Go SDK:**

  For Go developers, the **Milvus Go SDK** offers a lightweight solution to interact with Milvus. The performance benefits of Go align well with the requirement of Milvus for handling large-scale, low-latency queries.

- **Other SDKs:**

  Milvus also supports a variety of other SDKs, including C++, Node.js, and Rust, making it a flexible option for a wide range of programming languages and platforms.

Connection Protocols

Milvus supports various communication protocols to enable clients to interact with the server. The most common protocols used for client connections to Milvus are **gRPC** and **RESTful API**. Both protocols are designed to support high-performance, low-latency communication in distributed systems.

gRPC in Milvus: A Comprehensive Overview

In **Milvus**, **gRPC** is the high-performance communication protocol used between clients and Milvus services.

It enables efficient remote procedure calls so applications can perform operations like vector insertion, search, and collection management. Using Protocol Buffers and HTTP/2, gRPC provides fast, low-latency communication suitable for large-scale distributed vector search systems.

Introduction

Milvus is an open-source vector database designed for managing and searching massive volumes of vector data efficiently. To achieve high-performance communication between clients and servers, Milvus uses **gRPC** (Google Remote Procedure Call) as its primary protocol. gRPC is a modern RPC framework that leverages HTTP/2 and Protocol Buffers (protobuf) for fast, efficient, and cross-language communication.

The following sub-section explores how gRPC integrates with Milvus, the advantages it offers, its underlying mechanics, and what are the considerations for optimizing gRPC usage in Milvus-based applications.

Understanding gRPC

gRPC is a high-performance, open-source RPC framework developed by Google. It facilitates remote procedure calls between clients and servers using a binary protocol over HTTP/2. Unlike traditional RESTful APIs that communicate using text-based JSON over HTTP/1.1, gRPC uses:

- **HTTP/2** for multiplexed, bidirectional streaming communication.
- **Protocol Buffers** as the Interface Definition Language (IDL) and data serialization format.

This combination enables compact message formats, lower latency, and richer communication patterns compared to REST.

Role of gRPC in Milvus

In Milvus, gRPC serves as the primary communication protocol between clients and Milvus services.

It enables efficient remote procedure calls for operations such as vector insertion, search queries, and collection management.

By using Protocol Buffers and HTTP/2, gRPC ensures fast, reliable, and low-latency communication in the distributed Milvus architecture.

Primary Communication Protocol

Milvus utilizes gRPC as the default protocol for client-server communication, which is responsible for:

- Handling all client requests such as vector insertions, searches, updates, and metadata management.
- Enabling high-throughput, low-latency interactions with the Milvus vector engine.
- Supporting multiple client languages through SDKs that generate gRPC clients in Python, Java, Go, and the like.

Protocol Buffers for Data Serialization

Milvus defines its APIs using Protocol Buffers, which allows:

- Compact binary serialization of vector data and control messages.
- Strongly-typed messages reducing client-server communication errors.
- Easy auto-generation of client SDKs in various programming languages, ensuring consistent API usage across platforms.

Benefits of Using gRPC in Milvus

Using gRPC in Milvus provides high-performance communication through HTTP/2 and Protocol Buffers, enabling low-latency data exchange.

It supports efficient serialization, reducing network overhead when transmitting large vector data during insert and search operations. gRPC also enables scalable and reliable communication between distributed Milvus components and client applications.

Performance

- **Binary Serialization:** Protobuf messages are significantly smaller and faster to serialize/deserialize than JSON, reducing network bandwidth and CPU usage.
- **HTTP/2 Multiplexing:** Multiple RPC calls can occur concurrently over a single connection, eliminating the overhead of establishing multiple TCP connections and improving throughput.
- **Bidirectional Streaming:** It enables clients and servers to stream data independently, ideal for long-running queries or real-time data updates.

Scalability and Concurrency

- gRPC handles many simultaneous connections efficiently by multiplexing requests and responses over HTTP/2.
- Supports **connection pooling** and multiplexing, minimizing latency spikes under heavy client loads.
- Suitable for **distributed architectures** where multiple Milvus server nodes must handle diverse client requests.

Cross-language Support

- gRPC APIs defined via protobuf enable Milvus SDKs in Python, Java, Go, C++, Node.js, and others.
- Clients written in different languages can seamlessly communicate with Milvus servers without protocol compatibility concerns.

How gRPC Works in Milvus

In Milvus, communication between clients and internal services is implemented using gRPC, which allows remote procedure calls over the network.

First, the client sends a request such as vector insertion or similarity search through a gRPC API to the Milvus Proxy. The request is serialized using Protocol Buffers and transmitted over HTTP/2. The Proxy then forwards the request to the appropriate Milvus components like QueryNodes or DataNodes, which process the operation and return the results back to the client through the same gRPC channel.

Connection Establishment

- A client connects to Milvus by specifying the IP and gRPC port of the server (usually 19530).
- HTTP/2 connection is established with optional TLS encryption.
- The client and server negotiate streams for RPC calls.

RPC Lifecycle

- The client issues RPC calls such as Insert(), Search(), or CreateCollection().
- Each call includes serialized protobuf messages containing vectors, parameters, or commands.
- Milvus processes the requests, performs indexing or search operations, and sends back serialized responses.
- gRPC handles flow control, retransmissions, and error handling transparently.

Streaming

- Milvus leverages the streaming features of gRPC for efficient bulk operations and real-time updates.
- Clients can send batches of vectors as streams to optimize throughput.
- Servers can stream back partial results for large queries to reduce perceived latency.

Best Practices for Using gRPC with Milvus

- Use persistent gRPC connections to reduce connection overhead and improve performance during frequent vector insert and search operations.
- Batch multiple vectors in a single request to minimize network calls and improve throughput in large-scale workloads.
- Monitor request latency and configure appropriate timeout and retry policies to ensure reliable communication in distributed Milvus deployments.

Connection and Retry Configuration

- Use **connection pooling** to reuse existing gRPC connections and reduce overhead.
- Configure **timeouts and deadlines** to avoid hanging RPC calls.
- Implement **exponential backoff and jitter** for retries on transient failures to reduce network congestion.

Optimize Data Transfer

- Batch vector insertions to minimize per-request overhead.
- Use appropriate **search parameters** (for example nprobe in IVF indexes) to balance recall and latency.
- Enable **compression** on gRPC channels when transmitting large datasets over slower networks.

Security

- Use **TLS encryption** to secure client-server communication.
- Employ **mutual TLS (mTLS)** where both client and server verify the identity of each other for added security.
- Use authentication tokens or API keys integrated into gRPC metadata headers.

Monitoring and Debugging

- Instrument gRPC calls with distributed tracing tools to pinpoint latency or error sources.
- Use built-in metrics exporters of Milvus compatible with Prometheus to monitor RPC success rates, latencies, and connection health.
- Enable verbose logging during development to trace protobuf messages.

Limitations and Considerations

- gRPC requires HTTP/2-compatible infrastructure; older proxies or firewalls might need configuration.
- For simple or low-throughput scenarios, RESTful APIs may be simpler to integrate despite lower performance.
- Debugging binary protobuf messages requires tooling unlike textual JSON debugging.

gRPC is a cornerstone technology for Milvus, providing the performance, scalability, and flexibility required to manage large-scale vector databases effectively. By leveraging HTTP/2 multiplexing, protocol buffers, and cross-language client support, Milvus delivers low-latency, high-throughput vector search services suitable for modern AI-driven applications.

Understanding the inner workings of gRPC and applying the best practices for connection management, security, and monitoring empowers developers to build robust, scalable applications that maximize the power of Milvus.

RESTful API in Milvus

Although **gRPC** is the primary and default protocol of Milvus for communication, it also offers a **RESTful API** for clients that prefer an HTTP-based interface. This option is especially useful when integrating Milvus with web applications, microservices, or environments where HTTP/REST communication is the standard or more convenient.

Why Use RESTful API

The RESTful API provides a more traditional, widely adopted method of communication between clients and servers. It follows the principles of REST (Representational State Transfer), where clients send standard HTTP requests (GET, POST, PUT, DELETE) to interact with Milvus resources.

Advantages of RESTful API in Milvus

- **Ease of Use:** REST APIs are generally easier for developers to understand and implement because of their widespread use and reliance on simple HTTP semantics.
- **Stateless Communication:** Each HTTP request is self-contained and independent, which aligns well with microservice architectures and distributed systems that require loose coupling and scalability.
- **Wide Compatibility:** REST APIs can be easily accessed and consumed from almost any programming language or tool that supports HTTP. This makes it an excellent choice for web browsers, mobile apps, and services not natively supporting gRPC.
- **Human-Readable Data Format:** Unlike binary protobuf format of gRPC, RESTful APIs typically use JSON to transmit data. JSON is text-based, making it easier to inspect and debug during development.

How RESTful API Works in Milvus

- Clients send HTTP requests to specific REST endpoints exposed by the Milvus server.
- The requests may include query parameters or JSON-formatted bodies to specify operations such as vector insertion, search queries, or collection management.
- The Milvus server processes these requests and returns results in JSON format.
- Responses include search results, status messages, or error details, depending on the operation.
- RESTful APIs work well for applications with **low to moderate data interaction requirements** or when ease of integration outweighs the need for the highest throughput and lowest latency.

Establishing a Connection to Milvus

Connecting clients to the Milvus server is a foundational step that determines how efficiently applications interact with the vector database.

Connection Basics

- The client must know the **IP address and port number of the server** (default gRPC port: 19530, REST API port may vary).
- Using the respective SDK or HTTP client, the connection is initiated.
- For gRPC, this involves establishing a persistent, multiplexed HTTP/2 connection.
- For REST, each HTTP request is stateless, meaning a new TCP connection might be established unless HTTP keep-alive is used.

Connecting via SDK

Milvus SDKs abstract much of the connection handling complexity:

- Developers specify the server endpoint during client initialization.
- Authentication details (if any) are passed through SDK configuration.
- SDKs manage the underlying connection lifecycle, retries, and serialization/ deserialization.
- This allows developers to focus on business logic rather than networking intricacies.

Load Balancing and High Availability

In real-world deployments, Milvus often runs as a **distributed cluster** composed of multiple nodes for scalability and fault tolerance.

- A **load balancer or proxy** is usually placed in front of Milvus nodes to route client requests efficiently.
- The load balancer distributes client traffic based on node availability, current load, and health checks.
- This prevents any single node from becoming a bottleneck or point of failure.
- In case a node fails, high availability mechanisms redirect traffic to healthy nodes, maintaining service continuity without client disruption.
- Clients connecting via SDKs or REST should be aware of such infrastructure to leverage endpoint configurations optimized for load balancing.

Connection Pooling

To enhance efficiency, especially in applications with frequent Milvus interactions, connection pooling is recommended:

- Instead of opening a new connection for every request, **connection pooling** maintains a set of active connections that clients reuse.
- This reduces the overhead caused by TCP handshakes and TLS negotiations.
- Many Milvus SDKs support built-in connection pooling.
- Optimal pool size configuration depends on application workload and concurrency levels.
- Connection pooling improves throughput and reduces latency, especially under heavy loads.

Handling Client Queries in Milvus

After establishing a connection, clients interact with Milvus by sending queries and commands to manage vector data. These are studied in the following subsection.

Vector Search

- Vector similarity search is the core capability of Milvus.
- Clients submit a **query vector** and specify parameters like the number of nearest neighbors (k) and search precision controls.
- Milvus uses advanced vector indexes such as:
    - **IVF (Inverted File):** It divides the vector space into clusters for faster approximate searches.
    - **HNSW (Hierarchical Navigable Small World):** It is graph-based index optimized for fast search with high recall.
- The search operation returns the most similar vectors along with their metadata or IDs.
- This feature enables applications such as image recognition, recommendation systems, and NLP.

Data Insertion

- Clients insert vectors into collections, specifying vector dimensions, data types, and optional metadata fields.
- Milvus indexes the vectors upon insertion for optimized retrieval.

- Bulk insertion and batch processing are supported to improve throughput.
- SDKs and REST API handle serialization and network transmission of vector data transparently.

Updates and Deletions

- Clients can update existing vectors or their associated metadata.
- Deletion operations remove vectors from collections based on filters or IDs.
- Keeping vector data updated is critical for maintaining the accuracy and relevancy of search results.
- Milvus ensures index consistency and integrity during update and delete operations.

Best Practices for Client Connections

To maximize performance, reliability, and scalability when connecting to Milvus, the following best practices should be considered:

Optimize Connection Settings

- Configure **timeouts** to prevent clients from waiting indefinitely on stalled operations.
- Implement **retry policies** with exponential backoff to handle transient network errors or server unavailability gracefully.
- Use **connection pools** to maintain active channels, minimizing connection overhead.

Monitor Connection Health

- Continuously monitor latency, error rates, and dropped connections.
- Set up alerting on abnormal metrics to quickly detect and respond to issues.
- Leverage Milvus-provided metrics and logs to diagnose bottlenecks.

Use Efficient Data Formats

- For gRPC, always prefer **Protocol Buffers** over JSON because of its compactness and speed.
- For REST, optimize payload size by compressing large JSON responses or request bodies when possible.
- Efficient serialization reduces network bandwidth and CPU usage.

Leverage Load Balancing

- Deploy Milvus behind load balancers to distribute client requests evenly.

- Ensure the load balancer supports sticky sessions or client affinity if needed by your application.
- Implement health checks to automatically remove unhealthy nodes from the routing pool.

Security Considerations

- Use TLS encryption for client-server communication to protect sensitive vector data.
- Authenticate clients using tokens or API keys integrated into connection headers.
- Restrict network access to Milvus nodes through firewalls or private network configurations.

Milvus Python SDK (pymilvus)

The Python SDK, known as pymilvus, is the official and most mature client library for interacting with Milvus. It provides a Pythonic interface to perform all major operations: connecting to the server, managing collections, inserting/querying vectors, and performing index operations.

Installation

```
pip install pymilvus
```

Establishing a Connection

The connection process in pymilvus is simple and intuitive:

```
from pymilvus import connections

connections.connect(
    alias="default",
    host="localhost",
    port="19530"
)
```

- alias allows managing multiple Milvus connections.
- Optional parameters include secure=True, user, password for TLS and authentication.

Managing Collections

```
from pymilvus import CollectionSchema, FieldSchema, DataType, Collection

fields = [
```

```
FieldSchema(name="id", dtype=DataType.INT64, is_primary=True, auto_
id=True),
FieldSchema(name="embedding", dtype=DataType.FLOAT_VECTOR, dim=128)
]
schema = CollectionSchema(fields, description="Example collection")
collection = Collection(name="demo", schema=schema)
```

- Collections represent tables; schema defines fields and vector dimensions.

Inserting Data

Note: disable auto_id for the collection while inserting data.

```
import numpy as np
data = [[i for i in range(1000)], np.random.rand(1000, 128).tolist()]
collection.insert(data)
```

- insert takes a list of columns; order must match schema.

Indexing and Searching

```
collection.create_index("embedding", {"index_type": "IVF_FLAT", "metric_
type": "L2", "params": {"nlist": 128}})
collection.load()

search_vectors = np.random.rand(5, 128).tolist()
results = collection.search(search_vectors, "embedding", {"metric_type":
"L2", "params": {"nprobe": 10}}, limit=5)
```

- Index improves search speed; loading is required before querying.
- Search returns distance and entity IDs.

Querying Metadata

```
collection.describe()
collection.query(expr="id in [1, 2, 3]")
collection.num_entities
```

- Supports boolean expressions for filtering.

Best Practices

- **Batch inserts:** Group data to avoid memory overhead.
- **Connection pooling:** Use default alias or manage multiple using connections.
- **Timeouts and retries**: pymilvus handles retries for transient errors.

- **Memory management**: Unload large collections when not in use.
- **Logging:** Use pymilvus.logger for debugging client/server interactions.

Use Cases

- Machine learning inference pipelines
- Image and audio search systems
- Real-time recommendation engines using vector similarity

Milvus Java SDK

The Java SDK for Milvus is ideal for integrating vector search capabilities into enterprise-scale applications, Android apps, or any JVM-based backend systems. It offers robust support for connection management, data operations, and concurrent execution.

Installation (Maven)

```
<dependency>
<groupId>io.milvus</groupId>
<artifactId>milvus-sdk-java</artifactId>
<version>2.3.4</version><!-- check for latest -->
</dependency>
```

Connecting to Milvus

```
MilvusServiceClientmilvusClient = new MilvusServiceClient(
ConnectParam.newBuilder()
        .withHost("127.0.0.1")
        .withPort(19530)
        .build()
);
```

- Java SDK uses a `ConnectParam` builder to manage host, port, and security settings.
- Supports secure TLS connections and authentication (user/password).

Collection Management

```
FieldTypeidField = FieldType.newBuilder()
    .withName("id")
    .withDataType(DataType.Int64)
    .withPrimaryKey(true)
```

```
    .build();

FieldTypevectorField = FieldType.newBuilder()
    .withName("embedding")
    .withDataType(DataType.FloatVector)
    .withDimension(128)
    .build();

CreateCollectionParamcreateParam = CreateCollectionParam.newBuilder()
    .withCollectionName("demo")
    .withDescription("Java test")
    .withShardsNum(2)
    .addFieldType(idField)
    .addFieldType(vectorField)
    .build();

milvusClient.createCollection(createParam);
Inserting Data
List<Long> ids = LongStream.range(0, 1000).boxed().collect(Collectors.
toList());
List<List<Float>> vectors = generateRandomVectors(1000, 128);

InsertParaminsertParam = InsertParam.newBuilder()
    .withCollectionName("demo")
    .addField("id", ids)
    .addField("embedding", vectors)
    .build();

milvusClient.insert(insertParam);
```

- Batching is important for high performance.
- List<List<Float>> is used for float vectors.

Creating Index and Performing Search

```
CreateIndexParamindexParam = CreateIndexParam.newBuilder()
    .withCollectionName("demo")
    .withFieldName("embedding")
    .withIndexType(IndexType.IVF_FLAT)
    .withMetricType(MetricType.L2)
    .withExtraParam("{\"nlist\": 128}")
    .build();

milvusClient.createIndex(indexParam);

SearchParamsearchParam = SearchParam.newBuilder()
```

```
    .withCollectionName("demo")
    .withVectors(vectors)
    .withVectorFieldName("embedding")
    .withTopK(5)
    .withParams("{\"nprobe\": 10}")
    .build();
milvusClient.search(searchParam);
```

- Search returns results with IDs, scores, and matches.

Querying and Utility Operations

```
milvusClient.loadCollection("demo");
milvusClient.describeCollection("demo");
milvusClient.dropCollection("demo");
```

Best Practices

- Use connection pooling in multi-threaded applications.
- Optimize search parameters (nprobe, nlist) for latency versus accuracy trade-offs.
- Avoid excessive collection creation/deletion in short intervals.
- Use parallel execution for search-heavy applications.
- Enable logging for client-server diagnostics.

Ideal Use Cases

- Java-based ecommerce platforms with visual search
- Android apps needing local vector search (with a remote Milvus backend)
- Enterprise services with high-throughput, low-latency demands

Conclusion

Client connections with Milvus are fundamental to the overall functioning of the system. By offering robust SDKs, leveraging modern communication protocols such as gRPC and RESTful APIs, and supporting high-performance client-server interactions, Milvus makes it easy for developers to integrate powerful vector search capabilities into their applications. Understanding the methods of connecting to Milvus, optimizing connection configurations, and following the best practices will ensure that you can fully leverage the capabilities of Milvus to handle large-scale, real-time data processing and similarity searches effectively.

Index

D

E

F

G

H

I

P

Q

R

T

V

W